The
Birth
Order
Book

Other books by Dr. Kevin Leman

Making Children Mind without Losing Yours
First Time Mom
A Chicken's Guide to Talking Turkey to Your Kids about Sex
The Way of the Shepherd
Sex Begins in the Kitchen
The Perfect Match
Sheet Music: Uncovering the Secrets of Sexual Intimacy in Marriage
When Your Best Isn't Good Enough
Women Who Try Too Hard
Becoming the Parent God Wants You To Be
Becoming a Couple of Promise
Living in a Stepfamily without Getting Stepped On
What a Difference a Daddy Makes
Making Sense of the Men in Your Life
Adolescence Isn't Terminal: It Just Feels Like It
Say Good-bye to Stress
The Real You: Becoming the Person You Want to Be
Unlocking the Secrets of Your Childhood Memories
Keeping Your Family Strong in a World Gone Wrong
Ten Secrets to Raising Sensible, Successful Kids

Forthcoming birth order books for children:

My Firstborn, There's No One Like You
My Middle Child, There's No One Like You
My Youngest, There's No One Like You
My Only Child, There's No One Like You

The
Birth
Order
Book

*Why You Are
the Way You Are*

Dr. Kevin Leman

Revell
Grand Rapids, Michigan

© 1985, 1998 by Kevin Leman

Published by Fleming H. Revell
a division of Baker Publishing Group
P.O. Box 6287, Grand Rapids, MI 49516-6287
www.revellbooks.com

Sixth printing, April 2007
ISBN 10: 0-8007-5977-X
ISBN 978-0-8007-5977-3

Previously published in 1985 under the title *The Birth Order Book* and in 1998 under the title *The New Birth Order Book*

Printed in the United States of America

The Library of Congress has cataloged an earlier edition as follows:
Leman, Kevin.
    The new birth order book : why you are the way you are / Kevin Leman.
        p.   cm.
    Rev. ed. of: The birth order book.
    Includes bibliographical references (p.   ).
    ISBN 10: 0-8007-1759-7 (cloth)
    ISBN 978-0-8007-1759-9 (cloth)
    ISBN 10: 0-8007-5679-7 (pbk.)
    ISBN 978-0-8007-5679-6 (pbk.)
    1. Birth order. I. Leman, Kevin. Birth order book. II. Title.
BF723.B5L46   1998
155.9'24—dc21   98-28465

To my first born, lovable, perfectionist Holly. Your sense of fair play, creativity, love for God, and sensitivity to others make me proud to be your dad. I love you very much.

With special recognition to:

My first-born sister, Sally, with apologies for awakening her on at least one occasion by dangling a juicy night crawler under her nose. You are a very special sister.

and

Dr. John E. Leman Jr. (Jack), my second-born older brother and hero, whom I faithfully followed on more than one propitious childhood occasion when he tried to lose me in the woods. Thanks, Jack, for threatening to beat the tar out of the neighborhood bully for me.

and

My sweet mom and dad, May and John Leman. You did a great job of raising three pretty good kids, and we love you for it!

Contents

    Business   190

11 Birth Order Marriages Aren't Made
    in Heaven   207

12 I Only Count When . . .
    Taking a Look at Your Life-Style   231

13 Why Reality Discipline Works with Any Birth
    Order   250

14 Flaunt Your Imperfections
    Parenting First Borns and Only Children   268

15 Two May Be Company . . . or a Crowd
    Parenting the Two-Child Family   289

16 Taking Off the Squeeze
    Parenting the Middle Child   307

17 Helping the Family "Cub" Grow Up
    Parenting the Last Born   321

    Epilogue
    *There Is Still Only One Thing You Can't Do
    Without*   338

    Appendices
    A: U.S. Presidents and Their Birth Order   349
    B: A Review of *Born to Rebel* by Frank
       Sulloway   352
    Notes   357

Preface

MAYBE ABEL DID HAVE IT COMING

*W*ell, I lost again. Back in 1985 I submitted the original manuscript of this book to the publisher with the working title, "Abel Had It Coming."

They took one look at it and said, "Dr. Leman, you can't have a title like that."

I said, "Why not? It has a nice family ring to it—it's even biblical sounding."

But they stuck to their guns and said, no, I couldn't have that title—it would be too hard to understand, it wouldn't give immediate recognition to what the book was about, and so on, publisher ad nauseam.

Being a baby of the family, I threw a little temper tantrum: "Fine! You guys title it yourselves!" And so they gathered their most creative minds and went into what is called in the publishing world a "committee meeting." Several hours later, they came out with a classic camel-like piece of work that would do any committee proud: *The Birth Order Book: Why You Are the Way You Are.*

To be honest, I had to admit that the title did describe what is in the book and it did make best-seller charts. Indeed, in the past nineteen years many trees have given their all for *The Birth Order Book,* which seemed to hit a nerve all over North America and even around the world, as far as families were concerned. As people began to read about birth order and personality development, they experienced the "Aha!" phenomenon. I've been accused many times of peering in windows or tapping phones. I swear I'm not a voyeur or an eavesdropper—just an Adlerian psychologist who in over twenty-five years of practice has seen how birth order plays an important part in making you the person you are today.

When the Revell publishing house contacted me about doing an updated revision, I let them know I still liked my original title idea. I had hoped that maybe by now the public would be ready for "Abel Had It Coming"—my reference to the first struggle in all history between a first born and his baby brother.

But once again I was knocked on my last-born bumbum and told, "Leman, don't mess with success. The old title says it all. It ain't broke, so please don't try to fix it!"

But because this revision would include a lot of new material and updated information, the committee did meet again, starched collars and all, and decided to make a bold move. So now you are about to read a new edition of *The Birth Order Book,* and you may be wondering what's new?

Since the first edition came out, I've been able to do additional research to see how birth order ties into marriage, stepfamilies, vocation, and the business world. I've also done more work on the burden of perfectionism that is carried by almost all first borns and only children but can also affect individuals of other birth orders.

I've included material on all these topics, plus what I've learned from my own family as it kept growing (even though Sande and I weren't really trying). Since the first edition of *The Birth Order Book,* two more little Lemans have joined our den—Hannah and Lauren. So how does that affect birth order in the Leman family? Does that make our son Kevin, formerly the baby, now a middle child? Is Lauren a true baby of the family because she was born last? Read on and you'll see that birth order is not quite as simplistic as some doubters erroneously claim.

If you're a veteran birth order buff and you're choosing to read this book again, it's my hope that you will enjoy it more than you did last time. If you're a new reader who is a bit unfamiliar with (and maybe a tad skeptical of) how birth order really works, it's my hope that this revision will catch your imagination as the original did for so many thousands of others.

And if you're a last born like me, when you get to the part on Cain and Abel, keep in mind that you may want to walk just a bit more softly around the older ones in the family. Genesis doesn't say much about the natural rivalry that had to be there between Cain and his little brother. It only says that Abel outpointed Cain and in effect pulled the first role reversal on record. So maybe, in Cain's mind at least, Abel did have it coming!

Birth Order—Does It Really Make Any Sense?

i'm glad you asked. As North America's "pop" birth order psychologist, I get that question a lot. I'd really rather be called "one of North America's leading authorities on birth order, who makes a lot of sense." But, as a baby of the family with a strong drive to be entertaining and a little outrageous, I guess I can understand and put up with the "pop" label. After all, as I've crisscrossed the talk-show circuit countless times over the last twenty years, I often have to answer the question, Does birth order make any sense? My first response usually runs along the lines of "Does a bear go potty in the woods?"

Yes, birth order makes sense most of the time for a vast majority of people. The first thing that makes it intriguing is wrestling with the question: How can three or four or even eight little cubs be so different and yet come from the very same den? Yes, there are exceptions to the standard birth order rules but the exceptions are explainable when you understand how birth order works. Even the exceptions develop because of when you were born into your family. I call it your "branch on the family tree" and that branch has had a great deal to do with why you are the way you are today.

Nonetheless, as I give seminars or conduct counseling sessions, I still hear: "Birth order—isn't that like astrology? I'm a Sagittarius myself and my husband is a Libra— is that why he's driving me crazy?"

I smile and resist the strong temptation to say, "Astrology is really not my thing—I'm into pork bellies on the short term." Instead I reply kindly, "Birth order has no connection to astrology but it can give you some important clues about your personality, your spouse, your children, the kind of job you have, and even how well you get along with your Maker if you happen to believe you have one."

"Okay, okay," my questioner might reply, "so what is birth order then, and why should I be interested?"

I then explain that birth order is the science of understanding your place in the family line. Were you born first? second? third? or even farther down that line? Wherever you landed, it has affected your life in countless ways. Throughout my career as a psychologist, I've used the theory of birth order on a daily basis to help people understand themselves and solve their problems.

Which Traits Fit You Best?

To introduce my clients to birth order, I often give them a little quiz: Which of the following sets of personality traits fits you the best? (Anyone taking this quiz must understand that he or she doesn't have to be *everything* in a certain list of traits. Just pick the list that has the *most* items that seem to describe you and your way of operating in life.)

A. perfectionist, reliable, conscientious, list maker, well organized, hard driving, natural leader, critical, serious, scholarly, logical, doesn't like surprises, loves computers

B. mediator, compromising, diplomatic, avoids conflict, independent, loyal to peers, many friends, a maverick, secretive, unspoiled

C. manipulative, charming, blames others, attention seeker, tenacious, people person, natural salesperson, precocious, engaging, affectionate, loves surprises

D. little adult by age seven; very thorough; deliberate; high achiever; self-motivated; fearful; cautious; voracious reader; black and white thinker; uses "very," "extremely," "exactly," a lot; can't bear to fail; has very high expectations for self; more comfortable with people who are older or younger

If you noted that this test seemed rather easy because A, B, and C listed traits of the oldest right on down to the youngest in the family, you're right. If you picked list A, it's a very good bet you are a first born in your family. If you chose list B, chances are you are a middle child (second born of three children, or possibly third born of four). If list C seemed to relate best to who you are, it's likely you are the baby in the family and are not at all happy that this book has no pictures. (Just kidding—I like to have a little fun with last borns because I'm one myself, but more on that later.)

But what about list D? It describes the only child, and I threw it in because in recent years I have been getting more and more questions from only children who know they are "first borns" but want to know how they are different from people who have siblings. Well, one way they are different is that the only child is a super or extreme version of a first born. They have many of the same characteristics of first borns, but in many ways they're in a class by themselves. More on that in chapter 7.

Notice, regarding each major birth order, I always qualify the characteristics by saying "good bet" or "chances are." Not all characteristics fit each person in that birth order. In fact a first born may have baby characteristics, a last born can sometimes act like a first born in certain areas, and middle children may seem to be first borns. I've seen onlies who you would swear were youngest children. There are reasons for these inconsistencies, which I will explain as we go along.

What Do Presidents and Pastors Have in Common?

Birth order continues to be revealing when you look at who is in what occupation. For example, statistics show that first borns often fill positions of high authority or achievement. *Who's Who in America* or *American Men and Women in Science* both contain a high percentage of first borns. You will also find them more than well represented among Rhodes scholars and university professors.

As for presidents and pastors, you guessed it, a great number of them are first borns. The way I define a first born, twenty-three out of forty-one U.S. presidents (56 percent) have been first borns or functional first borns. I will explain what I mean by "functional" more completely in chapter 2. A number of our presidents were born later than number one in their families. In some cases, they were born last, but in all cases they were the first-born *males* in the family. That tells me they had excellent chances of developing first-born traits and *functioning* as first borns, which undoubtedly helped them be effective in their role of president and leader. (For a complete list of U.S. presidents and their birth orders, see appendix A.)

Of course, many of our presidents have been middle children, and a few have been last borns, including Ronald Reagan, the actor who made good in Washington. The big three of birth order—first born, middle child, and baby—was vividly represented during the 1992 presidential campaign when incumbent George Bush, Bill Clinton, and Ross Perot squared off in a televised debate. Clinton, the first born, was suave, confident, loaded with answers, and projected strong leadership abilities. Bush, the middle child, used a mediating negotiating style, even while in debate. Perot, the last born, was an outrageous baby and then some—hard hitting, outspoken, asked lots of embarrassing questions of his opponents, and often had the audience in stitches.

In regard to pastors, I was speaking to a group of fifty ministers and commented in passing, "Pastors, you know, are predominantly first borns." The skeptical looks on their faces told me that I might have wandered dangerously close to some kind of heresy, so I decided to poll the entire group and see if I was right. It turned out that forty-three out of the fifty were first-born sons or only children.

Research bears out that first borns are more highly motivated to achieve than later borns. A much greater proportion of first borns wind up in professions such as science, medicine, or law. You also find them in greater numbers among accountants, bookkeepers, executive secretaries, engineers, and computer specialists. And, oh yes, of the first twenty-three American astronauts sent into outer space, twenty-one were first borns and the other two were only children. All seven astronauts in the original Mercury program were first borns.[1]

Even Christa McAuliff, the teacher who died in the ill-fated *Challenger* space shuttle crash in 1986, was a first born who had four siblings.

> Research bears out that first borns are
> more highly motivated to achieve
> than later borns.

The point is, more often than not you will find first borns
in professions that take precision, strong powers of concentration, and dogged mental discipline.[2] In the 1970s I
served for several years as assistant dean of students at the
University of Arizona while also earning a doctorate. I
always enjoyed testing the birth order theories I was learning and I once asked a faculty member of the College of
Architecture if he had ever noticed where the college's faculty members came from as far as birth order was concerned. He gave me a blank stare and muttered, "Kevin, I
really have to run."

A good six months later he stopped me on campus one
day and said, "Do you remember that crazy question you
asked me about the birth order of our architectural faculty? Well, I finally decided to take an informal poll. It
turns out almost everyone of our faculty is either a first
born or the only child in the family."

My friend was quite impressed, but I was only gratified
to know that a basic birth order principle had proven out
again. People who like structure and order tend to enter
professions that are exacting. Architecture is one of those
professions.

How Birth Order Plays Out in Hollywood

At the other end of the birth order scale, you will find
a lot of later borns who are comedians. Babies of the family who are known and loved by millions of movie and TV
fans include Eddie Murphy, Goldie Hawn, Billy Crystal,
Joan Rivers, Leslie Nielsen, Danny DeVito, Drew Carey,
Jim Carrey, Steve Martin, and Chevy Chase. Other babies

of the family who kept us in stitches include the late comics John Candy and Charlie Chaplin.

It should be noted, however, that not all comics are pure last borns. While Steve Martin is the baby of his family, he had an older sister, which made him the first-born son. And while Jay Leno, star of the *Tonight Show,* is a baby, two other late-night stars are not—Johnny Carson and David Letterman. They are both middle children, born second of three.

Bill Cosby, one of the great comedians of all time, is a first born. Cosby, who holds a doctorate degree, is a perfectionist. He named all of his children with names beginning with "E"—to remind them to always seek excellence.

Other first-born entertainers and actors include Harrison Ford, Sean Connery, Clint Eastwood, Henry Fonda, Chuck Norris, Sylvester Stallone, and the late Humphrey Bogart. They all tend to be macho leading men.

Only children who are well known for their dramatic, and sometimes comedic, roles include Robert DeNiro, Laurence Fishburne, Anthony Hopkins, James Earl Jones, Tommy Lee Jones, Roger Moore, Gregory Peck, Tony Randall, William Shatner, and Robin Williams.

Newscasters and talk-show hosts on television are often first borns and only children. While on a tour of thirty-one cities, I did a little survey and learned that out of ninety-two talk-show hosts, only five were not first borns or onlies. Just a few of the more well-known first-born talk-show personalities are Phil Donahue, Oprah Winfrey, Sonia Friedman, Geraldo Rivera, Arsenio Hall, Sally Jessy Raphael, and the spokesman for excellence in broadcasting himself, Rush Limbaugh.

Rosie O'Donnell is not a true first born but she is the oldest daugher with two older brothers. An avid doll collector who shows the classic characteristics of a first born, she can pick out a flaw at fifty paces! "If you take one [doll] and put it in the wrong spot, she can pick it out in a second," Maureen O'Donnell says of sister Rosie.

As for newscasters, there is Walter Cronkhite, only child; Peter Jennings, first born of two; Ted Koppel, an only child; and Dan Rather, first born of three.

The Leman Tribe and How We Grew

In many families the three birth order positions—first born, middle child, and last born—are played out in more or less classic style. To give you one example that is close to home to me, I will introduce you to the family I grew up in. (You'll meet my own family, wife Sande, daughters Holly and Krissy, son Kevin II, and two latecomers—Hannah and Lauren—a little later.) My parents had three children:

> Sally—first born
> John Jr. (Jack)—middle child (first-born son), born
>   three years later
> Kevin (Cub)—baby of the family born five years after
>   Jack

Sally, eight years my senior, is a classic first born who lives in a small town in western New York. Because we have our own summer place on a lake nearby, we all get to drop in at her immaculate home from time to time every summer vacation. The first thing we notice when we come through Sally's front door is the *clear vinyl runner* leading to every room in the house. We get the message: "Thou shalt not walk on the blue carpet, except where absolutely necessary."

To say Sally is neat as a pin doesn't quite begin to tell the story. I suspect that from time to time she irons her welcome mat! Perhaps you use those garbage bags that have drawstrings? Sally does, too, and she ties bows on hers.

In short, whatever Sally does, she does it classy and she does it right. All her life she has been confident, scholarly, well liked (a cheerleader in high school)—a National Honor Society type all the way. In fact Sally, who is on the pastoral staff of her church and serves as director of children's ministries, has two books to her credit: *Making God Real to Your Children* and *Mommy Appleseed*, which deals with planting Scripture in a child's life in a natural way.[3]

Sally can even class up a camping trip. No one in the Leman clan can forget the time we all went camping high in the Sierra Nevadas. After a terrific day in the great out-of-doors, we were all ready to hop into our sleeping bags. Because at eight or nine thousand feet it gets rather nippy at night, even in the summer, most of us planned to sleep in our clothes.

Not Sally. She came out of her tent to say good night, attired in nighty and negligee and seemed puzzled when we all dissolved in laughter. But why not sleep in your negligee on a camping trip when you are a former home ec teacher turned preschool director? Why not add a little class to the campsite when you are creative, artistic, and neat in everything you do?

Sally has butterflies at least two days before giving a small dinner party. Bigger dinner parties cause butterflies for a week or ten days. Naturally everything must be color coordinated: The napkins match the napkin holders, which match the decor of the formal dining room. It's probably obvious that Sally is a perfectionist. I will explain more about perfectionists in chapters 5 and 6.

Born second in our family was my brother, Jack. Typical of a lot of middle children, his precise personality traits are a bit more difficult to pin down. Second children are known for going in exactly the opposite direction from the first born in the family. Typically the middle child is a mediator and a negotiator who avoids conflict. He can be a real paradox, independent, but with extreme loyalty to his peer group. He can be a maverick with many friends. He is usually the one to leave home first; at least he finds his real companionship outside the family circle because he often feels sort of left out of things at home.

In Jack's case, he didn't go in a completely opposite direction from Sally. He turned out to be extremely conscientious, serious, and scholarly. All of these traits are those belonging to first borns. So what happened to Jack? Well, he was a "functional first born"—first-born *male* in the Leman family. This often happens with the middle born, as we will see in chapter 8.

One classic middle-child trait that Jack possessed was to be a trailblazer who was willing to move far away from family roots in upper New York state. Sally followed the classic first-born trait of staying with tradition and still lives just a few miles from where we all grew up. But if Jack hadn't made the major independent breakthrough of traveling all the way to Tucson to take his graduate work at the University of Arizona, neither my parents nor I would have ended up living there. As it was, my parents followed Jack to Tucson. I came along as well and have lived here ever since, for more than thirty-five years.

And then there was little Kevin who came along five years after Jack, and a birth order rule of thumb says that when there is a five- to six-year gap, the next child starts a "new family," and you can make an educated guess that he or she will be a first-born personality type in some ways. When there is a gap of seven to ten years (or more), the next child falls into the "quasi-only child" category because there are so many years between him or her and the sibling above.[4]

Keep in mind, however, that these rules of thumb are subject to how the child is parented plus other influences that occur within the family constellation. In my case, for example, the rule of thumb sort of went out the window for one good reason. My brother, Jack, took all the heat because my parents expected a lot more from him than from his baby brother. Jack's given name was John E. Leman JUNIOR. He was to be the medical doctor my father had always wanted to be but couldn't because he was very poor and finished only eighth grade. Dad projected onto Jack his own dreams of a fine profession and his own fears of not being somebody. With that kind of pressure on him, you can see why Jack took on many first-born traits and, while he didn't end up a surgeon or an anesthesiologist, he did become an extremely conscientious Ph.D. in clinical psychology with his own private practice.

As for me, I was nicknamed "Little Cub" and the handle stuck. Instead of being ignored and left to myself, I became the family mascot who was always getting into something.

Babies of the family are very perceptive, and I learned very early that I had two superstars ahead of me. I quickly decided there wasn't a whole lot I could do by way of achievement to gain attention. My only real accomplishment from preschool up through high school was playing on the baseball team (that is, when I was eligible—usually the first six weeks of the spring semester before grades came out). Jack, a star quarterback, never bothered with baseball. In western New York, high school football was the major sport, while baseball was for hardy types willing to put up with freezing to death before small crowds in spring weather that often included late snowstorms.

But Little Cub wasn't going to be left out. What I lacked in achievement I made up for in mischievousness. I became a manipulative, charming, engaging, and sometimes devilish little show-off. At age eight, while trying to lead a cheer for my sister's high school team, I found my true calling in life. I learned that entertainers get attention. So entertain I did, especially for my classmates all through grade school and high school. I became something of a cross between terrorist and clown prince and gained incredible skill at driving teachers a little crazy.

It All Comes Back to That Family Tree

I have no way of knowing what kind of family you grew up in, but it's my guess you could come up with a cast of characters similar to the Leman kids: the good students, the athletes, the performers, the attention-getters, and the ones who are hard to pigeonhole. After about three decades of psychological study and practice, I am sure of only a few things:

1. *For a young child growing up, there is no greater influence than his or her family.* Yes, I know about all the time they spend in school, Little League, Brownies; it's really a drop in the bucket compared to what goes on at home. During those early years, parents and siblings make an indelible psychological imprint. This imprint greatly affects the development of one's basic personality, and later in life, family influence persists even across the miles when children grow up and move away.[5]

2. *The most intimate relationships you ever have in life are with your family*—the one you grew up in and the one you make for yourself through marriage. But the family you grew up in has the inside track. Think about how long you have been married. Now think about how long you have known your siblings. Some of us have known our siblings "all our lives," so to speak. Like it or not, you are tied to your siblings with bonds stronger than even the marriage bonds that tie you to your mate. And you have known your parents all your life as well.

Living in a family, then, is a unique and distinctive experience. The intimate relationships that develop in the family can be found nowhere else on earth.[6] And these relationships are created in great part by your order of birth.

3. *The relationship between parents and children is fluid, dynamic, and all-important.* Every time another child is born, the entire family environment changes. How parents interact with each child as it enters the family circle determines in great part that child's final destiny.

I'm not sure if that last remark sounds profound or just a bit pontifical. All I know is that my father never had the opportunity to go beyond eighth grade, something he always regretted. He wanted very much for at least one of his sons to be a medical doctor. I don't think he was partial to doctors because of any visions of saving the world from disease and death. He just knew that doctors were well educated and well paid. Education became a major value that he communicated to all of his children—even to bear cub Kevin, who didn't show as much promise as the older children.

I can still remember clearly how we would be riding in the car with my father and he would stop by the side of the road where a crew was doing jackhammer work or digging ditches. He would turn to us and say, "Do you want to do that? If you don't, then you go to the *big school*. Hear me? *Go to the big school*. You go to the big school, you don't have to do that, but if you don't, that's what you'll be doing all your life."

Did my dad's "big school" speech sink in? Well, the results tell their own story. First-born sister Sally got all As all her life, right up through a master's program. Brother Jack is a clinical psychologist, and somehow bear cub Kevin wound up a psychologist too. Sally and Jack were no great surprise. They had it right from the start. But how did Kevin, the clown prince, get a doctor's degree? One answer is, "With a great deal of difficulty!" For now let's leave it in the minor-miracle category. My high school teachers might even label it a *major* miracle.

What Reading This Book Will Do for You

As you read this book, you will find practical ways to use your particular birth order to your advantage in personal relationships, intimate relationships—particularly marriage—and even in the business world. In short, you'll receive a lot more insight into why you are the way you are, and there is nothing better than knowing yourself.

I believe that people don't spend enough time being aware of just how their branch fits on the family tree. First born or lonely only, middle child, or baby—all of us sprout in our own unique direction and make our own unique contributions.

I see it happen every day. As people understand birth order, they improve relationships where it counts—with friends and, most important, at home with the people who are nearest, but not always dearest. They even get some clues concerning why they hold the job they have and how to get along better with bosses and fellow workers.

Just a few questions that I often ask people reveal why a knowledge of birth order can help them. "Do people who are very much alike get along well in marriage?" As they think about it, they conclude that the answer more often than not is no. They're right. Statistics and my counseling load suggest that couples who get along best are different. Appreciating and understanding those differences is one of the things you'll learn from reading this book.

Another question, for those in the business world: "Are sales relational?" You might say, "Well, yes, I suppose so." You suppose so? Just think about how people buy in different ways. First borns read *Consumer's Report* before going to buy a new car. Babies walk on the car lot and ask, "Do you have a green one with leather seats, CD player, and gold wheel covers?"

And what about relationships with friends or people we know at church or in clubs where we are members? Isn't it interesting that birds of a feather do flock together? We identify with friends of the same birth order. For example, my wife, Sande; my sister, Sally; and Wendy, wife of my lifelong friend "Moonhead," are all first borns. During the summer, when our family is vacationing in upper New York state, they love to get together to go to yard sales, antique shops, and arts and crafts shows. They truly love to pursue the same kinds of treasures, which I, a baby of the family, prefer to call "expensive junk."

As I have counseled people over the last twenty years, I've used birth order again and again to help them turn their lives around. Understanding birth order and how it works helps Marsha finally grasp why her husband, John, is always so picky. And John gains insight into Marsha's "little girl" ways that are driving him more bonkers by the day. And when it comes to counseling parents and their children, birth order helps Mom and Dad get a handle on why ten-year-old Buford can go through life oblivious to his open fly and C+ average while thirteen-year-old sister Hortense has straight As—and a good start on an ulcer.

Birth Order Is Predictable—To a Point

Wherever I go, I make a hobby of guessing the birth order of waitresses, cab drivers, or people in the audience at the marriage and parenting seminars I conduct around the country. I don't have any strange supernatural powers when it comes to determining anybody's birth order but I do have an awful lot of research and plain old law-of-average odds on my side.

For example, during a seminar I take a quick look around and spot ten people who I believe are first-born or only-born children. In this case, I just go by physical appearance, nothing else. The folks I pick look as if they've stepped off the cover of *Glamour* magazine or out of an ad for Brooks Brothers suits. They're easy to spot because every hair is in place and they are color-coordinated from head to toe. Right there in front of everyone I go out on a limb and guess that each person I select is a first-born or only child. I usually hit nine out of ten, often ten out of ten.

This makes some people in the audience nervous. They think I'm giving some kind of short course on magic and other parlor tricks or that I'm a fugitive from a psychic hot line. Of course, that's not true at all. I have simply used a classic bit of birth order information to make a judgment.

The typical first born is usually neatly dressed and well groomed. Lots of research and my own personal observations in over twenty years of practice back this up. Admittedly, first borns are easier to recognize than middle children, who are probably hardest of all to identify.

When I can do what I call a "birth order demonstration" with someone out of a seminar audience, I have even more going for me. In Phoenix recently I picked a man out of the audience and in eight minutes I easily identified his birth order as well as that of his wife by asking only a few questions. When I asked him to describe himself, he said he was a loner and a reader and he appreciated order in his life (are you getting any clues yet?). Then I asked him to describe his mother and he said that she was *very* loving, *very* concerned about him, *very* intuitive, and a *very* good mom.

By now I knew I had a first born on my hands and the next question was whether or not he had married his opposite birth order (which supposedly guarantees more happiness) or whether he had possibly "married his mother." Oh yes, I had his mother pegged as a perfectionist, because she had been *very* loving and concerned about him. It was my guess that his wife was very loving but had a critical eye a mile wide and was as powerful as they come. So I went out on a limb a bit and speculated that his wife was quite protective, a perfectionist, and that there was a right way to approach her—and she probably liked to handle things herself. "My guess is, when you're driving, she's quick to criticize you," I ventured.

"Worse than that," he said, "she doesn't let me drive." The audience got tickled by that but it brought down the house when I said next, "Oh, *you're* the guy! I saw you go by the other day. You were in the back, buckled into your car seat."

To cap it all off, his wife, who was sitting back in the audience, clapped her hand over her mouth and said very loudly, "Oh, my gosh, I'm just like my mother!" No doubt she is. With birth order in families, what goes around comes around.

I Batted .500 on the *Today Show*

What about spotting babies of the family? They are often easy to identify; for example, while being interviewed by Katie Couric, cohost of the *Today Show*, I told her that she was a baby in her family, probably with two older brothers and two older sisters.

It turned out I was one brother off, but Katie's mouth still dropped open and she sort of stuttered, "Well . . . yes . . . but how did you know?"

I quickly explained that while she was beautifully dressed and perfectly groomed, her perky, affectionate nature gave her away. As she worked with Bryant Gumbel, she often touched him or grabbed his arm—her very engaging nature came across loud and clear. Off camera Katie let me know she didn't like being called "perky" very much but she had to admit I was right. It all still struck her as rather mysterious. I could tell the staff who had been filming the interview enjoyed it too—they were chuckling. Then a friendly gentleman stepped out of the group and said, "Are you Brother Kevin?"

I didn't quite know what he meant by "brother," but I said, "Hi, I'm Kevin Leman."

We shook hands and again he said, "No, you don't understand. Are you *Brother* Kevin?"

"Well, I'm Kevin . . ."

"No, are you the one who's on with Brother Randy?"

Then it hit me. This man listened to *Parent Talk*, a radio call-in show that I cohost with Randy Carlson, heard on more than six hundred stations—mostly Christian affiliates—throughout the nation every week.

We exchanged small talk for a few minutes and as we chatted, I observed, "Katie is obviously a baby, but Bryant Gumbel, he's got to be a first born, at least a first-born son."

"Bryant's not a first born," my new friend told me.

"He's got to be," I replied. "The expensive suits, one-hundred-dollar ties, confident, prepared to the teeth—a first born if I ever saw one."

"No, his brother, Greg, is the oldest by three years."

"It can't be," I (the birth order "expert") said in disbelief.

"It is, I'm telling you, it is," my new friend said. "I know his family."

As we talked, I got a better picture of what had faked me out. Clearly there had been a "role reversal" in the Gumbel family. Bryant had taken over as the "first born" while his brother, who today is a broadcaster and certainly no slouch in his own right, became "number two."

"Let me ask you a question," I said at one point. "Were Bryant and Greg's parents critical?"

"Extremely so," was his immediate answer and it spoke volumes. Here, indeed, was one of those exceptions to the birth order rules. Sometimes there are extenuating circumstances that tweak the natural birth order sequence. The result is that a later-born child may act like a first born or a first born can seem to have characteristics that are inconsistent with the way first borns are "supposed to act."

For some readers, my Bryant Gumbel story may be interesting, even a bit amusing, but for others it could be disturbing. You may be a precise, careful, conservative first-born or only child who isn't at all reassured when I have to admit that some birth order descriptions don't fit everyone. You may be like the guy who comes up to me and says, "Wait a minute, Leman. I heard a birth order talk (or read a birth order article) once. Those descriptions didn't fit my family at all. Furthermore, I'm the baby of my family and I'm the most responsible one of the bunch. Not only that, but I'm the only one who reads. The rest just stare at the boob tube. How do you explain that?"

Explain that I can, and a lot more. You see, sometimes a last born inherits the first-born role by default due to . . . but wait, I'm getting ahead of myself. All that is coming up in chapter 2.

2

But, Doc, I Don't Fit Your Birth Order Mold!

BIRTH ORDER VARIABLES—PART 1

*T*he so-called inconsistencies that occur when someone doesn't seem to fit into the typical birth order mold are only signposts pointing to what really is the most entertaining (and informative) part of birth order theory. To understand these signposts, we need to become acquainted with the psychological term, "family constellation." I prefer to simply call it the family zoo. Over the years much of my counseling practice has been with desperate mothers who have three or four little ankle biters, driving them up the wall. When I talk about the family zoo, these moms know exactly what I mean.

How two parents can have two, three, or more little critters in their particular family zoo who are so distinctly different is a question that birth order can help to answer. But you have to be aware of another bit of psychological jargon—the *variables* affecting each family constellation. *Variables* is a term all counselors learn in Psychology 101 and, without getting technical, it simply refers to different factors that can be examined while studying persons, families, or groups. When I use the term *variables* regarding birth order, I refer to different factors or forces that have an impact on each person, no matter what his or her birth order may be.

A lot of different things can be called a variable, but in my work over the past thirty years, I believe the most important variables that come into play when talking about birth order include:

spacing—the number of years between children

the sex of each child—and in what sequence males and females are born

physical, mental, or emotional differences—yes, genes are important

sibling deaths—which, if occurring early, cause the child below to be "bumped up" to the next birth order

adoptions—which may or may not have an effect on birth order, depending on how old the child is when adopted

the birth order position of each parent—first-born parents usually run a much different ship than later borns

the relationship between the parents—and the parenting style they use as they pass on their personal values to their children

the "critical eye" of a parent—constant criticism takes its toll *the blending of two or more families* due to death or divorce—in a stepfamily certain birth orders often get stepped on

Birth Order: Not As Simple As 1–2–3

The reason birth order looks inconsistent to some folks is they think it's some kind of simple ordinal system based on birth rank. First borns are supposed to be this, second borns are always like that, and third-born siblings are always another way, and so on.

But as we have already seen, some children act and appear very different from their ordinal birth order. And even when children seem to fit the typical descriptions of their ordinal birth order (number 1, number 2, etc.), they can exhibit characteristics of other birth orders, and that's where the variables come in. When variables take effect, they cause a child born in one birth position to *function*, at least in part, with characteristics of another birth position.

The point is that all birth orders have certain tendencies and general characteristics, but the real key to the whole thing is that there are dynamic fluid relationships existing between members of the family. And that's where the variables can cause functional birth order characteristics, when a child born in one birth order functions like a child who is born in another.

> All birth orders have certain tendencies and general characteristics, but the real key to the whole thing is that there are dynamic fluid relationships existing between members of the family.

In the remainder of this chapter, we'll look at the most obvious variables that can be seen in the children themselves—spacing, sex, and mental, physical, or emotional differences. And we'll also consider less discussed variables, like multiple births, the death of a sibling, and adopted siblings.

Spacing Can Create More Than One "Family"

An obvious—and crucial—birth order variable in any family is spacing—when each child arrives. Whenever you think of spacing, you should include the phenomenon called "dethronement" of the first born, which happens the minute a little brother or sister comes into the world. Until that moment, the first born has been number one and the apple of everybody's eye. Suddenly there is another little apple on the branch. The first born is no longer the special only one, and he may suffer some serious self-esteem problems if his parents don't make sure they let him know that he is still loved very much.

Many parents try to have their children two years apart (actually three is "ideal"), but these best-laid plans often go awry. When counseling, I often find there are gaps in the spacing of the children that can sometimes create "another family." I mentioned that there is a gap of five years between me and my older brother and I could well have started a second family, but other things—particularly my father's values—intervened. But to show you how a second family can actually occur, let's look at the example below:

Family A
Male—14
Female—13
– – – – – – –
Male—7
Female—5

The dotted line depicts the obvious split in this kind of birth order ranking. The gap of six years between the second- and third-born child could easily cause the third-born boy to develop first-born tendencies. This doesn't mean he would have no characteristics of a middle child (in a family of four children, numbers two and three are middle children). He could still become a negotiator; he could still have a lot of friends. But he also might be quite "adult"— conscientious, exacting—because he had so many older role models. Not only would his parents model adult characteristics for him but so would his much bigger (and more capable) brother and sister. And that's where he could learn to function in a number of ways as a first born.

To create one more example: Let's remove the male, seven, and the female, five, and insert a male, three, as shown below:

Family B

Male—14
Female—13
— — — — — —
Male—3

Now what do we have? When the gap between the last child and the one above becomes more than seven years, you have a very good chance of developing what we call a quasi-only child. The little three year old is "baby of the family," ordinally speaking, and he, indeed, may take on baby characteristics if his parents and those two older siblings dote on him. On the other hand, if he's left to himself and doesn't get much "cute little cub" treatment, he can easily become much like an only child, because he will be working extra hard, trying to emulate all those big role models above him who are so much more capable.

Meet the First Leman Family

The above examples of spacing are hypothetical, but I can give you another that is "real life" in every respect. I know the following family very well, because these kids belong to my wife, Sande, and me. Our "first" family included Holly, followed about a year and a half later by Krissy, who was followed four years later by Kevey (Kevin II).

Our first three followed the typical birth order patterns practically to a T. From day one, Holly was meticulous, perfectionistic, structured, hard driving, and bright—very bright. She was also a stickler for the rules and being precise. If she wanted to know what time we were going to leave, I couldn't say "around noon." I had to be clearer and make it, "We will depart the driveway by 11:55 A.M."

It was no surprise when Holly latched onto Judge Wapner's *People's Court* as one of her favorite TV shows. Today she's an English teacher who's a stickler for procedure and coming to class prepared. After graduating from college, Holly returned to Tucson to teach and joined the faculty of a local public high school where she taught English and creative writing to seniors. During her first year we would run across parents of students in her class who would tell us two things. They were essentially happy with Holly's teaching of their child, but then the next word out of their mouth was "detention." "Oh," I would reply, "your child doesn't always come to class prepared?"

"No, but he's learning!" would be the typical response.

Krissy, our second born, has also wound up as a teacher of second graders in a Christian school here in Tucson. She plans to become a counselor but has also been doing very well at teaching. After her first year of work, her principal told her that she was the first teacher to serve on his staff in twenty-five years to whom he had nothing to offer by way of suggestion on how to improve.

So, is Krissy the same kind of hard-driving, precise, stick-to-the-rules-and-get-your-work-in-on-time personality as her sister? Not really. But on the other hand, Krissy is in full control of her class because she's very *relational* with kids, the sure sign of a second born who has learned to negotiate, mediate, and go outside the family to make friends. From early on, this was Krissy's pattern. We still talk about her first day at kindergarten when she frightened her mother out of her wits by going to her "best friend's house" after school instead of coming straight home on the bus.

It's important to know, however, that Krissy was our baby girl for at least four years before Kevin came along. So she was the baby of the family for much of her early life when her life-style (the way she sees herself and the world) was being formed. Maybe that explains why she can't seem to shake the "Krissy" handle. I've suggested that sometime before she gets her AARP card, she should switch to Kris or her given name, Kristin!

Kevin, our third born, is the baby of the first Leman family. He is a classic last born—playful, great sense of humor, and very creative. I'd like to think he's going to be the next Gary Larson, creator of the cartoon *Far Side*. As this revision is being written, Kevin is finishing up art school and plans on a career in imagineering. He has worked for the Disney corporation part-time during the school year and full-time over the summer and has already come up with some design ideas for futuristic rides that someday may be part of Disney World or Disneyland.

For all of his last-born charms, Kevin is the first-born male in our family and has some first-born traits, as the following story illustrates. He is well liked where he attends art school, and one day a schoolmate who was struggling to get her life together asked him, "Kevin, can I ask you a question? Why are you always so happy?"

"Do you really want to know?" Kevin responded.

"Yeah, I certainly do!"

"Well, I love God and I come from a really neat family."

When Kevin told me that story, I was pleased but I was even more impressed when he added the sequel: "Dad, she still smokes pot but not as much. And she still rips things off sometimes. We went to Disney World together and when we came out of this gift shop she had that look on her face. I stopped her and said, 'Okay, let's have it.' She took it out of her pocket and handed it to me. I marched her right back into the store and she gave it back."

Kevin has a strong sense of responsibility. It's gratifying to be blessed with a kid like Kevin. As a teenager and now a young man of twenty, he's far ahead of where his father was at that point in life, and then some!

How We Got Our "Second Family"

When the first edition of *The Birth Order Book* came out, our children were all young:

Family Leman (mid '80s)
Holly—12
Krissy—10
Kevin—6

Sande and I thought our family was complete, but little did we know that a second family was on the way. In 1987, more than nine years after Kevin was born—and we were both in our early forties—a little "surprise" arrived, and we named her Hannah.

With such a large gap between Hannah and Kevey—nine and a half years—Hannah definitely started a second round of birth order for the Lemans. Today at age eleven, she's a budding artist, a skilled athlete, and a joy to raise. Her first-bornishness is definitely on the compliant side. For example, at age two she would try to get her parents organized, but always in a gentle fashion. When she needed a nap, she would come up, take our hands, and say, "Tired now."

But our second family was still not complete. Hannah was, indeed, a surprise but almost five and a half years later came our little "shocker," another toy princess we named Lauren. Learning that we were pregnant for a fifth time— in our *late* forties—was, indeed, a shock for me as well as my usually implacable first-born wife. After getting Hannah into preschool, Sande was finally seeing some daylight and having a little time for herself.

The pregnancy was a hard one for Sande, but when little Lauren arrived, she was as welcome and as loved as her siblings had ever been. Today at age six, Lauren is the baby of our second family and the true baby of our total family. Now we look like this:

Family Leman (as of late 1998)

Holly—26, classic first born, teaches English
Krissy—24, classic middle child, wants to be a
 counselor
Kevin—20, classic baby, fun-loving artist
- - - - - - - -
Hannah—11, a quasi-only child, exhibits many
 tender baby characteristics
Lauren—6, born last but a functional first born,
 very precise, cautious

For the first five years of her life, Hannah was a combination baby princess and quasi-only child. Because of the huge gap between her and her older brother and sisters, Hannah actually had five "parents" who doted on her. At least there were five very big and capable people she was trying to learn from and imitate. Then Lauren arrived and took the baby spot. And, again, because of a rather long gap between her and Hannah (five years), Lauren was not only the true baby princess of the family but also a candidate for functional first-born traits as well. We like to say that Hannah had five parents and Lauren had six!

And the first-born probabilities did develop. At two and a half, Lauren would take her little tape recorder, set it on the floor, and then line up all her tapes next to it in perfect order. To a baby of the family like me, who could hardly line up to go to the bathroom, this was almost scary.

But Lauren topped that not long ago when all of us gathered in the kitchen to discuss how our normal scheduling had been totally sabotaged. Sande had a doctor's appointment, so Krissy had to pick up Hannah after school. Holly would be late because of a teacher's meeting she had to attend, and I had a meeting that would make me late as well. And we were all due to meet for dinner at 7:00 at a certain restaurant. As we chewed on all the details together, five-year-old Lauren interjected, "My, my, my, this is very complicated." Everyone sort of froze and just looked at her.

I'm not sure where Lauren learned the word *complicated*, but obviously she knew what it meant. I suppose I sound like a proud parent but I rather doubt that's a typical observation for a five year old, particularly for a baby of the family. But that's where that variable of spacing comes in with Lauren. Whenever there's enough of a spread between your last born and the one above to create the functional first born, don't sell short the powerful imprint you and all of those older siblings are making on him or her. Granted, your little last born isn't a true first born, but he or she may carry some of the first-born burdens. We'll look more at first borns in chapter 4.

Why Southwest Is Such a Fun Airline

One other example of how spacing can create a first-born personality in a last-born child is Herb Kelleher, president and CEO of Southwest Airlines. As I was reading with interest a business column in our local paper one day, I learned that Kelleher and his staff had built Southwest into one of the most profitable operations anywhere. One of the reasons he gave was: "We defined a personality as well as a market niche. [We seek to] amuse, surprise, and entertain."[1]

I jotted a note next to that quote that said, "Herbie must be a baby." Later, when I telephoned him for an interview, he told me that, indeed, he is the baby of the family (fourth born of four), but that there is a *nine-year gap* between him and his next older brother. And the other brothers are thirteen and fourteen years older. With all that coaching and all those capable people to model after, it's no mystery that Herb Kelleher, baby of his family, made it to the top and became CEO of a prominent airline.

That's why Kelleher is a mixed bag. As a CEO he is in typically first-born company. At the same time, he loves to enjoy himself, and that's his baby side. You may have seen Southwest TV commercials where Kelleher is cast as a referee who calls unnecessary roughness penalties on luggage handlers who are a bit too careless with the baggage. While he doesn't force his employees to be amusing and entertaining, they often follow suit. If you've ever been on a Southwest Airline flight and have listened to the flight attendants singing their zany songs to the passengers, you know what I mean.

Kelleher says, "We don't force attendants to be entertainers. We just tell them if they feel comfortable doing things like that, great! And if they feel uncomfortable, don't bother. They actually come up with many of these things themselves."[2]

The Sex of Each Child Can Cause Pressure Points

Almost hand in hand with the spacing variable is the obvious variable of sex. We've already seen that a later-born child can become the first-born girl or the first-born boy. And I have mentioned how a number of U.S. presidents are functional first borns because of being the first male in the family. I always find it fascinating how often birth order plays a role in developing political leaders.

I was speaking to a Young Presidents group at a resort in Tucson, and the governor, Fife Symington, was present. I had gotten to the part where I was talking about how birth order impacts our lives and I spotted the governor of our state in a far corner of the room. When I asked for a show of hands on who was a first born, a middle child, or a last born, the governor put his hand up to identify himself as a baby of his family.

I caught the governor's eye across the room and said: "Governor Symington, excuse me, but you are not a baby of the family."

He looked at me as if to say, *What? I ought to know where I was born in my own family—I* **AM** *the baby.*

"I can see that you doubt me a bit," I said. "Would you tell me a bit about your family?"

"Well," replied the governor, "I've got three older sisters . . ."

"And you are the only son?" I interrupted.

"Yes, that's true."

"Bingo! I rest my case. Governor you are a first-born child—the first-born *male*—in the Symington family."

Symington went on to a star-crossed career as governor, which demonstrated that, while he was a functional first born, he also had weaknesses typical of some last borns.[3]

For one more illustration of how the sex variable affects birth order, let's consider a reverse of the Symington family and look at three boys followed by a girl. You don't have to be a certified psychologist to figure out that there will be something very special about one member of this family:

Family C

Male—16
Male—14
Male—12
Female—11

The fourth-born girl will definitely be a special baby princess. And in this kind of mix, which child is in the *least* preferable position? The third-born male—the twelve year old—has to be sweating a bit. When his younger sister was born, Mom had already been down to the hospital three times and brought home a boy every time. She and Dad were pulling for a girl each time, and then she arrived, only fifteen to eighteen months behind the third-born male. He was bound to hear her footsteps even before she could walk!

Who else in this family is in a favorable spot? A good bet is that first-born male who will likely excel at school. Of course, he will probably engage in plenty of rivalry with his younger brother, because any time the second born is of the same sex as the first born, there is bound to be more friction. If older brother is a scholar, second born is likely to be an athlete, or he may prefer the school band (maybe he'll form his own rock group) and leave athletics to the third-born boy. If the third born does become an athlete, it could be fortunate because it will help him work out frustrations caused by having to compete with his baby princess sister.

Family C is just one example of how the sex of each child can affect the family. The rule of thumb is: When sex differences create someone "special," it can put pressure on the child immediately above or below that special person.

When sex differences create someone "special," it can put pressure on
the child immediately above or below
that special person.

In This Corner, Burly the Bigger

Another variable that can turn the birth order factor upside down, or at least tilt it a bit, is a marked difference in physical looks, size, or ability. Little Chester, age ten, is the first born, but he's still called "little" because his brother, one year younger, is nicknamed "Burly" and is four inches taller and twenty-five pounds heavier. Because it's a two-child family, the two males are natural rivals, and Chester better be extra quick or extra smart or he's in for a lot of difficult days—and quite possibly a role reversal in which Burly will take all the first-born privileges and prerogatives by default while Chester slips back to second place. A role reversal is when two children do something of a flip-flop.

Another all-too-frequent example of this kind of variable is the two-girl family where one is extremely pretty and the other is extremely plain. If the plain one is first born, her pretty little sister may drive her into a shell from which she will never escape. If the first born is the pretty one, the plain baby of the family better figure out some kind of secret weapon—athletics or being family scholar—or she's in for a long and dreary career as the "homely little sister."

In the examples of Burley and the pretty second born, marked physical differences cause a second born to function like a first born and vice versa. Another physical difference that can flip-flop things in a hurry is when one member of the family suffers from serious disease or disability. For example, let's create a family where the first born has cerebral palsy:

Family D

Female—14, physically challenged with cerebral palsy
Female—12
Male—10

Here we have another case of a role reversal. The special person is born at the top, but her second-born sister is almost certain to take the role of the first born in the family because of her older sister's extreme disability.

A role reversal happens for other reasons, too, such as with the Gumbel brothers mentioned earlier. In their case, Greg, the oldest boy, was capable and bright and wound up in a very responsible position in television broadcasting. But three years below him was a younger brother named Bryant who achieved major fame in TV and stole the limelight from his brother. In this case, the variable wasn't disability or disease, it was critical parents who put pressure on Greg. That pressure somehow made him step into the background a bit while his younger brother thrived and jumped ahead.

Before we leave Family D, what about little last-born brother? He is, of course, the first-born male in the family and chances are that his cerebral-palsied sister will ace him out of the "baby" status. This last-born son may have a few baby characteristics but may act more like a first born than anything else.

One other difference that counselors see a lot more of in recent years is a combination of physical/mental problems that have come to be called ADHD (attention deficit hyperactivity disorder). A lot of people know this simply as ADD, but in 1987 the new term was introduced to include hyperactivity along with the problem of attention deficit.

Whatever you want to call it, ADHD can seriously affect the birth order factor. For example, suppose a family has a first-born boy with ADHD and a second-born girl who seems to be perfectly "normal." The almost classic response to this situation by the parents is that they will soon see the first-born son as something of the family black sheep—always a problem—while their second-born daughter takes over as far as gaining first-born privileges and plaudits.

Multiple Births Skew Any Birth Order

Another important variable in birth order is multiple births, which have been happening more often in recent years. The usual multiple birth that we've seen down through the years is, of course, twins. And twins are always special. Twins are usually very aware of who is the "first born." One of them will let you know that he is older, even if it's by as little as one minute!

No matter where twins may land in a family birth order, they wind up as something of a first-born/second-born combination and are usually competitor and companion. The first born often becomes the assertive leader and the second born follows along. This happens often, but not always. Some twinships can turn into real rivalries, particularly if the children are the same sex.[4] This is also a very common place to find a role reversal.

When it comes to the family constellation, a multiple birth is bound to cause pressure on anyone born above as well as anyone born below. Let's take a look at how this can work when twins arrive later, which is often the case because women in their forties are much more likely to have twins than women in their twenties.[5]

Family E
Female—12
Male—10
Males—7 and 7
Female—3

Here we have twins with a first-born female and a first-born male of the family above them. Those first borns can probably handle the special attention the twins are bound to attract, but that little sister at the bottom of the pack is going to have problems, even though she is supposedly the baby princess. At least she has a better chance than if she were a last-born boy. A last-born boy living under that seven-year-old "dynamic duo" would be even less special and he could become very discouraged while trying to compete for attention. Unless the parents became aware of what was happening, the twins could blow out their little brother's candle.

But pressure can come at the top of the family when a multiple birth occurs below. A graphic example of this occurred in November 1997 when septuplets were born to Bobbi and Kenny McCaughey of Carlisle, Iowa. The news reports revealed that the four girls and three boys had an older sister, Mikayla, who was twenty-one months old when they arrived and really didn't quite understand that all *seven* of them were coming home to stay. Talk about dethronement! You can bet your boots that little Mikayla soon started hearing the thundering hoofbeats of a stampede as all those little McCaugheys below her started claiming their share of the turf, and then some.

Shortly after the birth of the McCaughey septuplets, I had the pleasure of speaking to one set of grandparents (Bobbi's mother and father) during a *Parent Talk* show. Later during the show, we discussed how these septuplets were bound to dethrone their big sister. I suggested that when Bobbi and Kenny brought the "Magnificent Seven" home from the hospital, they needed to constantly remind Mikayla that: "You're a *big girl*. You take only one nap a day, but the babies have to take *this many* naps a day." One of the parents could hold up both hands—all ten fingers—to indicate for Mikayla that all her little brothers and sisters had to take ten naps a day— that's seventy naps!

Another obvious suggestion was that Mikayla be told that, because she is a big girl, she can be a helper and get diapers, powder, and other things for Mommy as she cares for all the babies.

I must say I will certainly be thinking a lot about the "oldest" of the McCaughey septuplets. While all of them were in the womb, little Kenneth Jr., the one nearest the cervical entrance, was literally "holding up all his brothers and sisters" because he was at the base of an inverted triangle that all of the babies formed inside the womb. Doctors nicknamed Kenneth "Hercules," not only because he had done a Herculean job in the womb, but because he was the largest of the septuplets at three pounds, four ounces, and was also first born. With all that going for little Kenneth before he ever appeared in this world, you can imagine the kind of expectations that may be placed on him.

Two Other Possible Variables: Deaths and Adoptions

Here are two examples of how death can affect birth order in a profound way: First, suppose a family has two sons and a daughter. At age four the older boy dies of spinal meningitis, leaving behind his two-year-old brother and six-month-old sister. The two year old takes over the firstborn role and grows up that way, while his little sister, who actually was born a baby of the family, grows up more as a first-born girl.

A second example: The oldest child in the family dies at age twelve in an automobile accident. His ten-year-old brother assumes the first-born role and is suddenly given first-born assignments and responsibilities. But is he really a first born? No, for ten years he grew up as a second born, content not to challenge his older brother for supremacy in the family. Now he is getting a lot of pressure that he really doesn't want.

Before the accident he had been in a fairly easy position because his older brother had been the ice cutter on the lake of life. All of a sudden older brother is gone and, while the trauma of losing him is bad enough, on top of that the second born suddenly feels as if the world is on his shoulders. He becomes the family STANDARD-BEARER; he has to live *his* life as well as his older brother's.

A classic illustration of this very scenario happened when Joseph Kennedy Jr. died at the controls of his bomber in World War II and his younger brother John had to become the family standard-bearer at the age of nineteen. For the rest of his life, even while in the White House, John Kennedy had to cope with the ghost of his older brother, Joe, who was the apple of their father's eye.

At seminars I'm sometimes asked, "How does adoption affect birth order?" The answer essentially is: It doesn't if the adoption occurs when the child is an infant. Today, however, many more people are adopting children who are a bit older—around three, four, five, and so on. Newly adoptive parents must keep in mind that a child adopted at age four has operated at a certain birth order level in whatever family he was part of before the adoption. Just because he may wind up to be the oldest or youngest in his new family, that doesn't necessarily make him a first born or a last born.

Also, there is another thing that adoptive parents need to watch out for, particularly if they are adding an adopted child to natural children already in the family. The obvious danger is to unconsciously favor a natural child over an adopted child. Also I advise parents not to adopt a child who is older than any natural children they may already have. The adopted "intruder" may have a negative effect on the child directly beneath him. For example, suppose a couple has a three-year-old natural child and they can have no more children of their own. So they adopt a five year old. What happens? Their three year old has just been knocked off his only-child mountaintop and now he has to contend with someone bigger and smarter. Always remember the principle, which applies in this case: Generally speaking, we are affected and influenced the most by whoever is directly above us in the family. When an older adopted child comes into a family, he or she is bound to collide with the natural child directly below in age.

As we have seen in this chapter, the typical birth order descriptions for onlies, first borns, middle children, and last borns can be modified or even flip-flopped by certain variables over which the children, and usually the parents, have no control.

3

What's Parenting Got to Do with It?

Birth Order Variables—Part 2

What's parenting got to do with altering birth order descriptions? A great deal.

So far, we have talked about birth order variables that have to do with the children—spacing, sex, physical or mental differences, multiple births, deaths, and adoptions. The parents of the children are also a major source of variables as well. In this chapter we will take a closer look at the birth order of the parents, the parent with the critical eye, parental values in general, and what happens in blended families. All of these factors are powerful variables that affect each child, particularly the first born or the only child.

Birth Order of Parents

Just how does Mom's or Dad's order of birth affect the children? One typical force at work is the tendency for a parent to overidentify with the child in the same birth order position he or she shares. This can lead to putting too much pressure on the child or spoiling or favoring the child.

To give you an example of the latter, in the 1970s I was an adjunct professor at the University of Arizona and was teaching a graduate class in child psychology. One morning we did a "family constellation demonstration" in front of two hundred students, most of whom were employed as teachers or counselors. I brought in a mother, a father, and three children and had an interesting time interacting with all of them in front of the class.

Afterward, when the family had gone, I asked the group for some feedback. Because the majority of those in the class were not neophytes but practicing professionals, I was curious about their reactions. There were different observations, but most of them agreed on one thing: "It seems as if you paid an awful lot of attention to the baby of the family—the four-year-old girl."

Without thinking too much about it, I said, "Yeah, wasn't she cute?" But then it hit me. Of course I thought the baby was cute! I had been the baby in my family too! I had made a career of being cute and funny all through school and beyond.

When I interacted with our first three children while they were growing up, whose antics did I enjoy the most? Kevin II, our baby, of course. For example, when Holly was thirteen and Krissy was eleven and they would come and complain about seven-year-old Kevey and his pestering ways, I would say, "Well, girls, let's remember he's the baby of the family. Little baby brothers do that kind of thing to sisters." I identified with Kevin and tended to favor him.

The Critical Eye Is Hard to Live Under

In my case, I was overidentifying with my last born in an indulging way, because, as a baby of the family myself, I loved to pester my older sister and brother when I was small. But let me be clear that overidentification can also be done in a nonindulgent, hard-line way, particularly when parents are both first born. This almost guarantees that the parents will have what I call "the critical eye." Instead of over-indulging their first-born child, they'll probably be extra hard on him or her as they exert their own exacting standards and learn how to parent at the same time. To show you what I mean, let's look at the following example:

Family F

Husband—first-born perfectionist dentist
Wife—first-born PTA president, known for getting
  people organized
Female—16
Female—14
Female—12

Who has the best spot in this family? Obviously it isn't the first-born girl for at least two reasons: First, she's the one Mom and Dad are going to have to practice on as far as parenting is concerned; second, she will have to perform under their critical perfectionistic eye.

The best position in the family could be the second-born girl because big sister has run interference for her to some extent and absorbed a lot of the perfectionistic energy that two first-born parents are likely to pour into their first child. But what about the baby of the family—the third-born girl? Will she be able to charm and manipulate her folks? That's doubtful because parents tend to identify with the child nearest them in birth order. Chances are the first-born dentist and his first-born PTA president–wife won't be too enamored with any baby-of-the-family preco-ciousness or manipulation.

What I hope is becoming very obvious to you is that in *any family* a lot depends on the personality and parenting style of Mom and Dad. If the parents are authoritarians who come down too hard and too unreasonably on their first born, they can turn her into a rebel who, instead of excelling in school as most first borns would, messes up just to foil the plans of her "perfect parents."

> In *any family* a lot depends on the personality and parenting style of Mom and Dad.

I have people call in to our show almost every week who tell me that they have this first born who isn't doing well in school at all. Often I can pinpoint the problem around mistakes the parents are making with that child. We'll talk more about authoritarian parenting style in chapter 13, as well as look at permissive parents and the happy medium, *authoritative* parenting, which uses reality discipline and a fair and reasonable approach.

For just one more look at how parenting style can make a real difference, let's consider Family G:

Family G
Female—10
Male—8

The key here is how Dad treats the ten-year-old daugh-ter and how Mom treats the eight-year-old son. Another key to any family is the cross-sexual relationships—Mom to son and Dad to daughter. If Mom pours too much into the ten-year-old daughter and doesn't have as much time for the eight-year-old boy, it will ensure that he'll be very different from big sister. It's very likely he'll take the role of first-born boy and be more aggressive, always ready to protect his turf.

But if Mom pays lots of attention to her younger son, he'll become more a baby of the family, fun-loving, affectionate, and probably understanding of women. If he has a healthy relationship with Mom—meaning that she is loving, kind, and gentle, but still does not take any guff from him—he will appreciate and respect women and be comfortable around them. As a rule, he will have an excellent chance to build a successful marriage.

But suppose the father has a critical eye and is very demanding and exacting. There is a good chance he could "destroy" his first-born daughter and his son will become the true first born in the family. First-born girls who grow up under a very perfectionistic, critical father are often hard on themselves and put themselves in situations that aren't healthy. When these first-born daughters grow up and marry, their husband pays the price for the sins of their wife's father.

What Made Lee Iacocca Run?

One of the most pervasive variables of all affecting birth order descriptions can be parental values, which can override almost everything else. Lee Iacocca of Ford and Chrysler fame is a good example. Lee is a second born with a sister, Delma, two years older. To understand him, however, you have to become acquainted with the values of the Iacocca parents—Italian immigrants who loved their children dearly but were always pushing them to "be the best you can be."

Lee was baby of the family but he was also first-born male and he got all kinds of pressure and prodding to perform, particularly from Dad. For example, Iacocca graduated twelfth in his class of more than nine hundred in high school, and what did Dad say? "Why weren't you *first?*" In his biography, Iacocca recalls, "To hear him describe it, you'd think I flunked!"[1]

This little anecdote sounds like a father who could ruin his son by always raising the bar too high but, fortunately, Iacocca and his dad were very close. Iacocca recalls:

> I loved pleasing him, and he was always terrifically proud of my accomplishments. If I won a spelling contest at school, he was on top of the world. Later in life, whenever I got a promotion, I'd call my father right away and he'd rush right out to tell all his friends. . . . In 1970, when I was named president of the Ford Motor Company, I don't know which of us was more excited.[2]

Later Iacocca was fired by Ford but he went on to mastermind a comeback from the dead for Chrysler. The values inculcated by his parents, particularly his father, gave him incredible resilience and steely resolve. Iacocca had style and all the tools to be a master CEO—aggressive, decisive, straightforward, compassionate, volatile, funny, and always someone who could tell it like it is. All of these traits can be traced right back to how a first-born son grew up in a loving Italian home in Allentown, Pennsylvania.

Lee Iacocca is only one example of the power of family values. The influence your family has on you as you grow up can reach across time and distance to touch you in profound and sometimes disturbing ways years after you think you've "grown beyond all that."

Another good example of how parental values had much to say about making a leader is Lute Olson. One of the most capable and successful college basketball coaches of

all time, Lute finally won it all when his Arizona Wildcats
took the NCAA crown in 1997.

When Lute came to the University of Arizona in 1984,
I noticed immediately that he was a natty dresser, with a
beautiful head of wavy white hair that was never out of
place. (Indeed, basketball fans may remember the moments just after Olson's team won the NCAA title in 1997.
His Wildcat players mussed his hair on national television!
For all I know, it was the first time anyone ever saw Lute
with messy hair, including his wife.)

So the telltale signs were there—Lute had to be a first
born and something of a perfectionist to boot. But while
Lute may look and act like a first born or only child, it
turns out he's really the baby of his family with three older
brothers!

Because I am a fervent Wildcat fan and have even served
as counselor to some U. of A. teams, I got to know Lute
and talked to him about how he simply didn't fit the pattern for his birth order. It turns out he got his meticulous
keep-things-organized-and-everything-in-its-place
approach to life from his Scandinavian parents. Lute grew
up on a farm where no excuses were accepted if you didn't
do your job. As Lute recalls, "You were expected to give
it your best shot."[3]

Blended Families

What happens when parents become stepparents? Another way to ask this question is, What happens when two
families blend because divorced or widowed parents
remarry? The answer is, *plenty!* The blended family variable can throw birth order (and the family) into chaos.
Through the years I have often commented to people contemplating remarriage, "Love is seldom lovelier the second time around." It's not that I'm cynical. As a coun-

selor, I can't be cynical but I am realistic, and the statistics on blended families are overwhelming.

In the '90s the divorce rate has hovered around 50 percent with odds being against or at best even for the survival of any marriage. But when you put a divorced mom and her kids together with a divorced dad and his brood, the odds get much larger. Sixty percent of second marriages fail.

And yet thirteen hundred new blended families form every day—and that's just in the United States. According to the Stepfamily Association of America, 40 percent of all marriages represent a remarriage of one or both parties. If remarriages continue at these rates, 35 percent of all children born will live in a stepfamily by the time they reach eighteen. As the third millennium approaches, one out of six children under the age of eighteen is a stepchild.[4]

On the nationally syndicated program for parents that I cohost, I often quote the equation: $E - R = D$ (expectations minus reality equals disillusionment). That little equation can apply to a lot of things in family living, but another equation I sometimes use fits blended families much more aptly: $N \times R = C$ (naïveté times reality equals chaos).

As one woman who married a father of two said, "The situation is just impossible. People go into these marriages with no idea of what is involved, and it's like falling off a cliff. There is never enough money to go around. . . ."[5] Not only is money short, so is time, energy, and patience. There is an old joke that applies all too well to stepfamilies:

Question: What's green and goes 100 MPH?
Answer: A frog in a blender.

It is not too much to say that one reason that blending a family is like putting a frog in a blender is because you are blending the birth orders of the children involved. One woman remarried and ended up with five children instead of her original two. She told me, "We went through months of premarital counseling, but it didn't prepare us for being a blended family. Until you live with someone every day, you and your children with him and his children, all together under the same roof, you don't know what you're going to cope with."

This woman was being brutally frank because she knew something about the brutal facts. To handle first borns, middle borns, and last borns in one family is challenging enough. But bring two families together into a *Brady Bunch* or *Eight Is Enough* setting, and things get complicated (usually chaotic) in a hurry.

And speaking of *The Brady Bunch* and *Eight Is Enough,* the writers of these popular TV shows, which still appear in reruns, created a plastic package where crises and problems always seemed to get solved neatly and easily as everyone continued to "blend happily ever after." In truth, people in a stepfamily seldom "just blend"—they collide.

I often tell people contemplating remarriage, "In a stepfamily you can get stepped on." But they go ahead anyway, sure that it will be "different for us." One of their most naive expectations is that there will be "instant love" among all members of the stepfamily. But instead of experiencing instant love, these stepparents acquire instant children and instant problems.

Men and women who are remarrying should first ask themselves, "Have we fallen in love, or have we fallen in need?" It is typical for people who have divorced or lost spouses in another way to say to each other, "You have two kids, I have one—why don't we get married and it will be easier for all of us." When it doesn't become easier but harder, they wonder why.

Men and women who are remarrying must stand shoulder to shoulder or they can easily disintegrate because of the simple factor of "length of relationships." There may be exceptions, but the relationship between remarried spouses is usually two years old at the most when they retie the knot. The relationship those spouses have had with their children is usually much longer. Is it reasonable to believe that a two-year-old relationship between a husband and wife who have remarried is going to outweigh parent/child relationships that have usually been in existence for several years at least, and in some cases, ten to fifteen years or more? To paraphrase the old saying: Blood in biological families is thicker than the punch served at the remarriage ceremony.

Granted, when children in a blended family are very young, Mom and Dad have a better chance. Suppose stepsisters, ages one and three, join stepbrothers, ages two and four. All their personalities are still in the formative stage and time is on the parents' side. But make those children a little older—beyond age five when the personality is formed—and instead of having instant love and harmony, what you can easily have is instant war!

Birth Orders Don't Change

The key to understanding how friction can develop in a blended family is to know that once the grain of the wood (the personality) is set after age five or six, every birth order is set as well. In other words, the first born is always a first born, a middle child is always a middle child, and so on. Blended families do not create new birth order positions. Because one first born suddenly has a stepbrother or sister who is older, that doesn't mean that first born stops being typically conscientious, structured, well organized, or perfectionist.

By the same token, a last born isn't suddenly going to change his personality because a divorce and remarriage make him a middle child in the family. He'll still lean toward being a show-off, an attention seeker, a manipulator, a charmer, and a little clown who likes to have fun, even though Mom and Dad would now like him to take on more responsibility.

So the key to the blended birth order game is this: When a child who is born into one birth order lands on another limb in his blended family tree, do not treat that child as something he is not. He may have to take on different responsibilities and play different roles at times, but never push or force him; never forget who he really is.[6]

Let's go down through the different birth orders and see what happens when they get "repositioned" in blended families. First, we'll take a blended family that winds up with almost all first borns in one way or another:

Family H

Mother—special jewel only child	Father—first-born perfectionist
Male—15	Male—16
Female—13	Male—14
Female—9	

According to what we've already learned about birth order and spacing, here we have a blended family whose name might be The Armageddons. Why? Because the family contains seven people with first-born characteristics. And at the top of the heap we have a father who is a perfectionistic first born who will be very demanding and critical of not only his own children but his stepchildren. And just for fun we've added in a mother who was a special jewel only child and will probably be extra sensitive about having things her way.

You don't have to go much deeper into this family to see how tension could arrive from many directions. There is bound to be natural rivalry between the two males at the top who are fifteen and sixteen. And the same could be true of the second-born female, thirteen, and second-born male, fourteen, who could easily vie for supremacy in their second-born roles.

What parents must remember is that these kids have nothing in common. Just seeing each other reminds them of something very hurtful—the divorce and separation from one of their parents. Before the stepfamily was formed, they were used to "making the calls." Now, if there is an ax to grind, they can easily find reason for doing so in each other. After a bad day at school, if all else fails, you can always pick on your no-good stepbrother or stepsister.

Another way the two oldest males may lock horns is if the mother's first born happens to be a "neat freak" who keeps his room clean (such things have been known to happen). He winds up having to share a room with his fifteen-year-old stepbrother, who is not that concerned about neatness and, in true first-born style, doesn't like surprises. What happens when the neat stepbrother decides he's had enough of a sloppy room and he cleans up the place and "puts a few things away"? What can we say? One word: Armageddon!

So what can stepparents do in the blended family when all these tensions and frictions arise? One recommendation I have made to many blended families is to run the family much like a small corporation. I urge them to have regular meetings where they all sit down and discuss the question, How does my behavior in this family affect all the other members of the family? And on top of that, If my behavior is causing problems, how can I change it?

But are all blended families with several first borns doomed to despair? Not necessarily. Let's look at one more schematic:

Family I

Father—amiable middle child	Mother—hard-driving first born
Male—14	Female—9
Female—12	Male—7
	Female—4

This family could have some problems, but not as many as Family H above. The oldest male on Dad's side is "king of the hill" in the new blended family and he's always gotten along quite well with his sister, two years younger. She is the first-born female of the family and has carved her own path quite nicely. Over on Mom's side, the nine-year-old female isn't going to challenge her fourteen-year-old stepbrother, and the seven year old (first-born male) is certainly not going to either. All in all, this family has a good chance of making it. If she plays her cards right, the little four year old on Mom's side may just be able to charm her older stepbrother and stepsister into treating her like baby princess.

That's not to say that there aren't some possible problems that could arise. For example, the twelve year old on Dad's side has been baby of the family all her life and, depending on how much her dad has spoiled her, she may or may not resent the three new "babies," all younger than she, who have suddenly moved in. And on Mom's side the oldest female has been ruling the roost in her family for as long as she can remember and suddenly she has been pressed into middle-child territory. She probably won't even think about taking on her fourteen-year-old stepbrother but if she's a feisty first born, she may decide the twelve-year-old stepsister is worth a try, especially if the girls have to share a room.

Blending Later Borns Is No Bargain Either

While trouble often arises in a blended family with first borns bumping heads, plenty of friction can occur down below as well. Let's look at how two later-born people got together and created a blended Brady Bunch:

Family J

Father—nonconfrontive middle child
Female—13
Female—10
Male—7

Mother—last-born baby princess
Male—14
Female—11
Male—8

Let's set aside for the moment the obvious friction at the top with the oldest female and the oldest male squaring off for king or queen of the hill. If they are both aggressive first borns, watch out! One or both of them, however, could be compliant first borns and that would make things easier.

What I want us to focus on here are the kids down below. The one in the worst position in this whole blended family is the ten year old on Dad's side. She has always been sandwiched between an older sister and a seven-year-old prince below her, so she's always felt the typical middle-child squeeze. Now all of a sudden, she has three more people to contend with, two of whom are older, so the squeeze gets even tighter.

On Mom's side, the one in the best position in the entire blended family is the second-born girl. She's always been the only girl in her original family, so she brings to the table a very positive attitude about herself and life in general. The bad news, however, is that she may resent the other two females—her stepsisters—and there can be lots of tension there.

The child the eleven-year-old girl may get along with best, strangely enough, is the seven-year-old stepbrother. This may be the case if she has always had her problems with her own brothers and still has an unfulfilled need to "mother" someone. These two could form what is called an "alliance" and get along very well.

Note that down at the bottom of this blended heap, we have two little guys vying for the title of crown prince (or maybe it's clown prince). Both of these babies have been used to the limelight and having things their way. Now they've got to share that limelight and there could be trouble. It would seem that there is room for only one baby in this family, so who will it be? The obvious choice is the youngest one of all—the seven year old on Dad's side. But that won't sit well with the eight year old on Mom's side. So both parents will need to work together to be sure that both of these "babies of the family" get their share of attention.

Note, too, the birth orders of the two parents. Dad is a nonconfrontive middle child and Mom was a last-born baby princess herself. That means that Dad has a contradiction working in his middle-child personality. Even though he may have learned some mediating and negotiating skills while growing up, he has decided on a life-style that is nonconfrontive because that's what makes him more comfortable. This means he won't want to do much mediating and negotiating with the children, so that leaves it to Mom. Mom is a last born who may have had a long history of being spoiled and wanting things her way. This will certainly spill over into wanting advantages and fair treatment for "her kids" instead of for "his kids."

Do you start to get a little better picture of why the blended family can become a blender in a hurry? If any blended family is going to make it, Mom and Dad need to follow this advice: Put yourselves first and the children second.

> **Put yourselves first and the children second.**

Birth Order Is Part of a Bigger Picture

This short course on the workings of what I call the family zoo is designed to tell you only one thing: When birth order is mixed with certain variables, you get a unique individual. In other words, birth order is not some cookie-cutter process that says first borns will all march in lock step this way, middle children will universally do something different, and last borns will all be like this or that. All birth order can do is give you some clues.

I have covered the most important birth order variables to help you understand just how birth order works. It is not "hard science" that can be measured in a test tube or computed to the tenth power with mathematical formulas. The variables, such as when the child is born or the child's sex, give birth order a subjective side. And additional variables, such as the values taught the child by the parents—who are certain birth orders themselves—come into play. It all combines to make a unique individual, who will *probably* have certain characteristics typical of his or her birth order, *but not necessarily.*

If I accomplished anything in the first three chapters, I hope I convinced you that in any family, a person's order of birth has a lifelong effect on who and what that person turns out to be.

> **In any family, a person's order of birth has a lifelong effect on who and what that person turns out to be.**

Despite my explanations about variables, over the years I have faced critics of all kinds. Professional colleagues as well as laypeople have on occasion assured me that birth order is only good for parlor games and that it has no real use in helping people figure out their lives. People attending my seminars come up to me from time to time to point out that "birth order doesn't work for them." But once I have a chance to explain the variables and just how certain factors work in individual families, they usually come around and see my point.

Professional colleagues, however, are tougher nuts to crack. Because everything does not always fit perfectly and consistently into neat statistical data banks, these scholars have turned their sixteen-inch guns on birth order, declaring that it is of little more value than the discredited science of phrenology (figuring out someone's personality according to the bumps on his or her head).[7]

In the early 1980s, a pair of Swiss psychologists—Cecile Ernst and Jules Angst—reviewed the results from two thousand birth order research projects and concluded that most of them had been done without enough controls on all the factors involved. They published a book on their studies, and at the end concluded *". . . birth order influences on personality and IQ have been widely overrated"* (emphasis theirs).[8]

A lot of my contemporaries jumped on the Ernst and Angst bandwagon and began saying things like you can "overinterpret the importance of birth order"[9] and birth order ". . . is significant only in families with more than seven children."[10]

Despite the Critics, I Know Birth Order Works

Since the 1980s I have used birth order theory with great success in counseling hundreds of couples and their children. In no case that I have handled in more than twenty-five years of psychological practice has birth order not applied to a substantial degree. That is not to say that birth order explains everything but it has always proved to be a helpful tool that my clients can understand and apply to their lives. So I have never let the carping of critics bother me as I have continued to use the theory of birth order to help people from every walk of life.

It's been gratifying—and a lot of fun—to get so many positive statements and even "testimonials" on the power of understanding birth order and the practical help in *The Birth Order Book*. One gracious woman, whose adult daughter was hospitalized due to a terrible auto accident that left her temporarily blind, told me personally that as she read aloud to her daughter from *The Birth Order Book*, not only did it make her laugh, but it helped her feel special and seemed to aid in her recovery. For the first time she really understood that she is one of a kind. Seeing her unique place among her siblings helped her make more sense of her family.

And I will never forget the letter I received from a man who runs a beautiful vacation resort in the Northeast. He invited my entire family and me to spend a month with him, compliments of the house, because of what he learned in *The Birth Order Book*. He wrote: "I spent hours in psychiatrists' offices trying to find out why my brother and I were so different. Then I picked up your book in an airport. By the time I landed, I had the answer."

The answer that he discovered was that, as the first born in his family, he had pursued a typical career: a financial consultant, detailed, precise, accurate—even a writer of financial manuals. His second-born, baby of the family brother was carefree, changed jobs at will, and couldn't save money because he was a big-time spender. People kept asking the older brother, "Why can't your younger brother shape up and be more like you?" *The Birth Order Book* gave him an explanation that made sense.

Birth Order Works for Businessmen Too

I get a lot of positive feedback on my birth order theory from the business world. One of my converts is Mike
Lorelli, a former Pepsico division president, who has also
held top posts at Pizza Hut and Tambrands, Inc. Lorelli,
a second child who "bumped heads" with an older brother
and came out on top in something of a role reversal,
became a believer when he read *The Birth Order Book* while
on a business trip. He contacted me and offered an invi-
tation to speak to a group of his top executives, which I
did with gratifying results.

Today, as a much sought-after business consultant, Mike
still orders *The Birth Order Book* by the case and distrib-
utes it to employees and clients. When I asked him why
he thought it was such a useful tool, he told me:

> Everybody who is important to me was born. And when
> you think about it that way, you can use birth order to cat-
> egorize people and try to figure out what's the best way
> to motivate your customers, suppliers, consumers, bosses,
> peers—whoever.
>
> In business it's not only I.Q. that matters; it's not nec-
> essarily great transactions that matter, but there are a lot
> of "softer sides" that can make a difference between suc-
> cess and failure. Birth order is one of those. It has, for
> example, helped me win people over and make them allies
> on my team to help keep the ship afloat.[11]

I believe Mike Lorelli is right when he talks about birth
order being one of the "softer sides" that can spell the dif-
ference between business success and failure. That's why
I do much of my speaking in such settings as the IBM
School of Management, the Williams Companies, Pepsi,
Pizza Hut, and Cincinnati Financial Insurance Company.
I've also talked to The Million Dollar Round Table, The

Top of the Table, and The Young Presidents Organization where salaries hit well over a million and more.

I love getting up to address a group of jaded vice presidents and sales managers who sit there, arms and legs akimbo, their body language saying in no uncertain terms, And *what* have they sent us *this* time? But a few minutes later the arms and legs relax, and blank faces light up as these high-powered business types get a handle on why it's so important to understand your own birth order as well as the birth order of people you have to deal with.

I also treasure a letter from Bruce Dingman, president of the Dingman Company, which specializes in finding the right executive for the right company. This letter says:

> About six years ago I read *The Birth Order Book* and since then I've used it as instructions and signs to watch for when trying to understand candidates for positions I am trying to fill. I don't assume someone has to be just as the book suggests, but I watch for the tendencies to be so. . . . Thank you for the wisdom you impart in your books.[12]

Michael C. Feiner, former senior vice president at Pepsico Europe, also has used birth order when filling positions in his firm. Here's what he told me about how he uses birth order when questioning a prospective employee:

> I usually ask one last question: "Can you tell me about your personal background—parents, siblings?" Then I just listen as tons of information begin to pour from the candidate. . . . Because getting things done in a large complex organization is so dependent on relationships, I probe quite extensively about family relationships and how the candidate carved out his/her own turf with his/her family.[13]

For more on how birth order principles apply to business, see chapter 10, as well as my book *Winning the Rat Race without Becoming a Rat*.

In Research, What Goes Around Comes Around

I share these testimonials to illustrate just how valuable birth order theory is in the practical world despite what some research critics say. But you know, it's a funny thing about scholars and research. What goes around usually does come around.

It was very gratifying (but not really surprising) when a scholarly, but very readable book came out in 1996 containing overwhelming statistical evidence that birth order theory does have credence and validity. That book was written by Frank Sulloway, a research scholar in the science technology and society program at the Massachusetts Institute of Technology. After twenty-six years of research on birth order, Sulloway published his findings in *Born to Rebel: Birth Order Family Dynamics and Creative Lives.*

Using an approach he calls "meta-analysis" (essentially the combining of many research studies by use of the computer), Sulloway amassed up to one million biographical points of information on more than 6,500 people who have lived during the last five hundred years. Included were 3,890 scientists who took part in twenty-eight scientific revolutions. Sulloway also studied hundreds of people involved in the French Revolution and the Protestant Reformation, as well as participants in sixty-one American reform movements.[14]

The bottom line to all of Sulloway's mental toil (it makes this baby of the family tired just to think about it) is this: Down through history first borns have been the ones who were conservative and willing to stick to the status quo and tradition, while later borns were the ones who wanted to change things and even start revolutions. According to Sulloway (who is a later born himself), later borns are more open-minded than first borns. They are "born to rebel," willing to take risks and do away with sacred cows. None of Sulloway's findings concerning the characteristics of first borns and later borns were news to me. They fit right in with what I've been saying for more than twenty-five years.

One area where I do not agree with Sulloway, however, is his contention that sibling rivalry is really based on Darwin's theory of survival of the fittest. Siblings use different strategies to compete with each other and in this way they secure their place or niche in the family and survive growing up. As Sulloway puts it, "Seen in evolutionary terms, the diverse features of personality represent different strategies for maximizing parental investment and getting out of childhood alive."[15]

Whether or not Sulloway is correct about evolution being a cause for sibling rivalry in humans is extremely arguable. Personally I believe that God created all of us in his own image and put his individual stamp on every one of us. For me, birth order is part of the explanation of why we are all so different. I repeat, it isn't the total explanation, but it is a part. Each of us is an individual, one of a kind; there are no duplicates of any of us. Even identical twins have different fingerprints.

Despite Sulloway's debatable theories about sibling rivalry and evolution, I do believe he has done a masterful job in coming to grips with the critics who claim that birth order is all hocus-pocus and worthless speculation. And what, you may ask, did Sulloway do about high-powered critics like Ernst and Angst who concluded that birth order didn't have a whole lot to do with personality development?

Sulloway went over the two thousand studies that Ernst and Angst had analyzed and learned that they had not been totally accurate in saying that all of them were flawed due to poor controls. Sulloway found 196 birth order projects involving 120,000 subjects where research *had been controlled in all areas*. When Sulloway analyzed these studies, he found birth order theory to be confirmed impressively, particularly in regard to last borns being nonconforming, adventuresome, and unconventional; and first borns being conscientious, responsible, and achievement-oriented.[16] If you'd like to know a little more about Sulloway's work and reactions to it pro and con, see appendix B.

4

First Come, First Served

A Closer Look at First Borns

*i*t's time to take a closer look at first borns—officially defined as oldest in the family. But don't forget the variables we just covered in chapters 2 and 3. First-born personalities can also be created by being oldest of your sex, having a five-year gap between you and the child above you of the same sex, or achieving a role reversal and taking over the first-born privileges and responsibilities. For the most part in this chapter we'll look at the first born who is oldest in the family, keeping in mind that other children born later can take on certain first-born traits.

If you are a first born (or an only child),[1] you are a much different person than you would have been had you been born later. If you are a later born, realize that a lot of things would be different—and so would you—had you been born first.

The "Four Corner" Birth Order Exercise

During family and parenting seminars, I use a favorite little "lab exercise" to help people get in touch with their birth order characteristics. At the same time, the exercise helps me get a better handle on the people I'm working with and how I can help them the most. Here's how it works:

I ask all seminar participants to join one of four groups: Only children in one corner, first borns in a second, middle borns in a third, and last borns go over in a far corner where they won't bother anyone but themselves. At this point I tell all four groups, "Just chat a bit but remain in your circle."

Then I move from one group to another and, as casually as possible, I leave a piece of paper in the center of each group, face down, containing identical instructions: "Congratulations! You are the leader of this group. Please introduce yourself to the others in your group, and then have each person do the same. As you talk together, make a list of personality characteristics that you all seem to share. Be prepared to report back to the rest of the seminar with your 'composite picture' of yourselves. Please start work immediately."

I return to the front of the room and all the groups keep waiting for me to give some kind of verbal instructions, but I say nothing. Instead, I pretend to look busy as I leaf through papers, waiting for "birth order nature" to take its course. Who will pick up the piece of paper first? Almost invariably, a person in the only-born and first-born groups picks up the paper and reads the instructions. Someone in the middle-born group soon follows suit. In no time, three groups in the room are busy with their assignments.

Oh yes, the fourth group? The last borns are usually still milling around, their piece of paper lying on the floor unread.

I wait a few minutes and make one more announcement: "You have only a few more minutes to finish your assignment. Be ready to report to the rest of the group at that time!"

The only borns and first borns look up like startled deer and then redouble their efforts to finish the assigned task. While the middles don't look quite as impressed, they do try to press on toward the finish. The last borns, however, are usually having such a good time they don't even hear what I said.

I recall one seminar when the babies all milled around in the far corner, their circle resembling a figure eight more than anything else. One man wound up standing on the piece of paper that I placed in the center of his circle, as totally oblivious to the proceedings as all the other last borns in his group.

Because I'm a last born myself, I am not trying to make fun of the babies of the family. No doubt if I were put through the same exercise, I'd be the guy standing on the piece of paper! But in the hundreds of times I've conducted this exercise, I can remember only one or two cases when the first person to pick up the piece of paper and start "obeying instructions" did *not* come from the first- or only-born circles.

Even the reports from the four groups bear out the classic birth order traits: The first borns report that a definite leader took charge. Among the confident only children, a power struggle often ensues over who will take charge but is finally settled. Of all the groups, the middle children probably enjoy the exercise the most as they get to know each other, have little trouble negotiating who will be leader, and do their assignment with no problem. As for the babies, what can I say? Life is a beach!

Everybody Has to Deal with First Borns

If you recall the little quiz you took in chapter 1, several typical characteristics of first- or only-born people are borne out in my lab exercise: They tend to be conscientious, well organized, serious, goal oriented, achieving, people pleasers, and believers in authority.

And when you add other signs of first borns and onlies, such as perfectionist, reliable, list maker, critical, scholarly, self-sacrificing, conservative, supporter of law and order, legalistic, and self-reliant, you can see why first borns usually get more ink in the write-ups of life. First borns are often the achievers because they are driven toward success and stardom in their given fields.

The world cannot ignore the first borns. If you aren't one, you have to deal with them somewhere along the line. It may have started early when your older first-born brother or sister wound up as your baby-sitter, something that didn't necessarily sit well with either of you. On the other hand, some first borns become the guardian and protector of their younger brothers or sisters. That's what happened with me. My first-born sister, Sally, eight years older, often went out of her way to care for her baby brother.

For example, when I started kindergarten I cried for the first two weeks because they had me in the afternoon session and I had to get to school by myself—a scary proposition for the little Cub. Sally couldn't take me because she was in school herself and my mom wasn't available because she was working as a superintendent of a convalescent home for children. We weren't your classic *Leave It to Beaver* family, which was so prevalent in those days. It seemed I was the only kid in the neighborhood whose mom worked and I still have a scar on my knuckle, which I cut on some kid's tooth when he teased me about it. After two weeks of hearing me sniffle, the kindergarten teacher relented and switched me to mornings so that big sister Sally could bring me to school.

One of my early memories is sitting on her bike, barely making the pedals turn because my legs weren't long enough, as Sally and her friend Martha walked beside me for over a mile, helping me steer.

Sally was always sacrificing for me. I'll never forget the time when I was about eight and Sally and I took the bus from our home to the Buffalo city limits, eight miles away. Our destination was a low-budget department store called W. T. Grants, which had a luncheonette. Sally offered to treat me to whatever I wanted and, as I looked at the menu, I saw hamburgers for thirty cents and turkey sandwiches for eighty cents. We seldom got real sliced turkey at our house, and my mouth watered.

"Can I have the turkey sandwich?" I asked.

"Of course you can. I'm treating," said Sally as she dug into her hard-earned baby-sitting money.

I have never forgotten how good that sandwich tasted and how she spent what was then "big bucks" to make me happy.

Sally also used to throw little tea parties with me as the honored guest. In the summers we'd have them on our lawn; in the winters we would stay inside, but summer or winter Sally did make her baby brother do something to help with the party. I had to make a one-mile round trip to Hildebrand's store on foot to get the goodies for the party, which were always the same: Pepsi and potato chips.

Now that we're adults, Sally still goes out of her way for her little brother. Every fall, after we have returned to Tucson for the coming school session, she goes out to our summer house on Chautauqua Lake, not far from her home in Jamestown, New York, and covers all the furniture for the winter.

There Are Two Kinds of First Borns

The Compliant Nurturers and Caregivers

Sally, you see, has always been what is called a "compliant first born." She wants to please. Because I have been painting first borns with some pretty broad brush strokes as organized, goal oriented, achievers, critical, and so on, you may think they are basically all bossy types who want to run the show. Many first borns do fit the description of "strong willed and aggressive." But there are plenty of first borns who are compliant—they're the model children who grew up to be pleasers of others. They still have all those first-born qualities, but they're always in a very reliable, conscientious, how-can-I-please-you? package.

Compliant first borns tend to be good students and good workers because they started out with a very strong need for Mom and Dad's approval. Then, of course, they need the approval of other authority figures: teachers, coaches, bosses. When asked to do something, their response is, "Yes, Mom . . . Yes, Dad . . . Yes, Sir . . . I'll be glad to do it." Who doesn't want a few children or employees like that around?

A classic example of a compliant first born is my wife, Sande. I have often shared the story of when we were at a five-star restaurant in Tucson and our meal had been served in the usual impeccable and precise manner. As I ate with gusto, I glanced over at Sande. She was simply picking around the edges of her poached salmon.

"How's your dinner?" I asked. "Does everything taste okay?"

"Oh . . . yes. Everything's great. Isn't this one of the nicest restaurants you could ever ask for?"

I went back to eating, but Sande continued picking and not really getting into that poached salmon. Finally I voiced my suspicions: "Honey, tell me, is your salmon really done to your liking?"

"Well . . . it's really not quite cooked in the middle . . ."

Actually, the "poached salmon" was so raw it should have still been swimming upriver to spawn. As a baby of the family, compliance had never been one of my strong suits. I quickly let the waiter know the condition of the salmon, and he as well as the maître d' and chef were horrified. In no time, an entirely new serving of salmon appeared, cooked to perfection. And a little later, the chef sent out a "peace offering" in the form of a giant baked Alaska dessert, "compliments of the house with apologies to Madam for the inconvenience."

The story of the uncooked salmon nicely illustrates Sande's "I'd-rather-not-complain-about-it-but-just-grin-and-bear-it" nature. Like my sister, Sally, Sande is a pleaser, a nurturer, and a caregiver, all classic characteristics of the compliant first born. And if you're thinking that Cubby Bear Leman was lucky to have two women like that in his life, you are absolutely right!

The downside of being a compliant first born is that you can attract the great white sharks of life. I often counsel compliant first borns who are getting chunks taken out of them by a spouse, a boss, or friends. The classic scenario includes a compliant first born working in middle management for a superintendent or manager who has a way of "piling on the work." As he drops little projects on this first born's desk, he also manages to mention that "evaluations are coming up soon."

While having a wife and four kids at home to feed and clothe is an obvious motivation, an even bigger one for the compliant first born is that psychological hammer that has been pounding on him ever since childhood. He's always been the responsible one that had to get everything done—take out the garbage, mow the lawn, wash the dishes—because his brothers and sisters were too little or perhaps undependable. Parents have a way of relying on (and taking advantage of) their first-born child. I call it the "let-Ryan-the-first-born-do-it syndrome."

Many other such scenarios could quickly be sketched. Team up the compliant first born with a selfish, narcissistic, or insensitive boss or spouse and you have the making of trouble in River City in a hurry. Compliant first borns are well known for taking it and being walked on by a world that loves to take advantage of them. They are also known for nursing their resentments quietly, and then venting with one grand explosion. And that's usually when they come to see me.

Aggressive First Borns Are the Movers and Shakers

While compliant first borns have a strong need to be conscientious, caregiving servants, there is another brand of first born who is assertive, strong willed, a high achiever, and a hard driver. These assertive first borns set high goals and have a strong need to be "king or queen pin." And along the way, they often develop badgerlike qualities— in other words, they can scratch, claw, and bite.

One classic example of the hard-driving, assertive first born is the executive who goes around uptight and immersed in his or her work for fifty weeks a year. Then, while on a two-week vacation, this same executive becomes a new person. I have had wives tell me, "When we go on vacation, Harry is just great. He relaxes and lets go. He's almost normal with the kids and with me. But about *two* days before vacation is over, he gets his game face back. Even before we get home, his old hard-driving personality is in high gear."

In recent years a growing part of my practice has included conducting seminars for groups of corporate executives. I make it a point to do a little surveying to see just how well first borns are represented in these groups. In one CEO organization, nineteen of the twenty attendees were first borns. In a meeting of the Young Presidents organization, some twenty-three of the twenty-six dynamic young men and women present told me they were first borns in their family.

First Borns Love to Be Exacting, Precise—and Picky

While some first borns become powerful leader types, others stay in the background doing exacting work like editing, bookkeeping, and accounting. Over the years while doing more than twenty books, I have had twelve editors, all first borns or only children with one exception. He turned out to be the second-born male in his family who had done a role reversal on his older brother and was, in effect, a functional first born.

Being a baby of the family, I deeply appreciate editors and what they can do to save me from disaster. But I really don't know much about them except that they love red pencils and ask lots of picky questions, such as, "What is this sentence that starts on page 33 and ends on page 35?"[2]

One of the most striking examples I ever saw regarding first borns and exacting professions occurred when I spoke to the Ohio Society of Accountants. After being introduced, I stood looking at 221 accountants, who were either giving me baleful stares or glancing at their watches. Deciding I needed to loosen them up a bit, I said, "Will all of you first borns and only children please rise." I wasn't too surprised when almost the entire room stood up! So I asked those who hadn't stood to stand up next and in that small group we counted nineteen middle children and last borns. Before letting them sit down, I had one more question: "What are *you* doing *here?*"

Everybody roared with laughter and had the evening ended right there it would have been a success. It isn't often that you can get more than two hundred accountants to smile, much less laugh aloud!

Accountants take their jobs seriously. In fact many a CEO will tell you that a company rises or falls, based on how careful a "bean counter" they have. Harvey Mackay, chairman and CEO of Mackay Envelope Corporation and author of many best-sellers on business including *Swim with the Sharks without Being Eaten Alive* believes that the first person you need to hire (after yourself) is a good accountant.[3] Mackay, first-born male in his family, could have specified a *first-born* accountant.

I had occasion to interview Mackay, and his powerful aggressiveness came out immediately. First borns are typically analytical and love to ask questions. My interview with Mackay occurred on the telephone and, while I couldn't see him, I quickly became convinced I was talking to a first born. After ten minutes he was still asking me the questions, and I was the one who was supposed to be conducting the interview![4]

Which Smothers Brother Is the Oldest?

You can find first borns as leaders in all kinds of situations. For example, if I asked you to name one of the Mandrell sisters, chances are excellent you will think of Barbara, and there is a good reason for that: She's the oldest, resourceful, outgoing, and definitely the leader. Few people mention Louise or "the other one"—Earlene.

Among contemporary actors working today are the four Baldwin brothers. Which one can you name? It's probably Alec, who is, of course, the oldest.

What about the Smothers Brothers? Did you think of Tommy? That's not surprising because he's the oldest even if he does act like a hypersensitive baby while on stage. My wife, Sande, and I have had dinner with the Smothers Brothers, and let me assure you, Tommy is the real leader of this duo. In fact Dickie confided that he had moved to the other end of the country just to get away from Tommy's "controlling nature." I looked at Tommy and he just smiled.

Here's one more example of two brothers—the ones who are credited with making the first successful flight in an airplane. If I asked you to name one of the Wright Brothers, the odds are well in favor of your saying, Wilbur. Strange, but he was the oldest by four years.

Among those 56 percent of U.S. presidents who have been first borns or functional first borns, there was Jimmy Carter, a serious, studious, overachieving governor of Georgia who out-and-out worked his way to the presidency of the United States. And standing in stark contrast to Jimmy was his baby brother, Billy, who got his own share of the spotlight for his beer drinking and rude, off-the-cuffs remarks, many of which were designed to embarrass his big brother.

First Borns Often Put Stress on Their Family

Outstanding leaders and achievers they may be, but hard-driving first borns often pay the price. If their bodies don't break down, relationships with family or friends usually do. I doubt if it's a coincidence that Lee Iacocca, one of the most capable and successful CEO's who ever lived, has had three divorces. In fact it's practically a birth order rule of thumb, particularly for first borns: The very traits and abilities that enable you to succeed at work, at church, or in other organizations will often work against you in your close personal relationships.

> The very traits and abilities that enable you to succeed at work, at church, or in other organizations will often work against you in your close personal relationships.

While on an American Airlines flight, I was fortunate enough to sit across the aisle from Robert Crandall, former chairman of the board and president of American Airlines. As we got acquainted, I learned that he was a first born, which didn't surprise me at all because of his well-known, hard-driving, levelheaded leadership abilities.

Later I had the opportunity to interview Crandall for a book I was writing for businesspeople called *Winning the Rat Race without Becoming a Rat*. When I asked him what he thought of the maxim, "Put your spouse first," he responded: "Yes, that's true. On the other hand, you have to have a spouse who recognizes that the number of times she can ask to be first is limited." He went on to say that putting one's spouse first doesn't have much to do with business, that it's more of a "personal values set" than a "business values set."

And there lies the rub. Trying to separate business from the family often results in the family getting the short end of the stick.[5]

Because I fly so much, I make it a habit to do informal surveys of airline pilots regarding their birth order. Because flying is such an exacting task that demands "perfection," it doesn't surprise me that pilots usually come up first born. In fact out of ninety-eight men and two women, my informal survey revealed that 88 percent were first borns or only children. On a recent United Airlines flight, the captain came out of the cockpit and came down the aisle greeting passengers, including me. So I asked him, "How is the first-born captain doing today?"

He gave me the strangest look and said, "Have we met?"

"No, but you *are* a first born, aren't you?"

"Well, yes, I am," he said, and in less than five minutes we were talking about a lot more than what a lovely day it was in the friendly skies. As the tears rolled down his cheeks, he told me about his third wife serving him with divorce papers. He was one of the best in the high-stress business called flying but at home he had crashed three times.

Sometimes the hard-driving first-born personality can go beyond neglecting family or friends and go all the way to the ultimate tragedy. Do you remember Cain, the first murderer in recorded history, according to the Old Testament? I referred to him and his brother Abel in the preface. Cain thought his sacrifice was every bit as good or better than Abel's. But God didn't and wouldn't accept it because it was the "fruit of the ground." Cain lured Abel out into the fields and killed him (see Gen. 4:3–8). When the first born, who is a goal-oriented achiever, starts thinking, "Winning is everything," he can shove aside values like being law abiding, loyal, or self-sacrificing. Instead, he will do anything to win.

What Makes the First Born Tick?

Whether compliant or powerful and assertive, there are at least two good reasons why first borns come in such downright upright (and often a little uptight) packages. Those two reasons are Mom and Dad. Oldest children serve as "guinea pigs" for parents who have never done this kind of thing before. Brand new parents are typically a bundle of ambivalence, one side overprotective, anxious, tentative, and inconsistent; the other side strict, disciplined, demanding, always pushing, and encouraging better performance.

Everything about a first-born child is important. While little Festus or Mildred is still on the way, the very air is charged with expectancy in more ways than one. With grand anticipation, young parents celebrate with baby showers, picking out names, choosing wallpaper for the nursery, buying baby clothes and toys. (And if the parents are first borns or only borns themselves, add to that list starting piggy banks, insurance policies, and college funds.)

Few will deny that the family sort of overdoes things with the first born. Parents, as well as grandparents, record every cry, look, whim, or move with a video camera or they're sure to fill the family photo album with dozens (hundreds) of pictures. Research indicates first borns walk and talk earlier than later borns. No surprise there. With all the coaching, prodding, and encouragement they get, they probably do it in self-defense!

As we've seen, first-born children often go on to become the leaders and achievers in life. This isn't necessarily their idea, but with only parents (and maybe grandparents, aunts, and uncles) for role models, they naturally take on more grown-up characteristics. This is why first borns are often serious and not much for surprises. They prefer to know what's happening and when; they thrive in being in control, on time, and organized—all characteristics that stand adults in good stead.

Remember that the child's personality is pretty well formed by the age of five. When the first born is very young—starting before he is even twelve months old—he is already observing his parents and noting *the right way* to do things. When you think about it, first borns basically learn only from adults—those big perfect people who do everything correctly. No wonder they're so willing to break their necks to be right, on time, and organized.

Perks and Privileges

As mentioned earlier, *anything* first borns do is a big deal for everyone in the family. All this attention encourages first borns to achieve. That was certainly true of my big sister, Sally, and older brother, Jack.

Because family and friends take the first born seriously, he or she often develops greater confidence. It's no wonder that first borns go on to become president of the club, the company, and even the country. While over 50 percent of U.S. presidents have been first borns or functional first borns, only three have been true babies. As I have contemplated why so few babies have made it to the White House, it occurs to me that maybe they just couldn't find it!

With their strong powers of concentration, patience, organization, and conscientiousness, first borns have a distinct advantage in many professions. I have often asked at seminars, "If you were manager of a bank and were hiring more tellers, whom would you choose?" Many answer they would take the last-born children, because they would be so friendly and outgoing as they work with the public. I always have to disagree, however, because, while it helps to be friendly with the public, it would be all too typical of a last-born bank teller to turn to the next teller over and say, "Helen, could you please take over for me? I've got to have a Coke and there are still fourteen people in my line."

And then there is that last-born problem of losing things: "Let's see, I know that $135,000 is around here someplace . . ."

Before I go any further with this illustration, let's remember the variables and the exceptions. I'm not saying that all babies of the family are automatically less conscientious or careless. I am saying that the law of averages reveals that the first born is a much better bet to be careful, conscientious, and perfectionist—all important traits for someone entrusted with a lot of responsibility. By their very nature, first borns hate to make mistakes. They are careful and calculating and sticklers for rules and regulations. In a fussy, precise place like a bank, these characteristics are not only useful, they are almost imperative.

Pressures and Problems

The other side of the coin for the first born, however, is that all that attention, the "ooh-ing" and "ahh-ing," the spotlight, and the responsibility add up to—PRESSURE! For one thing, ask any first born for memories of what he used to hear from Mom or Dad when he was a child and those other big role models he was always trying to emulate:

> I don't care what *he* did—you're the oldest!
> What? You don't want to take your little brother (sister) with you? Fine—stay home!
> Couldn't you keep your little brother (sister) out of trouble?
> What kind of example is that?
> Will you please act your age?
> When are you going to grow up?
> He's littler than you. You should know better!

Many first borns remember comments like these and smile wryly or just shake their heads and grin. Others aren't quite so easygoing about it. When I wrote *Growing Up First Born,* the editors added a subtitle: *The Pressure and Privilege of Being Number One.* Not long after the book came out, I received a letter from a woman who said she had read the book, but then she asked, "Excuse me, I remember all the pressure of being the oldest but where was the privilege? I seem to have missed that along the way."

All that attention, the "ooh-ing" and "ahh-ing," the spotlight, and the responsibility add up to—PRESSURE!

One thing many first borns can tell you is that, while they had to toe the mark, their younger brothers and sisters got off easy—or as I often hear, "got away with murder." First borns do take the brunt of discipline as parents work themselves into their parenting role.

Along with getting the most discipline, first borns also get the most work. When you need something done in the family, "who ya gonna call?" That dependable first born is likely to get the assignment, whether it's running down to the corner for a loaf of bread or picking up the dog flops.

And then, of course, there's the infamous task that most first-born adults can remember: being "left in charge" of younger brothers and sisters instead of being able to go off with their own friends. Invariably the first borns wind up being in charge a lot. Older sisters, particularly, are very dependable and conscientious as a rule, and many mothers take advantage of this. First-born girls often get labels like "mother hen" or even "the warden."

Yes, it's possible that some first borns do enjoy the baby-sitting role—for a while—but sooner or later, usually sooner, it turns into a drag. And it's not unusual for older children to try to ditch younger ones who tag along with them. In the dedication of this book, you may have noticed my "special recognition" for my brother, Jack, who often tried to lose his baby brother (me) in the woods!

Poor Jack. Sometimes I think he's still mad because Mom and Dad bought me a new Roadmaster bike, complete with kickstand, when I was six, and he had to make do with his old fenderless model. What really got to him, though, was that I wouldn't use my kickstand. I'd just throw my shiny new bike down on the driveway when I cruised into home base.

A good rule of thumb is not to expect your older children to be baby-sitters for the younger ones. I realize, of course, this rule is often broken—because of finances, unforeseen emergencies, or overloaded schedules. We'll talk more about that in the parenting section.

The bottom line is that parents expect too much of first borns. They are often forced to be the pacesetters and standard-bearers of the family and urged to follow in Father's and Mother's footsteps into professions or ways of life they really don't want. Today the age-old conflict between Father and first-born son still rages. The father wants the son to take over the family business or accomplish something he never accomplished. The son wants to start his *own* business raising earthworms, or maybe become a fry cook at Denny's, a shepherd, a chicken rancher, or just a vegetarian.

First-born boys are usually pressured to be the "crown prince" of the family and first-born girls get almost as much pressure to be the "crown princess." It's no wonder, then, that you can hear first borns saying as they are growing up or even after reaching adulthood:

> Everyone depends on me.
> I can't get away with anything.
> It's tough being the oldest.
> I was never allowed to be a kid.
> If I don't do it, it won't get done.
> If I don't do it, it won't get done right.
> Boy, if I acted the way my little brother does . . .
> Why do I have to do it? Nobody else does anything around here.

The First Born's Worst Nightmare

I've saved the worst nightmare for most first borns (and only children) for last. I will mention it here and then give it full treatment in the next two chapters. I'm talking about perfectionism. Ironically many discouraged first-born perfectionists challenge me, saying they can't possibly be perfectionists because they are so messy. These little scenarios often go something like this:

First-Born Frank   Your birth order system doesn't fit my
                          family at all—you say first borns are
                          neat. Well, I'm a first born and I'm
                          known for having the sloppiest desk in

	the office. In fact the last time anyone saw the top of my desk was the day before I started working for the company. So, what do you say to that, Doctor Leman?
Dr. Leman	That's interesting. What do you do for a living?
First-Born Frank	I'm an electrical engineer.
Dr. Leman	Sounds like a very structured area—lots of math and mental discipline?
First-Born Frank	True enough, but how do you account for the sloppy desk?
Dr. Leman	Your desk is sloppy—okay, but can you find what you need on it?
First-Born Frank	Of course. I usually know what's in every pile.
Dr. Leman	So, you have order within your disorder? You are in a very disciplined occupation—engineering. And while your desk is sloppy, you still feel you are organized. My guess is you are something of a perfectionist and perfectionists are known for having sloppy desks as a means of covering their discouragement for not always having life go just the way they want it. Another thing about perfectionists—when they find one thing that is wrong or imperfect they tend to generalize that one inconsistency and want to throw out the entire package. Maybe you're trying to throw out the birth order baby with the bathwater.
First-Born Frank	Well, I believe in being consistent and doing things right. I'm never satisfied—I always think I could do a little better job. I'm always trying harder . . .

Exactly. Frank has described a discouraged perfectionist (himself) to a T. But Frank is only one example of discouraged perfectionism. I get challenged by many others:

"You don't know my husband, Harry. He's the oldest in his family but he can't fix anything around the house. Every time he takes something apart he loses half the pieces. The only thing he has ever perfected is how to ruin the plumbing, the lawn mower—whatever he tries to repair is doomed."

"You should live with my wife, Gertrude. She's a first born, but the only way I can get her anywhere on time is to tell her we are due thirty to sixty minutes earlier than the actual appointment."

I still say that people like Harry, Gertrude, and, of course, first-born Frank, are odds-on favorites to be discouraged perfectionists. I'll even go so far as to say all first borns and only children are perfectionists—many of whom become discouraged. In twenty-five years of counseling, most of my clients have been first-born or only children and many of them have been *masking their perfectionism* with behavior that doesn't seem to fit.

I repeat that perfectionism is the major problem for almost all first borns and only children. At worst, it can be a curse and, at best, a heavy burden.

Assessing First-Born Strengths and Weaknesses

As we close this chapter on the characteristics of first borns, I would like my first-born readers to go over the chart below, which lists typical traits of first borns. Then consider each trait and decide if it is a strength or weakness as far as you are concerned. If it's a weakness, what changes could you make to improve in that area? If it's a strength, how could you capitalize on that strength or develop it even further?

Strengths and Weaknesses of First Borns

Typical Traits	Strengths	Weaknesses
Leadership ability	Take charge, know what to do	May undermine the initiative of those who lean on them too much or may come off as too overbearing or aggressive
Aggressive	Command respect; others want to follow their unflinching leadership	Can run roughshod over others; may be insensitive and tend to be selfish; too focused on the goal and not enough on the feelings of others
Compliant	Cooperative, easy to work with, good team player	Can be taken advantage of, bullied, bluffed
Perfectionistic	Always do things right and leave no stone unturned to do a thorough job	Tend to criticize themselves and/or others too much; never satisfied; may procrastinate because they fear they cannot do a "good enough job"
Organized	Have everything under control; always on top of things; tend to be on time and on schedule	May worry too much about order, process, and rules and not be flexible when it's needed; may show real impatience with anyone who is "disorganized" or not as meticulous; can be upset by surprises
Driver	Ambitious, enterprising, energetic, willing to sacrifice to be a sucess	Put themselves or those they work with under too much stress and pressure
List maker	Set goals and reach them; tend to get more done in a day than others, planning the day is a must	May become boxed in, too busy with the to-do list to see the big picture and what needs to be done right now
Logical	Known as straight thinkers; can be counted on not to be compulsive or to go off half-cocked	May believe they're always right and fail to pay attention to the more intuitive opinions of others
Scholarly	Tend to be voracious readers and accumulators of information and facts; good problem solvers who think things through	May spend too much time gathering facts when there are other things that need to be done; may be so serious they fail to see the humor in situations when humor is desperately needed

Being Honest with Your First-Born Self

1. Am I involved in too many activities? Which ones could I give up?
2. Do I know how to say no? Can I think of a recent example of saying no graciously but firmly?
3. How much of a problem is perfectionism for me? Can I state the difference between pursuing perfectionism and seeking excellence?
4. Am I a slave to my to-do lists or do I use lists to organize my life and keep it balanced?
5. Have I forgiven my parents for any pressures they put on me while growing up? Can I honestly say there were privileges to being first born as well as pressures?
6. Am I a compliant or aggressive first born? What are my best attributes? What are my key faults and what do I need to do to improve?
7. If I know I'm an aggressive first born, am I willing to ask my spouse, children, or fellow workers for feedback on my strengths and weaknesses? What would my family say to me about how much time I spend with them?
8. If I feel jealousy or any resentment toward any of my siblings, am I willing to confess and try to make it right? When and where could I do this?
9. Do I care too much about what others think of me? What has happened recently that can give me some clues?
10. How good am I at spotting flaws at fifty paces? Would my family or friends say I am too critical?

5

Just How Serious a Problem Is Perfectionism?

i've already mentioned perfectionism in less than approving terms, particularly because I see it so often in first borns and only children. But just how serious a problem is perfectionism? Isn't it true the world could use a few more perfectionists instead of putting up with all of the sloppy, slipshod work and service that goes on every day?

Regardless of your birth order, it could be interesting to see how you rate perfectionism as one of the "real problems of life." Which of the following describes perfectionism best for you?

A. a burden
B. a cause of stress and even disease
C. slow suicide
D. a strength

According to my counseling experience, any or all of the A, B, or C answers is correct. The incorrect answer is D. Perfectionism is not a strength, and if you think it is, I hope to convince you otherwise.

✓ Perfectionism is not a strength.

But first, you need to get a feeling for how much of a perfectionist you are. To do so, just fill in the blank next to each question below with 0 for never, 1 for seldom, 2 for often, and 3 for always. Then add up your score.

___ 1. Do mistakes—your own or others'—irritate you?

___ 2. Do you feel everyone should be as driven to do his best as you are?

___ 3. Do you use the word *should* a lot—as in "I should have taken care of that," or "We should meet on this immediately"?

___ 4. Do you find it hard to enjoy success? Even when something goes well, is it easy for you to find the things that could have been just a little better?

___ 5. Does one small mistake ruin your day—or at least your morning?

___ 6. Do terms like *good enough* and *just about right* bother you, particularly on the job?

___ 7. Do you tend to put things off because you feel you're not quite ready to do the job right?

___ 8. Do you find yourself apologizing for certain work because you could have done it better if you had had more time?

___ 9. Whether in a meeting, working in a team, or in any group situation in the workplace, do you prefer to be in control of what's happening?

___ 10. Realizing your deep need to have all your ducks in a row, do you insist that those around you have their ducks in the same row (think exactly the way you do)?

___ 11.Do you tend to see the glass half-empty instead of half-full?

Scoring:
11–16 mild perfectionist
17–25 medium perfectionist
26–33 extreme perfectionist (you're too hard on yourself and everyone else)

Perfectionism in the Personals

My favorite example of a person whom I would rate an extreme perfectionist appears in this ad I clipped from the personals in a daily newspaper.

CHRISTIAN, blond, blue eyes, 5'2", 100 lbs. prof., cauc/ female, no depend., wishes to meet Protestant Christian, prof. man in 30s with college degree who has compassion for animals and people, loves nature, exercise and phy. fitness *(no team sports)*, music and dance, church and home life. Desire nonsmoker/nondrinker, slender, 5'7"–6', lots of head hair, *no chest hair,* intelligent, honest and trustworthy, sense of humor, excellent communicator of feelings, very sensitive, gentle, affectionate, androgynous attitude about roles, giving, encouraging and helpful to others, no temper or *ego problems,* secure within and financially, health conscious, neat and clean, extremely considerate and dependable. I believe in old-fashioned morals and values. If you do, too, and are interested in a possible Christian commitment, write to PO Box 82533. Please include recent color photo and address.

A lot can be read into an ad like this. First of all, let me take a walk on the plank of life and suggest that this woman will be single for a long, long time. Can't you imagine her on a date with a Tom Cruise look-alike and she suddenly spots a chest hair peeking through his polo shirt? End of relationship!

My counselor's eyes suggest the odds are at least five hundred to one that this blonde, blue-eyed 5'2", 100 lb. professional female is a first born or only child. Surely she is a super extreme perfectionist who would score thirty or more on the above quiz. This kind of personality walks around holding up what I call the high-jump bar of life. She is always raising the bar a little higher and is a master at defeating herself at every turn.

A True Perfectionist at Eighteen Months

We all develop our particular life-style when we are very young, and that includes perfectionists. Sande and I saw the handwriting on the wall with our oldest daughter, Holly, when she was only eighteen months old. We were on an R and R trip to California and the seashore, and it was the first time on any beach for Holly. She soon discovered sand and came toddling over, holding up one finger with three or four grains of sand stuck to it.

"Ugh, ugh," she grunted, very displeased with all this "mess" and wondering if there wasn't something we could do about it. Before our eyes—at the tender age of eighteen months—Holly was displaying signs of the true perfectionist. Despite our best efforts to encourage and reinforce Holly rather than find fault or pick flaws, she has grown into a mature woman in her midtwenties, who seeks perfection in all she does. And that's why her high school literature students get detention when they come to class unprepared. Holly knows she would have her assignments in on time (she always did in high school and in four years of college) so she wants her students to do the same.

But while Holly is far from being a slob, she is hardly the neatest one in the family. That honor goes to her sister Krissy, our second-born middle child whom I'll be discussing later. But I don't find it odd at all that our perfectionist, first-born daughter acts a bit out of character and isn't always concerned about having a perfectly neat room. It's her own way of covering her frustration with life's less-than-perfect warts and bumps.

People who score in the medium-to-extreme perfectionist range on the quiz usually fall into the category I call "discouraged perfectionists." They go through life telling themselves the lie, "I only count when I'm perfect." It becomes their life-style. I'm not talking about life-style in the sense of what you wear, drive, eat, or drink. *Life-style* is a term coined by Dr. Alfred Adler, who used it to refer to how people function psychologically to reach their goals (more on this in chapter 12).

Beware the Ultracritical Perfectionist

When the discouraged perfectionist reaches a certain point, he or she can become ultracritical, not only of self but of others. The person in the want ad, for example, may somehow find a man who happens to meet all her "requirements" and is foolish enough to marry her. But after the honeymoon is over, he will almost certainly find he has an ultracritical discouraged perfectionist on his hands and he will pay a big price.

Ultracritical discouraged perfectionists hide behind a mask of "being objective." Their favorite motto is: "The good is enemy of the best!" They are such flaw pickers they can become a constant irritant to everyone. They can even become toxic, making fellow workers so angry or so worried about their performance that they can't do a job properly or safely.

I always tell managers and executives that if they have a severely discouraged ultracritical perfectionist on the payroll and he or she is working directly with other people, they should consider strong measures. First, this severely discouraged perfectionist needs a friendly warning and a chance to modify his or her behavior. If the extreme perfectionism continues, the best option is to transfer this person to another area—preferably where he or she can work mostly alone. And if that isn't possible, perhaps this ultracritical perfectionist should be advised to look for another line of work.

Speaking of looking for another line of work, if you are serving under an extremely critical perfectionist who happens to be the office manager, president, owner of the company, or some other position of tremendous power, do not get down on yourself because of the constant criticism. Instead, realize you could never please this person because he cannot please himself. Perhaps the job pays so well you can hang on and be hammered with the negatives while getting very little positive reinforcement. On the other hand, if self-fulfillment and job satisfaction are really important, it's best to consider moving on.

The Cycle of Perfectionism

Since writing the first edition of *The Birth Order Book*, I have come across some excellent studies that discuss the cycle of perfectionism, which can lead to extreme discouragement or, in extreme cases, defeat or failure. For the perfectionist, nothing is ever good enough and he or she is never quite finished with the task. The cycle of perfectionism generally follows these steps:

1. The perfectionist is the originator of the motto, *It's all or nothing.* He is sure he must be perfect in everything he does. He tends to be a streak performer;

when he's hot, he's hot, and when he's not, he's a mess.

2. This leads to biting off more than he or she can chew, perhaps the perfectionist's major problem. Perfectionists can always take on one more thing, even when his or her schedule is absolutely full and running over. This leads toward the next step in the spiral downward to defeat.

3. The hurdle effect causes the perfectionist to panic. He or she looks down the track and sees all those hurdles ahead. And each hurdle gets a little higher than the last one. The hurdles aren't necessarily there but they are perceived obstacles and they are overwhelming. *How did I get into this mess? How am I ever going to get out?* are the typical laments of the perfectionist.

4. As the hurdles seem to grow taller and taller, the perfectionist compounds his or her problems by maximizing failures and minimizing successes. If perfectionists make mistakes, they internalize them, chew on them, and go over and over in their minds what went wrong. If they manage to do something right, they think, *It could have been better.*

5. When the pressure becomes too great, the perfectionist may bail out, quitting the project or turning it in less than well done with the excuse, *There just wasn't enough time.*

6. Whether the perfectionist manages to finish his job or backs out of it because it simply proved too much, he is always left feeling he must try harder. He is the original victim of the Avis complex, sure that he is number 2 (or lower), never satisfied, and always shooting to be better.

The Avis complex doesn't haunt only "average people." It can be the bane of the celebrity, highly successful executive, or genius. Actor Alex Guinness admitted he was very insecure about his work and added, "I've never done anything I couldn't pull to bits."

Abraham Lincoln presented his Gettysburg Address and then described it as "a flat failure." Leonardo da Vinci, who was an outstanding painter, sculptor, scientist, engineer, and inventor, actually one of the world's true geniuses, said, "I have offended God and mankind because my work didn't reach the quality it should have."[1]

Figure 1
The Hopeless Pursuit of Perfection

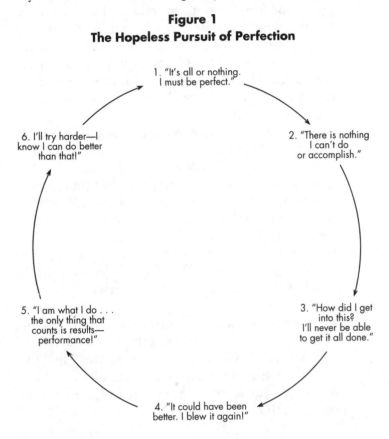

1. "It's all or nothing. I must be perfect."

2. "There is nothing I can't do or accomplish."

3. "How did I get into this? I'll never be able to get it all done."

4. "It could have been better. I blew it again!"

5. "I am what I do . . . the only thing that counts is results—performance!"

6. I'll try harder—I know I can do better than that!"

From Fritz Ridenour, *Untying Your Knots* (Old Tappan, N.J.: Revell, 1988), 112. Used by permission.

Skilled Procrastinators

This six-step cycle (see diagram above) can be repeated several times a day, depending on what the perfectionist is doing. While going through this cycle, the perfectionist often slips into the habit of procrastinating. Have you ever known a real procrastinator? (Perhaps you know one all too well.) The procrastinator has a real problem with time, schedules, and deadlines. A major reason behind the procrastination is the perfectionistic fear of failure. The perfectionist procrastinator has such high expectations he is afraid to start a project. He or she would rather stall and rush to get something done at the last minute. Then the procrastinator can say, "If there had been more time, I could have done a much better job."

Recently we did an entire *Parent Talk* show on the topic of perfectionism and feeling that you are not good enough, cannot jump high enough, and can never do anything really well. We had many callers that day who struggle with perfectionism, procrastinating, and just feeling like they don't measure up in life. One of them was Michael who complained that he never got things accomplished, never finished things (a sure sign of a procrastinating perfectionist). He started projects with his wife or his kids and didn't finish them. He felt overcommitted and admitted he had been definitely biting off more than he could chew.

Michael sounded like the very person I had in mind when I wrote *When Your Best Is Not Good Enough*,[2] a book that zeros in on perfectionism and how to conquer it. While we were on the air, I told Michael I could describe him and his family without ever seeing any of them. Here is what I said:

"Sometimes you'll be asked to do something and you'll say no because you'll look at the big picture and say, *This is impossible, I can't do it*. And then you'll move on to something else. Or, as you've already admitted, you will do some things to a certain degree or a certain point and either lose interest or turn left or right at the last minute.

"My big guess is, Michael, that you grew up in a home where criticism reigned. In other words, you had a critical-eyed parent and you protected yourself from criticism by not finishing things. Your thinking was, *If I don't finish it, how can anybody criticize me?* This, of course, is where self-deception comes in and we become great at lying to ourselves."

Michael replied: "That's almost exactly who I am and what I do. Some days I'll look at the problem and say, *You know, this has eight or nine steps. I can't do this.* Or some days I'll even do two or three steps and then, as you said, turn right or turn left and I just walk away from the problem. And that's one of the biggest issues I have—that walking away. I need to stop and say, *I've committed to this. This is something that needs to get done.*"

As is so often the case, Michael knew the answer to his problem. It was simply a matter of following through and changing his behavior. I asked him if he had liked building models as a kid, and he said that indeed he did, ". . . model cars, stuff like that." I told Michael I often found that guys who really struggle with procrastinating and perfectionism usually loved building models or assembling puzzles—anything where all the parts come together.

"Here's the kicker, Michael," I added. "You are a very competent person, more competent than you've ever believed yourself to be. If I talked to people who know you well, I believe they would say, 'He's a guy with such great potential. It's unbelievable!'"

Michael's reply: "Have you been hiding in my closet?"

It turned out Michael was production manager of a ceramics shop—a very exacting kind of work that is a natural for a perfectionist. I said I was quite sure that people had told him he had done beautiful work on certain ceramic pieces, but inside he was saying, *If you only knew about that little flaw.*

"Very, very true," Michael answered. "You know, I recycle a lot of ceramics because of that . . ."

Because *Parent Talk* goes out mainly over Christian radio stations, it turned out that Michael was, indeed, a believer so I gave him the following advice: Perfectionists need to understand that God is described in Scripture as a God of grace who doesn't demand perfection. Michael needed to give himself permission to be imperfect. I urged him to flaunt his imperfections before his children and be the first to say to them or to his wife, "Honey, I'm sorry. I was wrong. I shouldn't have said that."

As for getting things done, Michael needs to set some time limits for finishing projects. He must make the limits reasonable but at the end of the time, stop and accept the job the way it is without trying to "perfect it."

Finally, I urged Michael not to be so quick to put himself down. So many people who struggle with perfectionism will say things like: "It's no good," or "Oh, it isn't much—it's really nothing." Those are sure signs of a perfectionist who is fending off criticism. Instead, Michael needs to start telling himself the truth—that he has really been given a wonderful gift and he needs to use that gift in the most positive way he possibly can.

Perfectionism Got George in Trouble with the IRS

One of the most unusual procrastinators I ever counseled was a man we'll call George. He came to me because he had not filed his income tax for the last four years. I asked him why. It turned out he had such an elaborate system for keeping records and receipts that reporting his income tax had become an insurmountable task. His family room contained several picnic tables nicely covered with shelf paper. Overflowing on each table were neatly stacked piles of receipts, notes, and bills of sale.

George kept telling himself the lie that he was dedicated to details and getting things right. Meanwhile, he couldn't sleep because of having all those unpaid taxes hanging over his head. (More precisely, the IRS was hanging over his head!)

I wasn't surprised to learn that George's wife was the critical kind (and a perfectionist) who was always on his case about getting things fixed around the house. When Alice asked him to fix the toaster or the doorjamb or whatever, his reply was standard: "Don't worry, honey. I'll do it tomorrow." Of course, tomorrow came, and the toaster and other things remained unrepaired.

George had so many uncompleted tasks staring him in the face that all he could do was tread water in the swimming pool of life. But no one can tread water forever, and finally George came to see me. He knew he was in trouble and he wanted some help. After a number of sessions, I finally got him to attack his problems one at a time. He had to commit to fixing the toaster on a Monday, doorjamb on a Tuesday, and so on.

We agreed on one inviolate rule: He had to finish one job before he could start another. That's always the key to helping the discouraged perfectionist who procrastinates. He has to commit himself to finish one thing before he starts another. I know this sounds overly simplistic but it's a basic principle that can do wonders if the procrastinating perfectionist has the commitment to carry it through. As I told George: Beautiful cathedrals are built one brick at a time.

Beautiful cathedrals are built one brick at a time.

George must have heard me because he did manage to change. He even committed to a definite schedule for cleaning up his taxes, one step—and one picnic table—at a time. The final irony of this story is that, after paying necessary penalties, George learned that the government owed *him* some money!

Perfectionists Can Spot a Flaw at Fifty Paces

Remember my first-born sister, Sally? I think you could tell from my description of her that she's something of a perfectionist. I have several stories about how Sally tries to keep the world straightened up, cleaned up, or shaped up, but perhaps this one will suffice:

A few years ago I bought a new boat. It wasn't a yacht or cabin cruiser—just a nice nineteen-foot ski boat that I had delivered to Chautauqua Lake in upstate New York where our summer home is located.

I was as proud as any last born could be as I backed my new toy into the water and then secured it to the dock. I couldn't wait to show my big sister what I'd purchased and I didn't have to wait long. Sally drove out from her home in nearby Jamestown and quickly came down to the dock to take a look at baby brother's brand new toy.

I didn't say a word. I just stepped back and beamed, waiting for her comments on my beautiful new boat.

Sally looked into the boat and the first words out of her mouth weren't "Gorgeous!" or "First class!" or any number of other things I could have thought of had I been gazing on such a beauty for the first time. No, Sally's first word was "Footprints!"

Footprints? What was she talking about?

Then I looked down to the boat and, yes, there they were—muddy footprints on the maroon carpeting. While launching the boat, I had apparently stepped into some mud and then tracked it on the carpet and on some of the seat cushions as well. Now if anyone else but Sally had made this rather critical appraisal on seeing my boat for the first time, I would have been irritated. Instead, I just did my best impression of Mr. Rogers and said, "Yes, Sally, those are footprints. Can you say footprints?" And then I bent down and brushed the dried mud away with my hand.

My sister and I had a good laugh about it then and we still do every time we remember the story. We both know that it's her tendency, as a perfectionist first born, to pick out the flaw in any situation. It isn't that she's mean or disrespectful. She just can't help it and she's actually trying to help.

Handling Failure

Fortunately Sally's perfectionism really leans more toward seeking excellence, even though she does have that flaw-picking quality. She hasn't become a discouraged perfectionist by any means. But a lot of perfectionist flaw pickers *do* become discouraged and depressed, especially if they fail in any regard.

How about you? When you spot a flaw in your performance or appearance, do you equate it with failure and get down on yourself? Do you tell yourself that you've done it again or that you'll never amount to anything?

What I try to tell perfectionist clients (usually first-born or only children) is that every human being who ever lived has failed at one time or another. It doesn't matter how intelligent, talented, or fortunate you may be; the only way to avoid failure is to sit back and do nothing. But that's a form of failure too and it's often what happens when a perfectionist becomes incapacitated by his fear of messing things up. What you do with occasional failure is strictly up to you. You can see failure as your deadly enemy, which holds you back and threatens your very existence, or you can see failure as a teacher and, in some cases, a blessing because it leads down another trail that brings you to success.

Being Objective

The key to handling failure and making it a teacher rather than a destroyer is to look at it in a detached, objective way. Now I know that's easier said (and done) by a last born who doesn't have a perfectionist cell in his body. So if you're a first-born or only child and failure really bugs you, you have to attack it systematically with what I call cognitive discipline.

The first thing you must do is refuse to use negative self-talk. Don't respond with: "I knew this was going to happen! It always happens to me!" If you hear yourself thinking that kind of thing, stop and instead look closely at the situation. What caused the failure? What was your first mistake, which led to the second and so on? Did you go against your better judgment? What can you do differently next time? As you analyze your failure or mistake, you will automatically be learning and setting yourself up to improve in the future.

Of course, it's hard when you fail and you get fired on by critics—your spouse, others in your family, your boss, friends, or that busybody neighbor who seems to know everything you do. Remember that you're under no obligation to believe or even listen to the people who are criticizing or even condemning you.

If you're a first born, keep in mind that you've been busy all your life living up to everyone else's standards. You may have never even stopped to figure out exactly what you want out of life. You've been living up to your parents' expectations, your teachers' expectations, your spouse's expectations, and so on and so on. When you try to live up to everyone else's expectations, you tend to believe what everyone else says about you. We would never have heard of some of the world's most famous people if they had listened to their critics early on:

Sir Winston Churchill, the prime minister who kept England afloat during World War II strictly on the strength of his brilliant oratory, was at the bottom of his class in one school and failed the entrance exams to another.

Pablo Picasso, the brilliant painter whose works command mind-boggling prices, was barely able to read and write at the age of ten when his father yanked him out of school. Then a tutor came in to instruct him but gave up and quit in disgust because Pablo just didn't have it.

There are many other examples. Louis Pasteur was not the top student in his chemistry class. Publishers told Zane Grey he could never be a writer. Thomas Edison's teachers concluded he was a few bricks short of a full load and tossed him out of school. His mother ended up home schooling him. Then there was that composer named Beethoven, whose teacher called him a "hopeless dunce." And let's not forget Albert Einstein, whose theory of relativity changed the scientific world. He performed badly in almost all of his high school courses and even flunked his college entrance exams![3]

I have often imagined how it was for Einstein while growing up. The teacher would be leaning over little Albert at his school desk, saying, "Albert! What *are* you doing? You're supposed to be practicing your multiplication tables. What on earth is this capital E and that equals sign and the little mc with a ^{2} after it? Can't you handle six times seven?"

Refusing to Feel Guilty

One more thing to remember as you battle failure: You are almost certainly battling guilt as well. Just ask yourself, *Do I feel guilty much of the time?* For most perfectionists the answer is almost always yes. I have counseled many people whom I sometimes call "the guilt gatherers of life." The common mistakes that they make include:

- They pile one infraction on top of another.
- They let their children manipulate them.
- They take the blame when others are responsible.
- They give in to depression.
- They believe they deserve to suffer.
- They judge themselves by what others think of them.
- They would rather suffer than take steps to change things.

I have written extensively on dealing with guilt in other books. For more information, see *When Your Best Isn't Good Enough* and *Women Who Try Too Hard: Breaking the Pleaser Habits.*[4]

Moving from Perfectionism toward Excellence

THERE IS A WAY OUT OF THE PERFECTIONIST SWAMP

ll right, reading the last chapter has convinced you that perfectionism is not a healthy way to live. You are aware that you are a perfectionist to some degree and you're concerned that you may be in some trouble or even on thin ice.

Congratulations! You have made the first step toward making a change that could literally save your health or your life. It may even save you some friends. Discouraged perfectionists are often stubborn, opinionated, and strong-willed types who become known for telling it like it is. And what happens when you tell everyone like it is? People suddenly are too busy for lunch—and for much of anything else. Even your enemies don't want to hang around long enough to insult you.

And unless you can change your perfectionistic attitude, it won't do any good to tell yourself you'll just keep your mouth shut and put up with it. Try that and you will really lose your health. Your perfectionism will cause anxiety and whether anxiety is conscious or unconscious it's got to come out somewhere. Certain parts of your body will pay the price. That's why so many first-born or only children wind up going to see psychologists, and the first symptoms they notice are migraines, stomach disorders, or backaches. They are the worriers of life, the ones who develop colitis, ulcers, facial tics, and cluster headaches.

Now right here you may be thinking, *C'mon, Dr. Leman, you're laying it on a bit thick, aren't you?*

Well, yes and no. I admit that not all perfectionists wind up with serious medical and psychological problems. Some perfectionists function very efficiently, but underneath the polished, seemingly flawless exterior is usually a person who wonders how long he or she can stay ahead of the posse, continually frustrated, perhaps wondering, "Why do I do these compulsive things over and over?" Whatever your degree of perfectionism, I know it is a burden and certainly a source of stress. And I also know from working with hundreds of perfectionists that the answer lies in controlling your perfectionism and turning it in an entirely new direction.

When the Light Began to Dawn for Edwin

One of my most prized letters comes from Edwin, a former newspaper reporter who rose to become one of five vice presidents with a publicly traded telecommunications company. I'm going to quote a great deal of Edwin's letter because it is such a choice example of a perfectionist who begins to see the light:

> Can't remember when I laughed so much while reading a nonfiction book. Laughed? I howled at some paragraphs in *The Birth Order Book*. And then I threw the book across the room when you answered a question that has been bugging me for years.
>
> So, this is a thank-you letter for answering, in fact, several questions that have haunted me for a long time. . . .
>
> Want clues to my birth order? I bought your book after wandering into a New York bookstore last Saturday, while fretting that the scarf I purchased a month earlier was navy blue—not black as I thought—and didn't match my new black top coat. . . .
>
> If that's not enough: in my closet, dress shirts are on blue hangers, dark shirts on the left, lighter-colored shirts on the right; sport shirts are on brown hangers. I'm laughing so much thinking about this, I can hardly continue writing.
>
> Surely you've guessed: I have no siblings. But here's something curious that I discovered several years ago and wanted to alert you to: Virtually all of my close friends are first-born or only children. And with two exceptions, all fall in the much-younger, much-older groups—something that has always been apparent to me, but I never understood until reading your book.
>
> Of course, I've always known that I was not a perfectionist—far from it. Proof: my desk has, throughout my career, been a mess most of the time (but I can find anything within sixty seconds). And then I read your book and converted it into a Frisbee! I could never figure out why I lost control of my desk so often. Thank you for telling me the answer to something that has bugged me for years.
>
> Nonetheless, it is a bit spooky having a stranger—you—know so much about my personal life. Good grief! Dr. Leman, you will never know how much enlightenment your book has given me. Thank you.

Needless to say, I treasure Edwin's letter. Being a baby I always love strokes but I'm also a counselor and it's great to hear that I've helped someone learn something about himself and be able to make some changes. The changes will be long in coming, but at least Edwin can understand why he does what he does and take small steps toward doing something about it.

The Big Difference between Perfectionism and Excellence

Of course, many perfectionists would stop me right here and say, "Yes, just what do I do about my perfectionism? Shoot for mediocrity and failure?"

Of course not. The key is to learn the difference between the hopeless pursuit of perfection and the satisfying seeking of excellence. Following is a little quiz I put together to help clients learn the difference. Each question has two statements, one of which identifies the perfectionist and the other the seeker of excellence. Read each pair of statements and label one of them E (for excellence) and the other P (for perfectionism).

> Learn the difference between the hopeless pursuit of perfection and the satisfying seeking of excellence.

1. I aim for the top. ____
   I strive to do my best. ____
2. What counts is the bottom line. Everything else is just talk. ____
   I did my best, and whatever happens, I'm happy with me. ____
3. What's the use? I can't do what I know I am capable of. ____

This one hurts, but I'm staying with it. ____
4. I blew it! How could I let this happen? ____
   What a bummer! But I see what went wrong. Next
   time . . . ____
5. What if I slip up again? What if something happens
   I can't control? Everyone will laugh. ____
   Here I am with the same opportunity. This time it's
   going to be different. ____
6. I play to win. Nobody remembers who finished second. ____
   I strive to do my best. I'm happy with that. ____
7. Why do people have to be so negative? Don't they
   know how long I've worked on this project? ____
   They may be right. I don't like it, but there may be
   something in what they say. ____
8. Let's not kid ourselves. They love me around here
   because I produce. ____
   Everybody likes to win but it's playing the game and
   being part of the process that counts. ____

It isn't too hard to see that in each pair, the first statement is that of the perfectionist and the second statement
that of the seeker of excellence. Here's why:

1. Those who chase perfection are always reaching
   beyond their grasp—for the top. They set impossible goals. Pursuers of excellence set goals too, according to their own high standards, but they put those
   goals within reach.
2. Perfectionists base their value on their accomplishments. They have to produce or else. Seekers of excellence value themselves simply for who they are.
3. Perfectionists are easily dismayed by disappointment
   and will often throw up their hands in total defeat
   because if they can't be perfect, why even try? Seek-

ers of excellence can be disappointed and hurt by a setback but they don't give up. They keep moving toward their goal.

4. Perfectionists regard failure as the ultimate evil and let it devastate them. Pursuers of excellence are always learning from their mistakes and failures so they can do a better job in the future.

5. Perfectionists remember their mistakes and chew on them the way a dog gnaws a bone. They are sure everyone else remembers them too and are ready to pounce. Seekers of excellence correct their mistakes and let them fade from memory so they aren't inhibited in the future.

6. Perfectionists can settle only for being number one. Pursuers of excellence are happy with themselves as long as they are sure they tried as hard as they could.

7. Perfectionists fear and hate criticism and will either avoid it or ignore it. Seekers of excellence don't enjoy criticism but they welcome it because it may help them improve.

8. Perfectionists have to win or their self-image plunges to zero. Pursuers of excellence can finish second, third, or even lower and their self-image remains strong.

How to Control Perfectionism by Seeking Excellence

Following are some suggestions I have seen work wonders in the lives of perfectionists I have counseled.

1. *Take perfectionism seriously.* Perfectionism isn't some little "psychological glitch" in your makeup. It is your deadly enemy. I call it slow suicide, and that's not even half facetious.

The perfectionist is always trying to avoid criticism or failure, both of which he sees as totally unacceptable. My advice is realize that you will always have critics with you, and everybody fails now and then. When you don't succeed, analyze the situation. What is the worst that can result from your failure to do what you had hoped to do? Maybe you need to fine-tune your goal setting and not reach so high. Remember, there are many major league baseball players in the Hall of Fame who failed seven times out of ten. In other words, they batted .300 and made the Hall.

A good hitter—someone who bats at least .300—doesn't get down on himself if he strikes out or if his sharp line drive is speared by the shortstop and he's robbed of a base hit. Instead, he hitches up his pants and tells himself, *Next time I'll get a hit.* Whatever you're doing, the moral is clear: Give it your best shot and then *live with your best shot* and be satisfied. Or to put it another way: The real winners in life take their cuts, and even if they strike out, next time up they get back in the batter's box of life and keep swinging.

> The real winners in life take their cuts, and even if they strike out, next time up they get back in the batter's box of life and keep swinging.

2. *Recognize that you have an almost desperate need to be perfect.* And at the same time, recognize the fallacy in this kind of thinking. Since you are *never* going to be perfect, why not give yourself permission to be *imperfect*? Do it one day at a time. Every morning start off by giving yourself permission to be imperfect.

Of course I'm not suggesting that you settle for mediocrity. I am a firm believer that the world needs a certain number of perfectionists who are very good at their job. For example, last summer I was enjoying myself in our summer place in upstate New York when my stomach began acting up. The pain wouldn't go away and I wound

up in the emergency ward headed for a gall bladder operation. Just before they put me under, I told the anesthesiologist (whose last name sounded like Rumpelstiltskin
backwards) that we were going to talk about his birth
order. He said to me in broken English, "Birth order? I
am unfamiliar with term 'birth order.'"
    I said, "You are the first-born son, aren't you?"
    "No," he replied.
    "Noooo...?" I responded, flabbergasted.
    He said firmly, "I'm the ONLY son."
    I said, "Proceed!"
    And, as you know, I like to poll airline pilots to see if they
are first born, and they usually are. One day, however, I had
to take a small commuter plane to a parenting seminar in
Santa Maria, 140 miles up the California coast from Los
Angeles. The commuter plane was so small that I wound up
sitting barely three feet from the two guys flying the plane,
and I couldn't help noticing the lead pilot's digital watch.
    "You're a first born, aren't you?" I said comfortably.
    "No, actually, I'm a baby of the family," he replied.
    I started getting a little nervous and inquired, "How
about your buddy?"
    After conversing briefly with his copilot, he turned and
said, "He's the youngest too!"
    We were taxiing for takeoff and two babies were flying
the plane! I almost bailed out right there, but the day was
saved when I learned that the pilot had a gap of twelve
years between him and the next oldest child in the family.
And the copilot had a six-year gap between him and his
older brother, who was a pilot as well.
    I calmed down and decided to stay in my seat. The law
of variables may have put two last borns in the cockpit of
the plane but they were really a functional only child and
a functional first born, and that was good enough for me.
(P.S.: We made it to Santa Maria with no problem and

both pilots did a beautiful job, even when the air got a little rough.)[1]

My point in telling you about the anesthesiologist and the two pilots is that some personality types are better fitted to certain jobs than others. So I don't mind if anesthesiologists, pilots, surgeons, and the like allow themselves to be imperfect, particularly at home with the wife and kids, just so they're seeking excellence while on the job!

3. *Make a conscious effort to go easy on criticizing yourself and others.* In fact start going easy on others first. If you have to give someone feedback, try to separate the deed from the doer, which is not easy. A good approach is not to say, "*You* did this" or "*You* did that," but practice talking about what happened instead. Say, "Now you're getting it. That looks great!" A strange thing will happen. As you lighten up on others, you will learn to lighten up on yourself!

The destructive feeling that many perfectionists have is self-directed anger. That is why they are so self-critical. You can learn to be less critical if you add a margin for error to your tasks and remind yourself that everyone makes mistakes.

4. *Have the courage to admit out loud, "I was wrong."* This may be the most difficult sentence any perfectionist has to utter because your whole code goes against the idea of ever being wrong, "less than," or not perfect. And as you make progress on "I was wrong," also try two other short sentences that may be even more difficult: "I'm sorry," and "Will you forgive me?"

These three sentences total nine words—the toughest nine words any birth order has to utter, but particularly hard for first-born perfectionists. When perfectionism is your goal, admitting that you have missed that goal is difficult. It's an admission of failure, and failure is anathema to the perfectionist. But admitting mistakes makes you human and approachable.

5. *Work on developing a thicker skin.* Be aware that perfectionists are sensitive, admit that this is an ingrained pattern, and deal with it, but don't expect to get rid of it overnight. Instead, watch for those times when you catch yourself being very sensitive or being defensive about criticism, whether it comes from others or from within yourself.

You will do a lot of the "two steps forward, one step backward" shuffle. At the end of the day, you may look back and say, *I really didn't need to get so upset over forgetting to mail that important letter or to make that call.* But even to be aware of how upset you got over something that really wasn't worth it is making progress. Ingrained patterns are not changed overnight.

I often tell sensitive perfectionists to be sure to do nice things for themselves. As the hair color ad puts it, "You're worth it." But perfectionists have a hard time believing that. One of my clients had a habit of going to the local department store, buying new clothes, and then returning them a few days later. This woman was an extremely discouraged perfectionist who always returned whatever she bought, giving the excuse that something "just wasn't quite right." I told her that what wasn't quite right was that she thought she wasn't worth the new clothes because she wasn't meeting her perfectionistic standards.

We had to work on two problems: (1) She really needed new clothes. (2) She really needed to understand that it was okay to buy something new and keep it. Finding fault with what she bought was really a cover-up for her belief that she didn't deserve a new dress.

Finally we had a breakthrough. She bought a new dress and actually kept it. Then she got a new sweater and kept that. I knew we were out of the woods when her husband finally called me and complained about all these bills he was getting for his wife's new clothes!

6. *Bite off smaller chunks of life.* In other words, don't take on so much at once. That's when the big picture becomes overwhelming—a typical plight of the perfectionist. So work at doing one thing at a time. Finish A before going to B. Yes, there will always be those things that come up—phone calls or emergencies, minor or major. The thing to do is avoid putting a major task into a tight schedule (a typical problem for the perfectionist because he or she is always doing too many things and thinking there will be time for all of them). Always leave room in your schedule for the interruptions and the emergencies.

7. *Expect less of yourself.* Perfectionists are famous for unrealistic expectations and for setting goals that are way out of human reach. What you may want to try is what I call "negative motivation." I once worked with a professional baseball pitcher who was an extreme perfectionist. As long as he was ahead in the count, he could usually get batters out, but if he got behind—three balls and one strike, for example—he would more often than not walk the hitter. And if someone made an error in the field behind him, he'd usually fall apart.

After I worked with him for several sessions, he got traded to another team. One day I was fortunate enough to be in the same city where this player's team had a game. I went to the ballpark and managed to get down near the dugout and get his attention. He was pleasantly surprised to see me, and I was pleased to learn he was five wins and no losses to that point in the season.

"Don't worry, Doc," he said with a grin, "I never forgot what you told me. Every time I walk out to the pitcher's mound, I tell myself, 'Maybe today's the day I'm going to blow it.'"

That may sound like crazy advice, but for this extreme perfectionist it worked. It helped him acknowledge that there were going to be days when he would go out there and blow it. Once he accepted that, he was able to relax and pitch up to his potential because he literally expected less of himself and wasn't paralyzed by his perfectionism.

8. *Become skilled at saying no.* This is especially important if you are a first-born or only child who wants and needs the approval of others.

Perfectionists get trapped in situations where they say yes, when they really want to say no. Not being able to say no raises the perfectionist's frustration level to the point where he or she is literally ready to explode.

But if you can't say no, you'll never be able to say yes to life. In other words, you'll not have a life of your own because too many people will be taking advantage and pulling you in a dozen different directions to get what they want out of you. I'm not talking about fair-weather friends or even enemies. These people who make unreasonable demands on your time are often your own family. And, of course, it's hardest to tell a husband or a child, or maybe your mother or father, "No, I can't do that," or, even better, "No, I really don't want to do that—it's not me."

But it's amazing what will happen if you learn to say no in a very respectful and gentle way. You will stop saying yes to headaches and stomach problems, and people will start backing off and will not try to take advantage of you as much.

9. *Work on becoming an optimist.* Perfectionists usually see the proverbial glass as half-empty. Change this pessimistic view to one that sees the glass as half-full. Positive thinking is not just a cliché that turned Dr. Norman Vincent Peale's books into best-sellers. It really works because it can be one of the most powerful psychological forces on earth. So start using it in simple ways. Think about and

meditate on things you are thankful for. More important, think about people you are thankful for and why.

When you are tempted to think about what went wrong today, remind yourself of at least three things that went right. If you can't think of anything that went right today, go back a day or two. The key is to focus on the good, not the bad. And think about what can happen during the coming days and coming weeks that will be enjoyable.

10. *Change your self-talk.* I mentioned this in chapter 5, but it bears repeating because it's a key to controlling perfectionism. Here are some examples of changing negative self-talk to positive self-talk:

> Instead of saying, "I hate these staff meetings," say, "I'm not much for staff meetings but I'm looking forward to this one because I may learn something."
> Instead of saying, "I can't do this, I'll make a fool of myself," say, "I can do this. I don't have to be afraid because the other people there won't be judging me."
> Instead of saying, "I can't talk in front of a group," say, "Talking to groups isn't my favorite sport but I am prepared and what I have to say this time is important."[2]

Positive self-talk is a great tool for dealing with feelings of inadequacy and not being liked. Instead of dwelling on your weaknesses, make a list of your strengths and dwell on those. As for your imperfections, keep telling yourself that imperfect people can be very approachable and likable. Also try praying into a mirror, saying aloud, "Lord, help me love me as I know you love me."

11. *Get rid of grudges.* So you were insulted, or your lovely work was not appreciated as much as it should have been. A grudge is a heavy burden and all it does is sap your energy. Realize that people make mistakes and they sometimes say things they don't mean or regret. The world still

goes on, so why waste your time and energy carrying that grudge?

Another way to put it is, learn to forgive and quit living by the letter of the law. My counseling practice includes many first borns and only children who see God as a judge, policeman, or at best a referee, who is trying to keep the game honest. These first borns get this kind of perception because of how they related to their parents, especially their father. The first born grows up with adults as primary role models and he or she buys deeply into the whole concept of authority and the idea that authority figures are always right and must be obeyed to the very letter.

Ironically, as I counsel Christians who place their faith in Jesus Christ as their Savior, first borns and only children, particularly, have difficulty with the concept of God's grace and forgiveness. They just can't understand that they don't have to earn God's forgiveness; they have only to accept it.

When first borns and only children pray, they tend to address God by using what I call their "ideal self." Their prayers reflect how they would like to act or be or how they want the world to see them. When it comes to forgiveness, the ideal-self kind of prayer sounds like this: "Lord, please help me be more tolerant of little Buford" (or my husband, or whomever). Ideal-self prayers don't get down to the *real me* and telling it like it is: "Lord, I have a lousy temper. Forgive me for the way I chewed out my kids today."

We'll look further at the "ideal self" versus the "real self" in the next chapter on only children, because the only child more than any other personality tends to rely too much on his or her own ability.

Whether you are an only child or even a last born, perfectionism can suck you into acting as though God isn't really big enough to forgive you. Some perfectionists like to control God and decide what he can forgive and what he can't. Even more typical is the perfectionist who believes he has to do something to earn God's forgiveness. The difference between Christianity and all other faiths on this earth is that Christians know they can do nothing to earn forgiveness. Their salvation is God's gift to them. They cannot be perfect enough for God, because only God is perfect.

12. *Don't let life blow out your candle.* One of my favorite counseling techniques with adults is to ask them for five to ten early childhood memories. They may recall only faint glimpses, scenes that flash across their mind, but these little glimpses still mean something. If not, they wouldn't have stuck in their memory for all these years. Part of Adlerian psychology says that early childhood memories are consistent with the way a person sees life as an adult. In fact these early recollections of life—what happened good or bad—are usually symbolic of a person's entire life-style.

I recall a client who was in his twenties when he came to see me. When I asked him for an early childhood memory, he spoke of looking out the window and watching the other boys flying kites in a stiff breeze. It seemed to him that ever since he could remember, he had been standing on the sidelines watching other people have fun. That was one of the reasons he had come to see me. He was still basically watching life go by and not doing much with his potential, even though he was gifted in several areas. He was always wishing he was like others who were involved, active, successful—the people he admired and envied.

Of course, you already guessed the young man's birth order. He was the oldest in his family, and you've probably already guessed what his parents were like—perfectionists and overly demanding. The reason this man lacked self-confidence to try much of anything was obvious. His parents had blown out his candle at an early age.

Not all first borns and only children wind up like this young man. But he is a good example of how first borns or onlies can become discouraged perfectionists. They have so much going for them—ambition, strong power of concentration, excellent organizational and planning skills, and creative thinking. They are precise, meticulous, with excellent memories. They usually come across as leaders and are looked up to by the rest of us. In short, they have it together.

But having it together is not a guarantee that you can't get out of balance and become a victim of your own perfectionism. Perfectionists constantly have to work at being open, tolerant, and patient—with others and themselves. They can't accomplish this in a weekend seminar or by reading one or two books.

Over the years, however, any first born or only child can mature and grow emotionally and spiritually. It wouldn't hurt for every perfectionist (of any birth order) to keep the following paraphrase of a well-known bumper sticker firmly in mind: I must learn to be patient (with myself and others). God isn't finished with me yet!

> I must learn to be patient
> (with myself and others).
> God isn't finished with me yet!

That's an excellent motto, particularly for only children, who face several major challenges, not the least of which is perfectionism. I'm convinced that few onlies ever completely lick their propensity to be intolerant or impatient toward the mere mortals with whom they have to deal. Many only children might prefer a bumper sticker saying: God, grant me patience, but hurry!

7

Lonely Only, Super First Born

A Closer Look at Only Children

*i*f you are a typical only child perfectionist, you may have turned to this chapter muttering, "About time—it's already page 130 and the only child has been barely mentioned—just sort of lumped in with first borns like some kind of vestigial organ."

If that's what you're thinking, I understand. Lonely onlies tend to be critical—and even more than a bit self-centered. After all, the only child has a unique advantage/ disadvantage: He or she has never had to compete with siblings for parental attention, favor, or resources. In this distinction there is good news and bad news. The good news is that it helps make the only child more confident, articulate, and seemingly on top of things. The bad news is that because the only child has never had siblings, he or she has never learned to deal with brothers and sisters. The only child doesn't have to share with siblings or to sometimes go second. It leaves the only child self-centered by default and, depending on how he or she was parented, the confident outer shell may hide someone who feels inferior, rebellious, and always trying to prove he or she is good enough. And that brings us right back to the classic signs of being a discouraged perfectionist.

Only Children Used to Get Bad Press

Up into the '80s and '90s, only children got a bad rap. One survey of college students seemed to prove that only children are perceived as more self-centered, attention seeking, unhappy, and unlikable than those who grew up with siblings.[1] This survey, done in the 1970s, seemed to echo the label put on only children back in the 1920s by none other than Alfred Adler, the pioneer psychologist who made birth order such an important part of his school of thinking. In one of Adler's most important books, he penned the infamous judgment, "The only child has difficulties with every independent activity and sooner or later they become useless in life."[2]

With all due respect to a patron saint of my profession, I must challenge Adler's statement on two counts. First, it has a slight grammar problem (which to a baby of the family like me is no big deal), but far more important is that what he says about only children as a total group is simply not true.

Exactly how and why Alfie Adler came to this conclusion is hard to say. Perhaps he had just had a long day counseling an only child—perhaps several only children. Whatever happened, he put a very erroneous blanket label on a birth order that has turned out some of the more outstanding names in all walks of life.

If Adler really believed that only children as a rule would turn out having difficulties with being independent and would wind up useless, he would have had a hard time explaining U.S. presidents Gerald Ford and Franklin D. Roosevelt, the only man to be elected four times; premier journalists Ted Koppel and Walter Cronkite; singing star Lena Horne; film stars Brooke Shields and Gregory Peck; magician extraordinaire David Copperfield; and football greats Roger Staubach and Joe Montana, legendary quarterbacks in the National Football League.

Other only children who lived fairly useful lives include Leonardo da Vinci, the Duchess of Windsor, Charles Lindbergh, Indira Gandhi, and Isaac Newton.

If we care to look into the business world, we need certainly to consider Robert E. Allen, CEO of AT&T; Carl Icahn, architect of some of the biggest corporate takeovers in history; and T. Boone Pickens, billionaire oil tycoon.

T. Boone Pickens: "Birth Order Makes Sense"

The first time I met T. Boone Pickens, we were on the same TV talk show, pushing books we had just written. As we sat in the green room waiting to go on, he saw me holding a copy of *The Birth Order Book*.

"What's birth order?" Boone wanted to know.

Since walking in, I had been watching Boone and I thought I'd take a shot at guessing his birth order: "Well, you're probably an only child, aren't you?"

Boone looked at me rather strangely and said, "Why, yes! How did you know? Have we met?"

"I'm a psychologist and birth order is something I use in my work."

We started talking about birth order, and after ten minutes of my instruction, Boone was suggesting uses for birth order I'd never thought of, and I'm the guy who supposedly wrote the book!

A typical only child, Boone has a mind like the proverbial steel trap. He travels with his wife, Bea, and an entourage of several other people, but something occurred that day that had never happened before, or since, for that matter. Boone went on first and, after his six-minute spot on the show, everyone got up and was ready to board his limo and head for the airport. But this time Boone said, "Everybody sit down. Dr. Leman's on next, and we're going to learn something about birth order."

When I finished with my segment, Boone said something I'll never forget. In fact I remember it as though it were yesterday: "You know, this makes sense. Big business and industry would be smart to pay attention to everyone's birth order, I would think—especially when assigning certain jobs within the organization."

Needless to say, my encounter with T. Boone Pickens made my day and then some. In a few minutes he had grasped what I had been trying to tell people for years. Boone could see that the first person you want to understand completely is *you*.[3] It's too bad T. Boone Pickens and Alfred Adler couldn't have met and had a chat about only children being doomed to a useless life.

The bottom line is that it's never a good idea to stereotype any birth order into some kind of slot or rut because of what you've heard, read, or even observed. Of course, some only children do come out spoiled, selfish, lazy, aloof, and even dependent and useless. But I've counseled middle children in that boat and not a few last borns who fit the same description.

Some Lonely Onlies I Admire

Although I'm a last born (and nothing like an only child), certain lonely onlies are among people I admire most in this world. One is Ted Koppel, the succinct, do-things-exactly-right host of *Nightline.* In my opinion Koppel has done more outstanding TV interviews of news makers than any man or woman alive. I also have the highest regard for humorist and songwriter Steve Allen, who has turned out something like ten thousand tunes; and Dick Cavett, another excellent talk-show host with acerbic wit. America's leading developmental psychologist, Dr. James Dobson, is a person I've known and admired for years. Listen to his program and you'll never hear a mistake. As an only child, he doesn't allow them!

Nor can I forget to mention Charles Gibson, former cohost of *Good Morning, America,* where I have been a frequent guest as "family psychologist."[4] Gibson goes by "Charles" or "Charlie," and it's easy to see why he can't quite make up his mind. According to his ordinal birth order, he is the last born in his family and that accounts for the "Charlie" who is easygoing and engaging. But the sibling just above him is more than ten years older, which automatically qualifies him for functional only child. And that accounts for the "Charles," who has such a confident, in-charge manner.

And right here in Arizona we have Pat McMahon. Those of us who reside in the Grand Canyon state know he is one of the best radio/television personalities in the business. I've been on literally hundreds of TV and radio stations and have been interviewed by some of the best, but I have to say McMahon is a marvel.

Other lonely onlies I admire are Lauren Bacall, Nancy Reagan, Joe Montana, and Carol Burnett.

Key to Understanding the Only Child

I could go on with my only-child hall of fame but perhaps I need to stop and ask some obvious questions: (1) Where has all this criticism of onlies come from over the years?

(2) What is the only child's downside, or should I say dark side? The key to understanding an only child is knowing *why* he or she is an only. There are two major reasons, either of which determines the only child's fate to a great extent.

> The key to understanding an only child is knowing *why* he or she is an only.

The Special Jewel

You may be a "special jewel" only child, meaning that your parents wanted more children but could have only one and all their energy and attention (along with a certain amount of doting and spoiling) went into you. If you're a special jewel, remember you were probably sheltered and kept from reality in your earlier years. And you may well have developed a typical trait of many only children—feeling overly important. Now that you're an adult, you may have to cope with what could be a lifelong problem—being self-centered—because it's hard to break that pattern molded long ago by Mom and Dad. Special jewels often arrive when parents are older—usually in their thirties—and they make their only child the "center of the universe."

I tell special jewels not to take the self-centered label too hard. They must keep in mind that they never had to learn how to share with siblings, so it's natural enough to feel overly important. Adult only children need to balance two extremes: believing they really are more important than others and thinking they are being treated unfairly when things don't go their way.

Parental Plan

The other reason you may be an only child is that your parents planned for only one. In the late '60s, when I was getting started in counseling, the planned-for only child was often the victim of very structured, tightly disciplined parents. They treated their lonely only as a little adult, always pressuring him or her to be "grown up," mature, responsible, and dependable. This kind of only child can appear very confident, cool, and calm on the surface, but just beneath, he or she is seething with inner rebellion. All your life you may have resented having to be the "little adult" and now, having reached adulthood, you may be ready to (or are in the midst of) indulging yourself in one way or another.

In the late '80s and throughout the '90s, families have been growing ever smaller and many parents are opting for only one child. These only children aren't as pressured as they used to be. They're the beneficiaries of better parenting and often turn out to be well-adjusted, pleasant people with great initiative and high self-esteem. U.S. Bureau of Census statistics reveal that from 1980 to 1990 there was a 76 percent increase among women near the end of their childbearing years who still had only one child. What that tells me is that there was a very good chance that these families would have no more children—that one was all they planned on.[5]

One social psychologist, who teaches at the University of Texas at Austin, says, "The view of only children as selfish and lonely is a gross exaggeration of reality."[6] The more recent assessment of the only child is that he or she may have great initiative and good self-esteem. It's also often the case that the only child never felt all that lonely either.[7]

Perfectionist Only Children Want to Do It Right

Whether special jewels or planned, only children are excellent candidates for growing up to be ultra perfectionists. They want things just so and when things don't go their way, they get frustrated, antsy, and even angry. They become very impatient with, or very intolerant of, people who don't measure up to their standards. Only children often quietly (sometimes not so quietly) wish they could move in, take over, and "do it right."

Only children are excellent candidates for growing up to be ultra perfectionists.

The single personality type I see far too much of in my office is the "discouraged perfectionist," the person who thinks he or she has to be perfect (see chapter 5). These people are very structured, with high expectations for themselves and others. Only children suffer the most severely from this problem, but first borns are not far behind.

Discouraged perfectionists come in different makes and models, but one of the most prevalent is the woman who wants to be everybody's rescuer. She agonizes over the problems of others and always wants to move in, take over, and solve everything. I call this the "nurse mentality" and it is no coincidence that nurses are often only children, or at least first borns in their family.

When I believe I have a discouraged perfectionist on my hands, I ask the client to complete a little exercise that compares her "ideal self" with the "real self." In other words, I want her to contrast the self she would like to believe others see (the ideal) with the kind of person she believes she actually is (the real). Below is an exhaustive example of how a forty-one-year-old discouraged perfectionist only child, whom I will call Kathleen, completed this exercise.

Ideal Kathleen	Real Kathleen
organized and efficient	inefficient and unorganized
happy and cheerful	negative and grumpy
uplifting, able to bring out the best in those around me	nitpicky, discouraging to those around me
have realistic view of time and how much can be accomplished	begin things that won't fit in time slot—can't possibly finish

(continued)

Ideal Kathleen	Real Kathleen
good housekeeper	always behind
able to manage household efficiently	can't get it together or get others to help
energetic and eager	mostly tired and force myself to do things
sexually aggressive and expressive	tired and mechanical
have realistic love expectations	have unrealistic romantic expectations, wanting to be pursued like before we were married
beautiful on the inside so the beauty can flow out	full of anger inside
self-confident no matter what others think	wonder what others are thinking
make steady progress toward goal	procrastinate, put everything off till the last minute
finish projects	have many unfinished projects
have clean closets at home	too much clutter, can't part with anything
short and to the point	could go on and on and on
self-assured	need approval of others
feel secure	need to be needed

As I said, Kathleen completed this in exhaustive fashion and let me know she could have gone on—and on! For a nonperfectionist baby of the family like myself, it was not only exhaustive, it was exhausting! The above lists are the most thorough I had ever seen concerning the comparison of the ideal versus the real person. But on the other hand, it didn't surprise me, because Kathleen was, indeed, a classic discouraged perfectionist. She knew exactly what she was supposed to be like, but she couldn't measure up.

Her husband, Russ, described her as depressed, full of guilt, much too sensitive, a worrier, under a lot of pressure, constantly on the go, always catching up on projects, always having to do the right thing, always biting off more than she could chew—and always feeling like a failure.

After I looked at Kathleen's real/ideal exercise, I gave her a suggestion for the next time she began to think discouraging thoughts: Take off her high-heeled shoe and rap herself on the side of the head a few times. "I'm sure you've heard of the best-selling book *How to Be Your Own Best Friend*," I chided. "Kathleen, you could easily write *How to Be Your Own Worst Enemy!*"

Kathleen was wallowing so deeply in her discouraged perfectionism that she didn't even see the humor in what I was trying to tell her—or the truth. I went on to explain that she was her own worst enemy because she let several different enemies live right there inside of her head. The first thing she had to understand was that by comparing the "ideal" with the "real," she could get to the very crux of the defeated perfectionist personality. One of Kathleen's enemies was the idealism that had made her set extremely high goals. When she couldn't reach those goals, her *perception* of her real self made her feel like a failure on every count. She really wasn't as bad as her "real Kathleen" column seemed to say, but she *thought* she was and that trapped her in her own prison of unfulfilled perfectionism.

Kathleen's Father Was a Flaw Finder

Kathleen's prison had been created mostly by the way she had been parented. You may have guessed that Kathleen—an only child—grew up in a family with a very detached father who would never praise her for anything. In fact he was very good at finding her flaws. Kathleen always felt as if she had to measure up but she never could no matter how hard she tried.

For example at age thirteen she single-handedly built a brick wall that went around the back of her home and encircled a small bricked-in patio. It was a major task for anyone and practically impossible for a thirteen year old.

But in her own way she pulled it off and did an exceptionally good job. Everyone who saw the wall marveled at her work—except her father.

When Dad came home from a business trip and found the wall, he was enraged. Everything Kathleen had done was wrong. He couldn't find one thing right with the wall or with her.

Things were bad enough growing up, but Kathleen fortified her perfectionist prison by choosing to marry Russ. He was smart, good at his job, and very successful. He was also a first-born child and very insecure, because he always felt as if he couldn't quite measure up either. Russ was an interesting combination, almost a paradox in that he was very critical and flaw-finding but at the same time he didn't want to have any conflict. The result was that he disapproved of Kathleen but never said much. Communication was almost zero.

And so Russ was absolutely inept at providing what Kathleen really needed in life: a husband who could share intimate thoughts and feelings with her. Kathleen's forte, however, was getting her hopes high and then having Russ fall short of her expectations. But instead of confronting Russ, she turned the evidence on herself and became all the more convicted of not being a good person. Whenever Russ didn't measure up to her lofty expectations for a husband, she didn't tell herself Russ was terrible; she told herself she was terrible and if she could be a better person, Russ would behave differently!

As part of the counseling program, we brought Russ into the office, and I helped him learn how to articulate his feelings, first with me alone and then later in front of Kathleen. It was a revelation to him as he became aware that he was full of feelings but had just never learned to let them out. He had always quietly "disapproved" of Kathleen, and she had sensed it, only driving her deeper into

discouraged perfectionism. When they finally got to talking, a lot of things cleared up fast.

One thing they learned together was that Russ was a
controller and that Kathleen was a pleaser. One of the reasons behind Russ's reluctance to show feelings was that he
was afraid if he ever told his wife how he felt, she would
reject him. This is a classic characteristic of some controllers
who have a hard time sharing their feelings, because they
are afraid if they ever do they'll be rejected. (See chapter
12 for more on controllers and pleasers.)

On the other hand, as a pleaser Kathleen was sure she
could never say no to anyone, that she had to do everything for everybody, and continually put herself second and
the entire world first. It was exceptionally gratifying to help
Kathleen and Russ find out they could share feelings with
each other and love each other just the way they were.

Because Kathleen was such a super pleaser, an important
part of her therapy was getting her to learn the word *no*.
Her inability to say no led her into the overwhelming propensity to commit herself to more than she could handle.
I had to literally argue her into agreeing to weed things out
of her life that were really too much for her. Kathleen was
extremely active in her church. She served as a Sunday
school teacher and was on every possible church board. In
addition, she had decided to home school her two children
and hold down a part-time job of twenty-two hours a week!

There was, of course, no way any human being could do
all this very satisfactorily. Kathleen had no time for herself,
not to mention time for Russ. But it was her style, and she
drove herself to the brink. That's when she came to see me.

"How will I ever catch up?" Kathleen asked me in one
of our sessions.

"My general prescription, Kathleen, is that you drop
some things or you will drop dead yourself."

I got her to agree to give up teaching her kids at home,
as well as quit her part-time job. I also suggested she cut

back on some of her church work, where she was doing far more than one person should. It was extremely difficult for Kathleen to resign any of her positions at the church because her faith meant a great deal to her. But I tried to sell her on the idea that if she were really going to serve God well, she had to start by serving her husband and family well. I also advised her to start treating herself better.

One of Kathleen's allies was her only-child propensity to follow directions and she became one of my star clients. Of all the changes she made, the ones that I felt were the most significant centered around backing off and saying no to a world that was constantly pressuring her with typical requests like, "I know you're busy, but you're really the one person we know who can handle this."

Before she sought help, Kathleen was in danger of fulfilling Alfred Adler's prophecy that only children feel useless and lack independence. I find it ironic that, while Adler was so negative on only children, one of my clients—an only child—fulfilled another one of his claims: It isn't important where you were born in your family. Your particular birth order only means you have had a certain environment in which to develop. As an adult you can recognize your characteristics and take practical steps to emphasize your strong points and strengthen your weak ones.[8]

Kathleen, the discouraged pursuer of perfection, became a much more relaxed seeker of excellence. She proved there is *always* hope even for an only child whose unfeeling, critical father turned her into a totally discouraged perfectionist. I count Kathleen as one of the real victories of my counseling career.

How Edwin Got over the Hump

Another success story, in which I like to think I played a part, is that of Edwin, the super perfectionist only child you met earlier.

After Edwin read the first edition of *The Birth Order Book*, he wrote to thank me for explaining why and how he was such an only-child perfectionist: He strived to be color-coordinated, even to the point of hanging different shirts on different colored hangers; and he had the classic messy desk with piles everywhere from which he could extract whatever he was looking for in sixty seconds. Later I wrote back to ask him if he would care to contribute some thoughts to a new book I was planning to write on using birth order principles in the business world. He didn't reply for several months, and I thought probably he had been busy or perhaps he had forgotten about it. So I dropped him another note to renew my request.

About two weeks later Edwin wrote back, listing in breathless fashion an incredible array of assignments, tasks, and crises that he had been handling as a busy vice president and that my first letter had been resting safely in one of his piles, this one being next to his couch. But now the deadlines and crises had passed, including his housekeeper hanging his dress shirts on *blue* hangers instead of *brown* hangers! He had kept the housekeeper despite this glaring error and had gotten rid of all of his brown hangers so that now all his shirts, dress or sport, were on blue hangers. Finally he was ready to deal with the questions I had sent and I would "hear from him soon."

Frankly I wasn't too optimistic. It was obvious that Edwin was still going at a frenetic pace and he was still saying yes to too many of life's insatiable demands. And he seemed to be enjoying all of the pressures, which is often true of perfectionists, until they start to reach burn-out. Still, I could see Edwin was making a little progress. Switching to all-blue hangers for all of his shirts sounds humorous and a little eccentric, but I saw it as a baby step toward less structure.

It turned out that "soon" took several more months, suggesting that Edwin was still hanging on to the perfectionistic habit of procrastinating. Finally he did send answers to my questions, including this one: "You're a vice president. How do you see your perfectionism helping or hurting you on the job?" Here is his insightful reply:

> It helps to strive for perfectionism because you quickly build a reputation for doing quality work. When the boss has an especially important assignment, to whom is he/she going to assign it? That's right, the person who will—based on past experience—do the best job. . . .
>
> Early in my career I recall being given a series of assignments. I was not able to complete them in the normal, eight-hour work days, and put in a considerable amount of noncompensated overtime. I was criticized for this by coworkers. I thought nothing of the additional hours—I simply wanted to do the best possible job I could. I honestly didn't even think about this work leading to a promotion or a raise (which it did). I was just trying to do the best job that I was capable of doing.
>
> Perfectionism hurts, however, because you demand the same (perfection) from your coworkers and subordinates. Occasionally, resentment can result. I used to be easily disappointed and upset when I saw that someone just didn't give 100 percent. Now I realize that, for whatever reasons, not all people have the same motivation.

When I asked Edwin if he thought he was making any progress with his messy desk (and couch), he said:

> Until I read *The Birth Order Book,* I thought that I lost control of my desk because I switched from project to project during the day, putting files on top of other files in a desperate attempt to keep the flow of work moving and not interrupting the momentum by taking time to refile things.

However, now I understand that this is merely my defense mechanism to try to convince the world that I am not really a perfectionist. That way I am less likely to be criticized. Only children, you know, don't want to be criticized even if it is for being a perfectionist! And don't criticize me for a messy desk either. I've improved my desk since I've read *The Birth Order Book*.

Edwin will always struggle with perfectionism but he's making real progress that goes beyond improving his "messy desk." When he took the perfectionist quiz (see page 98) Edwin scored in the high 20s, meaning that he was close to an extreme perfectionist, but when he did the comparison of perfectionism and excellence exercise (see page 117), he clearly showed he knew the difference and was coming down on the side of excellence much more often than he used to. He told me:

> I seek excellence, not perfection. There is a difference. I strive for excellence, knowing that perfection means flawless.
>
> Let's say we are considering an acquisition, and time is short. My "briefing report" for the acquisitions group will be thorough and complete—covering all of the research and facts—but it may not be perfect. I may include my hand-drawn charts (I'm a lousy artist), not slick, computer-generated charts; some of the T's may not be crossed, but the information will be correct, thorough, and timely. That will be an excellent report, but not a perfect one.

The last line of Edwin's note above clearly tells me he is over the perfectionistic hump. He can do a less-than-perfect report that includes a typo or two and even hand-drawn charts and still call it excellent, because it does what it is supposed to do—deliver information. Edwin finally sees the point. His goal is to do the best job possible with high standards rather than turning every job into a monument that glorifies his perfectionism.

If I ran a larger operation that needed Edwin's skills, I'd hire him in a heartbeat. Any company would be lucky to have him as vice president or even as CEO because his struggles with perfectionism—and less than perfect coworkers—have made him a more understanding, well-rounded personality, who still wants to do the best job he can.[9]

But, of course, Edwin isn't perfect. If you want a bloody nose, just try calling him Eddie. It's interesting—when you think about first borns and only children, a Kathryn, a Robert, or a Suzanne may come to mind who loathe being called Kathy, Bobby, or Susie.

A Final Word for Onlies and Other Perfectionists

A piece of advice that I give to all perfectionists and especially to only children is: Lower your high-jump bar of life.

Lower your high-jump bar of life.

Others haven't put that bar up so high—*you* have, as you have reached for perfection and made real success impossible. When you learn to settle for excellence, however, life will be more satisfying, happier, and more fulfilling, as you clear the bar and then some!

Assessing Your Only-Child Strengths and Weaknesses

Go over the chart below, which lists typical traits of only children. Consider each trait and decide if it is a strength or weakness as far as you are concerned. If it's a weakness, what changes could you make to improve in that area? If it's a strength, how could you capitalize on that strength or develop it even further?

Strengths and Weaknesses of Only Children

Typical Traits	Strengths	Weaknesses
Confident, self-assured	Trust own opinion, not afraid to make decisions	May be self-centered from being treated by parents as "center of universe"; also fearful, ambivalent about trying new things
Perfectionist	Always do things right and leave no stone unturned to do a thorough job	Tend to criticize themselves and/or others too much; never satisfied; may procrastinate because they fear they cannot do a "good enough job"
Organized	Have everything under control; always on top of things; tend to be on time and on schedule	May worry too much about order, process, and rules and not be flexible when it's needed; may show real impatience with anyone who is "dis-organized" or not as meticulous; can be upset by surprises
Driver	Ambitious, enterprising, energetic, willing to sacrifice to be a success	Put themselves or those they work with under too much stress and pressure
List maker	Set goals and reach them; tend to get more done in a day than others; planning the day is a must	May become boxed in, too busy with the to-do list to see the big picture and what needs to be done right now
Logical	Known as straight thinkers; can be counted on not to be compulsive or to go off half-cocked	May believe they're always right and fail to pay attention to the more intuitive opinions of others
Scholarly	Tend to be voracious readers and accumulators of information and facts; good problem solvers who think things through	May spend too much time gathering facts when there are other things that need to be done; may be so serious they fail to see the humor in situations when humor is desperately needed

Being Honest with Your Only-Child Self

1. Am I learning to bite off less and not expect so much of myself? What recent examples can I think of?
2. Am I building time and space for myself into my schedule? How do I know?
3. Am I developing friends among younger or older people rather than only my own age level? (List ages of your friends. Who gives you strokes? Who argues with you?)
4. How selfish and self-centered am I really? What can I do to put others first, help others more, be less critical?

5. Do I understand and really believe that no one is perfect?
6. Do I understand and really believe that my naturally high standards need to be more reasonable and less excessive?
7. Do I understand I really can't do it all myself? What recent examples of depending on others can I think of?
8. I am working on my self-talk. What recent example of turning negative self-talk to positive self-talk can I think of?

8

I Never Did Get No Respect

A CLOSER LOOK AT THE MIDDLE CHILD

*W*e've been spending a lot of time on first borns and only children and their nemesis, perfectionism. But if you're later born and fall somewhere in that nebulous "middle child" category, you're probably not too upset with the lack of attention. You may even be saying, "I'm not surprised. He's likely to get to me *last*. What else is new?"

It is quite normal for middle children to feel left out, ignored, and even insulted. After the first edition of *The Birth Order Book* came out, I received several letters of mild complaint from middle borns. Here's a sample:

Dear Dr. Leman:
I counted the number of pages in *The Birth Order Book*
and fewer are devoted to middle children than any other
birth order! What gives?

> Feeling ignored,
> Middle Child Reader

Going along with what I always thought was a middle-
child attempt to poke a little fun, I would respond to these
complaints by writing back a bit tongue-in-cheek:

Dear Middle Child:
So what? What's the big deal? Besides, you're used to it!
Get a life!

> Happy family photo albums,
> Dr. Leman

Middle Borns Are a Bit Mysterious

I suppose the middle child does get fewer pages in this
book than the other birth orders.[1] One reason for this little oversight is that we psychologists don't know that much
about middle children. They are, in fact, a bit mysterious.

Although I counsel fewer middle children than last borns
or babies, I have talked to enough of them over the years
to see a classic pattern emerging: The official definition of
a middle child is a person born somewhere between the
first or oldest in the family and the last—the literal baby of
the family. This results in the middle children feeling they
were born *too late* to get the privileges and special treatment the first born seemed to inherit by right. And they
were born *too soon* to strike the bonanza that many last
borns enjoy—having the parents lighten up on discipline.

I'm not alone in saying that middle children are a mystery. Many articles and books have been written about
them, one of the best being *First Child, Second Child* by

Bradford Wilson and George Edington. These authors admit that of all birth order positions, "'middleness' is the most difficult to define, let alone describe or generalize about in any meaningful way."[2]

One reason for all the fogginess is that the term "middle" can mean many things. The typical middle child can be the second of three, or the third of four, or the fourth of five, and so on. Some authors go into great detail on categorizing different middle-born children. In my own counseling, however, I have discovered that middle-born children and *second borns* have a great deal in common and are often one and the same because many families stop at three. For the purposes of this chapter, we will group the second-born and middle child together and refer to them as "middle children." In chapter 15 we will go into the second born of two children in a more thorough way when we talk about parenting the two-child family.

Middles and the "Branching Off Effect"

When talking about the middle child, the most critical factor is the "branching off effect" that is always at work in the family. This principle says the second born will be most directly influenced by the first born, the third born will be most directly influenced by the second born, and so on. By "influenced," I simply mean that each child looks *above*, sizes up the older sibling, and patterns his life according to what he sees.

The second born has the first born for his role model and, as he watches the first born in action, the second born develops a style of life of his own. Because the older brother or sister is usually stronger, smarter, and obviously bigger, the second born typically shoots off in another direction. If, however, he senses he can compete with his older sibling, he may do so. If he competes successfully enough, you can have a "role reversal," something we discussed earlier in the variables of birth order.

The second born can, for all intents and purposes, take over the first born's prestige, privileges, and responsibilities. That's what happened with Richard Nixon, second born of five boys. Because his older brother by four years was sickly, the mantle of responsibility often fell on Richard's shoulders. But in another sense, Nixon retained several "middle child" qualities that stood him in good stead later in life.[3]

The point is, any time a second-born child enters the family, his life-style is determined by his perception of his older sibling. The second born may be a pleaser or an antagonizer. He may become a victim or a martyr. He may become a manipulator or a controller. Any number of life-styles can appear but *they all play off the first born*. The general conclusion of all research studies done on birth order is that second borns will probably be somewhat the opposite of first borns.

> Any time a second-born child enters the family, his life-style is determined by his perception of his older sibling.

When You Say "Middle Child," Think "Contradictions"

Because later-born children play off the ones directly above them, there is no sure-fire way to predict which way they may go or how their personality will develop. I have looked at many charts listing characteristics of middle-born children and found them to be an exercise in paradox. An example of one of these charts appears below, containing two columns with words and phrases that can all be very typical of the middle child. The left- and right-hand columns have been arranged to illustrate some of the direct contradictions you can find in this birth order:

The Middle Born: Inconsistent Paradox

Loner, quiet, shy	Sociable, friendly, outgoing
Impatient, easily frustrated	Takes life in stride, laid-back
Very competitive	Easygoing, not competitive
Rebel, family goat	Peacemaker, mediator
Aggressive, a scrapper	Avoids conflict

The bottom line is that the middle child is "iffy"—the product of many pressures coming from different directions. More than any other birth order, you must look at the entire family to understand a particular middle child. How he or she finally turned out is about as predictable as a Chicago weather report. In many ways, the middle child remains a mystery.

Middles Know How Rodney Feels

One thing, however, that is not such a mystery about middle children is that they usually feel the squeeze from above and below. You may have noted that the title of this chapter paraphrases comedian Rodney Dangerfield's famous line: "I don't get no respect!" Many middle children would say they understand.

I have counseled many middle borns who have told me they did not feel that special growing up. "My older brothers got all the glory, and my little sister got all the attention, and then there was me," is a very familiar assessment.

Somehow there just doesn't seem to be a great deal of parental awareness of the middle child's need for a spot in the pecking order. The following scene comes from a work of fiction, but it is all too true for many middle borns:

When Mama introduced Sylvie, she always said, "This is Sylvie, my oldest child."

When Mama introduced Rufus, she always said, "This is Rufus, the baby in the family."

When Mama introduced Joey to people, she would say, "This is Joey, my oldest son."

When Mama introduced Jane, she just said, "This is Jane." Because Mama had not figured out that Jane was the middle Moffat. Nobody had figured this out, but Jane.[4]

If I want to get a rise out of middle-born children at a seminar, all I have to say is, "family photo album." They laugh, but it's usually sardonic laughter. The family photo album often contains solid proof that Mom and Dad relegate the middle child to the background. There will be two thousand pictures of the first born, and thirteen of the middle child. Second-born children, in particular, seem to fall victim to this strange phenomenon. It's almost as if Mom and Dad had their first child and snapped pictures left and right. Then, when the second born came along, they either went on welfare and couldn't buy film or the camera got broken and wasn't fixed until "Baby Princess" arrived.

Picture (no pun intended) the scene. Thirteen-year-old girl falls in puppy love for the first time and wants to give her boyfriend her picture. She goes to her mother and says, "Hey, Mom, are there any pictures of me without *her?*" Mom looks a little chagrined and has to shake her head no. So the new boyfriend gets her photo—carefully trimmed so older sister's armpit barely shows!

Middles Find All the Friends They Can

Middle-born children often hang out more with their peer group than does any other child in the family. That's really no surprise because middles often feel like fifth wheels who are out of place and misunderstood at home or like some kind of leftovers that always get bypassed and upstaged by the younger or older siblings.

No wonder, then, that friends become very important to the middle child, because friends make him or her feel special. At home the first born is special because he or she is first. The last born is special because he or she means the end of the line. The middle child? He's "good old John," or "just plain Mary."

There is a psychological theory that says human beings operate according to three natural motivations:

1. To obtain rewards and recognition
2. To avoid pain and danger
3. To get even[5]

Every birth order has these three motivations operating in life but it is especially interesting to trace their effect on the behavior of the typical middle born.

To obtain rewards and recognition, the squeezed-out middle born goes outside the family to create another kind of "family" where he or she can feel special. First borns typically have fewer friends. Middle children often have many.

How sad, you may say, that the middle-born child has to go outside the family to get recognition and feelings of acceptance. But weep not for our social butterfly. All these relationships will pay off later, as I'll explain in a moment.

So to avoid the pain and frustration of being an outsider in his family, the middle child leaves home the quickest. I don't mean he runs away or volunteers for boarding school, but he makes friends more quickly at school and in the neighborhood. Tired of being told, "You're too young," when he seeks the same privileges as the oldest, and weary of hearing, "You're too old," when he whines for a little TLC like that given the youngest, the middle child goes where he is "just the right age"—to his peer group.

And to get even, at least a little bit for those feelings of rootlessness, the middle child becomes a bit of a free spirit.

He gives himself the right to reject the family's do's and don'ts, at least in part, by choosing some other group's values for a measuring stick. It may be a team (middle children are great team players), a club, or a gang of kids who hang out together. The important thing is that the middle child experiences the group *as his,* something his family can't control or squeeze in any way.

Because of this early search for friends and recognition outside the home while growing up, the middle child may be the one who moves away from the family as an adult. This was graphically illustrated during one of my guest appearances on *Oprah.* Three young women were also on the show as an example of how birth order plays out among three sisters. When I happened to make the point that the middle child is most likely to move away from the family, the oldest and youngest sisters howled with delight. They had always lived in New Jersey, close to their parents and the rest of the family. The middle daughter, who it turned out had many friends, had taken off to make a life for herself in California.

Middles Are Often Good Mediators

Of course, some middle children choose other ways to meet their needs for obtaining recognition, avoiding pain, and getting even. They may prefer becoming mediators and even at times are manipulative. Because they couldn't have Mom and Dad all to themselves and get their way, they learned to negotiate and compromise. And these, obviously, aren't such bad skills to have for getting along later in life. (If you are getting the message that middle children just may turn out to be the best-adjusted adults in the family, you're right, but more on that later.)

But if the middle child is very compliant and not at all interested in confrontation or conflict, the propensities to negotiate and compromise can backfire. I've had more than one middle-child super mom and super wife come to me for counseling with the same problem: The husband is having another affair (with a younger, more attractive woman, of course) but second-born wife is sticking it out—again.

She has many options: moving out, serving papers, confronting the other woman, but she doesn't really want to do anything. She grew up a pleaser, always trying to avoid rocking the boat. Now she has become a victim and indulges in victim thinking. She will hang tough with her cheating hubby until the bitter end, and he knows it.

Donald Trump: Deals Are His Art Form

On the other hand, the aggressive, competitive middle child may use his negotiating/mediating skills to become a skilled entrepreneur. Possibly the most outstanding example of this is Donald Trump, one of the more flamboyant real estate wheeler-dealers of the twentieth century.

Trump is the fourth born of five who looked above at two older sisters and a first-born big brother, Freddy Jr. Father Trump was grooming Freddy Jr. to take over and follow in his footsteps as a hard-driving builder and manager of huge apartment buildings in New York City, but there was a problem. Freddy Jr. was a complacent, compliant first born who wanted to please people rather than manage or control them. Donald, eight years younger than his oldest brother, took over the position of successor to his father more or less by default, and his career in real estate was launched.

This sounds like a "role reversal" but it is not. To have a true role reversal, Donald would have had to be within two years of Freddy. Instead, because there was an eight-year gap between Freddy, the first-born son, and Donald, the next son to be born in the family, Donald was able to develop a lot of first-born qualities of his own despite having those two older sisters above him. The Trumps are a good example of how a large gap between same sex children can make a huge difference in the roles they eventually play in the family.

When I'm doing a seminar, people sometimes come up to me and say, "I'm a middle child, but I feel I have an awful lot of first-born qualities as well." When I start to probe a little in their family relationships, I usually discover a situation with similarities to what happened with Donald Trump, who became a functional first born due to certain variables at work in his family.

In his autobiography, Trump speaks of making deals and says:

> I don't do it for the money. I've got enough, much more than I'll ever need. I do it to do it. Deals are my art form. Other people paint beautifully on canvas or write wonderful poetry. I like to make deals, preferably big deals. That's how I get my kicks. . . . The real excitement is playing the game. I don't spend a lot of time worrying about what I should have done differently, or what's going to happen next. If you ask me exactly what the deals . . . all add up to in the end, I'm not sure I have a very good answer. Except that I've had a very good time making them.[6]

Nixon and Bush: Skilled in Diplomacy

If I were to ask you to name two U.S. presidents of the latter twentieth century who were considered skilled in foreign affairs and diplomacy, who would come to mind? If you know much about our presidents at all, you may well have thought of Richard Nixon or George Bush, who most political observers say were very adept on the foreign affairs front. It just so happens, of course, that both men were middle children.

You may recall that I mentioned how Nixon did a role reversal on his older brother because of the older brother's ongoing illness. Nonetheless, Nixon also grew up learning how to negotiate and mediate. A major reason for this may have been that his younger brother was born only twelve months after him, which meant that baby Richard got very little experience at being the baby of the family. Instead, he was quickly thrust into the middle-child role.

More Insights on the Middle Child

Although middle children are not as easy to paint in clear and vivid colors as first borns or only children, we do know some things that can help adult middle children function with better understanding of themselves and how they relate to others:

1. *You are more of a closed book than an open one.* Studies show middle children are the most secretive of all birth orders.[7] If this applies to you, realize you could be displaying the "burned child" reaction. The burned middle child experiences the world as paying him less attention than it did his older or younger siblings. This leads you to "play it closer to the vest" with your relationships.

As a rule, you do not choose to confide in very many people. This is not necessarily a minus; in fact in some cases it may be the wise thing to do. But it can also backfire. It's interesting to note that President Nixon got into all kinds of Watergate troubles because of being secretive. His effort to cover up what had gone on eventually led to his impeachment.

I appear from time to time on the Leeza Gibbons TV talk show, and not long ago she invited me to take part in a program dealing with birth order, which her producer had entitled, "Born First, Born Last . . . What's My Destiny?" One of the families that appeared on the show included a mother and four daughters who fit into typical birth order stereotypes right down the line. The third-born girl was shy, a peacemaker who didn't want anyone in the family to be fighting or mad at one another. She was also very secretive, something I've seen borne out in so many middle children over the years.

This child's destiny will more likely than not include being very secretive in her marriage, and I hope she chooses a man who is very patient and willing to listen and draw her out. Being secretive and closed is not the best quality to bring to a marriage. I have counseled too many middle children who were simply not communicating with their spouse.

2. *You are likely to be mentally tough and independent.* While in graduate school, I often heard that middle children are the last to seek the services of helping professionals, such as psychologists, counselors, or ministers. After I got out into the real world and began counseling people, I quickly saw that my own caseload bore out exactly what I had learned in school.

Who would show up more often in my office? First-born engineers, doctors, people in professions that are demanding and exacting. Why would first borns (and only children) top the list? One reason, of course, is that first borns and only children have the most hang-ups (usually caused by overly demanding parents). At the same time, they are logical, scholarly, organized people who are much more likely to analyze their plight and seek help. Because first borns have always bought into authority figures, they have no problem with coming to psychologists, counselors—people who *know*—for help.

The next largest group on my client roll is last borns—the babies who are used to being cared for and helped. And, finally, my smallest group of counselees is middle children. But I am not surprised. The reason could lie in the burned child reaction coming out (or perhaps the burned child wants to stay in hiding?). Another explanation is that middle children tend to be mentally tough and independent, qualities they acquired while learning to cope with feelings of rejection and "being a fifth wheel" while growing up.

Since I don't need more clients, I can say with all objectivity to the middle child, it's fine to be tough and independent. It is foolish, however, to refuse to get the help you may need. I urge any middle child, who is in a situation where counseling might do some good, to sit down and think it through carefully. You might be cutting off your nose to spite your face because you're nurturing a grudge you got way back on that day when your older sister got to go to the beach and you didn't, and then a couple of hours later, you got grounded for a month when you clobbered your little brother for being such a pest.

3. *Teenage middles often run with the pack.* If you're a middle-born parent with teenagers, you may well understand why your own children are out "running with the pack." Possibly you gave your own parents fits by going along with what they thought was the wrong crowd.

I counsel many families where parents are worried about a child who seems to be "hanging with the wrong crowd." Granted, not all these children are middle born, but middle borns seem to turn up with this problem more than do those of other birth orders. In my own experience, I see first borns as being the least inclined to run with the pack, mainly because they are such natural leaders. Last borns may run with the pack strictly because they like to explore and take risks, but middle children have deeper reasons. Because of being squeezed and feeling they don't really fit in at home, middle children have a deep need to belong and the pack fills the bill.

4. *You're likely to be the most faithful marriage partner.* Studies also show that middle borns rate as the most monogamous of all birth orders.[8] There is no surprise here.

Middle children grow up feeling they don't fit in that well at home, so when they start their own family, they are extra motivated to make their marriage work.

Another way to say this is that middle children are loyal. They are far more prone to stick to their commitments. While this is an excellent quality, it can lead to a lot of pain for a middle-child spouse who is being taken advantage of by a mate who is unfaithful, abusive, or dominating.

5. *You probably embarrass easily.* Again we can't lay a blanket judgment on any birth order, but studies show that middle borns are much more prone to embarrassment, but of course they will never admit it.[9] Why would the middle child admit to embarrassment? That in itself would be embarrassing!

This is one of the areas where the paradox of middle children becomes most apparent. While they are prone to embarrassment, middle borns are often rebellious as far as convention is concerned, something that could obviously put them in embarrassing situations. Alfred Adler characterized the first born by saying he "likes . . . the exercise of authority and exaggerates the importance of rules and laws." As for the second child, "he will be inclined to believe . . . there is no power in the world which cannot be overthrown."[10]

Middle Ground: Not a Bad Place to Stand

Like any other birth order, being a middle child has its pluses and minuses, but when you add it all up, the middle ground is not a bad spot at all on which to stand. All the research shows that middle borns do not have as many hang-ups or problems as first borns or only children (and that's obviously one reason why they don't show up in great numbers in counseling offices). Yes, I realize that you may be a middle born who thinks your siblings got all the privileges or the breaks or the spoiling while you had to toe the mark. But did it really hurt you that much? Maybe it did you some good!

> **All the research shows that middle borns do not have as many hang-ups or problems as first borns or only children.**

Breaks and privileges are not necessarily that great. There are almost always strings attached. That's why studies show that later-born children are less fearful and anxious than first borns. While new parents are handing out all those breaks and privileges to the first born, they are also transmitting their fears and anxieties as they wrestle with problems and crises they've never seen before. In addition, they usually have high expectations, which put pressure on their first-born child.

So by the time you—the middle child—came along, your parents almost certainly were more relaxed than they were when your older brother or sister arrived. That first-born sibling of yours ran interference for you—what I call "snowplowing the roads of life."

Granted, not all first borns simply "snowplow the roads of life" for their little brother or sister. They may charge down the road so hard and so fast they leave the middle child feeling left in the dust. It is interesting that Alfred Adler, the father of birth-order psychology, was a middle child himself. And while he thought being a middle child was a fairly safe spot, he did admit that he often felt "put in the shade" by his older brother, a true first born who always seemed to be outdoing him at every turn. At one point Adler said: "My eldest brother . . . is a good industrious fellow—he was always ahead of me—and for the matter of that he is *still* ahead of me!"[11]

Even if you had to live in the shadow of a crown prince or princess, there is no point in wasting time in self-pity. With true middle-born resourcefulness, be thankful for the experience. At least it gave you empathy for people who don't always get to be the star. Kathy Nessel, a fellow psychologist, is a middle child herself. I like the way she sums up the advantages of middledom:

> Middle children are tenacious adults because we are used to life being rather unfair. Our expectations are lower; consequently, we are more accepting in a relationship. The middle child may say, "Well, this isn't perfect, but it is kind of nice." We are not as driven as first borns, but then again neither are we as compulsive.[12]

I had a middle-child client echo Kathy Nessel's words recently when he said: "Being a middle child of three wasn't easy, but as an adult I really believe I can cope with problems better because I got a lot of good training in give-and-take while I was growing up. I'm glad I wasn't first, and I'm glad I wasn't last. I'm glad I'm me!"

All of this suggests that perhaps the best word for the middle child is "balanced." And in this topsy-turvy world, being balanced is not a bad way to fly.

Assessing Your Middle-Child Strengths and Weaknesses

Go over the chart below, which lists typical traits of middle borns. Keep in mind that a lot of these may not apply to you at all—middle children are known for paradox and contradiction. When you do find a trait that applies, decide if it is a strength or a weakness. If it is a weakness, what changes could you make to improve in that area? If it's a strength, how would you capitalize on that strength or develop it even further?

Strengths and Weaknesses of Middle Children

Typical Traits	Strengths	Weaknesses
Grew up feeling squeezed and rootless	Learned not to be spoiled	May be rebellious because they don't feel they fit in
Reasonable expectations	Because life hasn't always been fair, they are unspoiled, realistic	Being treated unfairly may have made them suspicious, cynical, even bitter
Social lion	Relationships are very important; they make friends and tend to keep them	Friends can be too important and not offending them may cloud judgment on key decisions
Independent thinker	Willing to do things differently, take a risk, strike out on their own	May appear to be bullheaded, stubborn unwilling to cooperate
Compromising	Know how to get along with others; can be skilled at mediating disputes or negotiating disagreements	Can be seen as willing to have peace at any price; others may try to take advantage of them
Diplomatic	Peacemakers; willing to work things out; great at seeing issues from both sides	May hate confrontation; often choose not to share their real opinions and feelings
Secretive	Can be trusted with sensitive information; know how to keep secrets	May fail to admit it when they need help—it's just too embarrassing

Being Honest with Your Middle-Child Self

1. Is being a middle child comfortable for me? How do I know?
2. Would my family and friends call me secretive or open?
3. How willing am I to seek help from counselors, doctors, and other authority figures?
4. How do I recall my older sibling or siblings? Did they snowplow the roads of life for me or did they make the roads even rougher to travel? If the latter, have I made peace with that—and them?

5. In the process of give-and-take (at home or at work), I would rate myself as A—excellent, B—good, C—fair to poor. What are my reasons for that rating?

6. If while I was growing up, I felt squeezed and that life was not always fair, how have I adjusted to that as an adult? Is that legacy a strength or a weakness today?

Born Last
but Seldom Least

A Closer Look at the Baby
of the Family

first of all, I want all you babies of the family to know that I'm on to you. I know you have just skipped the first eight chapters and started right here. I understand. Like any last born, I would have done the same thing. I hope you'll go back later to read some pretty important stuff you missed, but meanwhile let's begin with a little story of how Cubby Leman found his true calling in life.

The year is 1952. The scene is a hot, sweaty gymnasium at Williamsville Central High School in western New York. A hard-fought basketball game is in progress and a skinny little eight-year-old kid is out on the floor during a time-out trying to lead cheers. Pinned on his sweater is an image of the team mascot—a billy goat.

The game is as close as the air. The place is packed with screaming fans but at the moment the fans aren't screaming for the "Billies." They're all laughing at this little kid, who has gotten the cheer completely backwards and forgotten what comes next. His big sister, captain of the Williamsville cheerleaders, looks embarrassed, but she has to laugh too, because this little kid is pretty funny.

But is the little eight-year-old guy embarrassed? He doesn't seem to mind at all. In fact he is looking up at the crowd and kind of enjoying the fact that they are all laughing!

Last Borns Often Love the Limelight

I was that little kid—born last in a batch of three—nicknamed "Cub" when I was eleven days old. The name stuck and as I became a toddler and a preschooler, I instinctively became aware of how to always be the "cute little Cubby" in the family. The youngest may have been born last but he has a sixth sense that tells him he's not going to be least!

Youngest children in the family are typically the outgoing charmers, the personable manipulators. They are also affectionate, uncomplicated, and sometimes a little absentminded. Their "What? Me worry?" approach to life gets smiles and shakes of the head. Last borns are the most likely to show up at the elementary school concert or the Sunday school picnic unzipped or unbuttoned in some delicately obvious area. Without doubt, they can be a little different.

It stands to reason, then, that the family clown or entertainer is likely to be the last born. Nobody told me that—I just naturally assumed the role. That was my thing in life—getting people to laugh or point or comment.

No wonder, then, that when I turned eight and my cheerleader sister, Sally, invited me to become the mascot for the high school team, I jumped at the chance. Hundreds of people came to those games and they would all be looking right at me! I loved every minute of it, even that embarrassing scene when I forgot the cheer and the crowd roared with laughter. In fact at that moment in the Williamsville High School gym, I made a decision. In my eight-year-old mind, at least, a star was born. I decided to be an entertainer.

Yes, I know I came out a psychologist who is practicing family therapy. I enjoy my chosen profession and get deep satisfaction from helping families, but my cherished avocation is making people laugh, and I do it whenever and wherever I can—in seminars, conventions, and during television and radio talk shows.

The "Clowns" Also Have a Dark Side

A typical characteristic of the last born is that he is carefree and vivacious—a real people person, who is usually popular in spite of (because of?) his clowning antics. Get the family together for the big Thanksgiving or Christmas photo. Work tenaciously to maneuver everyone into place and to snap the shutter when everyone looks halfway sane and—whoops! Who's that over on the left with the crossed eyes trying to touch his nose with his tongue? Yes, it's last-born Buford (who in this picture may be twenty-six years old) doing his thing for a laugh.

Or maybe Buford is doing his thing for other reasons. There is another strain of characteristics in most last borns. Besides being charming, outgoing, affectionate, and uncomplicated, they can also be rebellious, temperamental, manipulative, spoiled, impatient, and impetuous.

I can relate to this dark side of the last born. Without question, part of my motivation for being "clown prince" of the Leman family was that I wasn't born crown prince or princess. Sally and Jack had beaten me to it. It seemed to me they had all the talent, ability, and smarts. Five years older, Jack was 9.75 in everything he did. Eight years older, sister Sally was a perfect 10.0. Ever since I could remember, it seemed that I scored around 1.8 in comparison to their abilities and achievements. In short, they had all the firepower, and I was a dud.

So it's no surprise that I took the Dennis the Menace route to get my share of the attention. As a five year old, I went to a relative's wedding and became forever established in her memory bank when it came time to throw the rice. Everyone was throwing rice but Kevin. I was throwing gravel.

These are typical feelings and actions of the last-born child. Last borns carry the curse of not being taken very seriously, first by their families and then by the world. And many last borns have a "burning desire to make an important contribution to the world."[1] From the time they are old enough to start figuring things out, last borns are acutely aware they are youngest, smallest, weakest, and least equipped to compete in life. After all, who can trust little Festus to set the table or pour the milk? He's just not quite big enough for that yet.

Those Born Before Cast a Long Shadow

I like the description of last borns by Mopsy Strange Kennedy, a family therapist who has written on occasion for various magazines. Mopsy is a last born herself and that's no surprise. Only a last-born baby of the family is likely to grow up, get a degree, become a therapist, and still keep a handle that sounds like a nickname or pet label of some kind. And so Ms. Kennedy speaks from experience when she observes that the babies of the family "live, inevitably, in the potent shadow of those who were Born Before."[2]

I understand when Mopsy recalls how her early achievements (tying shoes, learning to read, telling time) were greeted with polite yawns and murmurings of, "Isn't that nice," or worse, "Horace, do you remember when Ralph learned to do that?" Ralph, of course, is the big brother born first. Last borns instinctively know and understand that their knowledge and ability carry far less weight than that of their older brothers and sisters. Not only do parents react with less spontaneous joy at the accomplishments of the last born; they may, in fact, impatiently wonder, *Why can't this kid catch on faster? His older brother had this down cold by the time he was two and a half.*

Part of the reason for this is that the parents get all "taught out" by the time the last born arrives. The tendency is to let the last born sort of shift for himself. It's not unusual for babies of the family to get most of their instruction from their brothers and sisters in many areas. The parents are just too pooped for any more pedagogy.

Obviously, receiving instructions from older brothers and sisters does not ensure that last borns are getting the facts of life (or anything else) very straight. Last borns are used to being put down or written off. The older kids always laugh at the babies, who still grope blindly with fantasies like Santa Claus and the Tooth Fairy. It's no wonder the last born grows up with an "I'll show *them!*" attitude.

It's no wonder the last born grows up with an "I'll show *them!*" attitude.

The Checkered Academic Career of Kevin the Clown

In *First Child, Second Child,* Wilson and Edington comment:

> Some last borns become very adept at charming the world
> in various ways, while others grow up with a feeling that
> the only way they can gain anybody's attention is by mak-
> ing a mess; by being a problem child or a pest or a rebel
> who enjoys shooting spitballs at City Hall. If you are a typ-
> ical last born, you have a fair share of both the charmer
> and the rebel in your makeup, and other people are often
> caught off guard by the fact that you can be endearing one
> minute, and hard to deal with the next.[3]

The above paragraph describes me to the last untied
shoelace. To "really show them I mattered" was one of my
main motivations while growing up, and I was indeed a
charmer one moment and a spitball shooting rebel the
next. I have to say that Sally and Jack didn't make fun of
me a lot. Indeed, Sally became something of a second
mother. But both of them certainly had it all over me in
the achievement categories. I often describe the three of
us in the same terminology used for reading groups at
school. Sally, the A+ student, and Jack, the B+ student,
were the "bluebirds" of the family. I took one look at all
this and decided to become the "crow." Reading bored
me and studying anything was the last thing I wanted to
do—and I usually did it last, or not at all.

But I wanted—and desperately needed—attention and
I got it by clowning, teasing, and showing off. I wasn't
your classic juvenile delinquent. I could actually be quite
diplomatic, which probably saved my life a few times when
I went too far with big brother, Jack.

When I could tell that he was getting ready to land on
me, I'd go into one of my cute little self-deprecating

speeches and say things like: "C'mon, Jack, you're so hand-
some, you're the king, you're the best. You wouldn't hurt
a poor little guy like me, would you?" My ploys usually
worked—at least they reduced Jack's wrath to a sharp
punch on the arm instead of something more serious that
might have rearranged my teeth.

Another thing you will read on the characteristics charts
for last borns is that they are suckers for praise and encouragement. A little pat on the head, a slap on the back, and
a "Go get 'em—we're counting on you" is enough to keep
a last born going for hours, if not weeks.[4]

That was certainly the case when I was the mascot for
the high school team. One of my most legendary feats
involved a sneak attack on another school's mascot. Am-
herst Central High School was our mortal enemy in athletics, and their cheerleading squad included two guys who
dressed up in a tiger suit and danced around on the sidelines during the basketball and football games. One night,
as I watched from our side of the gym, a fantasy formed.
What if I could sneak up on the tiger, yank off its tail, and
run as fast as my eight-year-old legs could carry me back
to our bench before anyone could stop me? Well, I did just
that and made the high school paper with the banner head-
line:

Demon Leman Defeats
Amherst Tiger in Halftime Bout

With that kind of clipping, a last born barely needs food.
He's living on praise.

But it's hard for a leopard (or a billy goat) to change its
spots. Once I started getting all that reinforcement as a
kid, I went on to develop clowning (as well as being a problem child) into a fine art. By the time I hit (literally) high

school I was a master of sorts at getting laughs while driving teachers crazy.

I did all the dumb tricks: crawling out of class on my hands and knees, setting wastebaskets on fire, getting everyone in school to bring alarm clocks set for 2:00 P.M. and put them in their lockers. Today principals and teachers would shake their heads and go back to worrying about the newest dope pusher or gang member seen on campus. But in the 1960s, wastebasket arson was a big deal and that kind of caper got me all kinds of laughs. It got so the other kids would come into a class on the first day of the term, see me, and start nudging each other and smiling. Yes, this class was going to be a blast. Leman was in it!

No Joy to Have in Class

When some birth order charts talk about a last born's charm, they mention that he or she can be "a joy to have in a group or a class." Not for my teachers, I wasn't. Not only was I a constant disruption, I refused to learn anything either.

As a high school senior I took a course called Consumer Math, a fancy term for bonehead arithmetic. They stuck me in there because it was the last term of the year and they didn't know what else to do with me.

The first six weeks I got a C and the second six weeks I pulled a D. During the third six weeks I was getting an F and was thrown out, but not before I had driven the teacher out as well. And I didn't just drive her out of class; I drove her out of teaching. She quit and didn't come back!

The poor woman just didn't know how to handle powerful attention-getters like Leman. She thought I was out to get her. Not really—I was out to get laughs, admiration from my schoolmates, and the limelight. Very few of my teachers understood this, but one exception was an English instructor who kept me in line quite easily. He was so direct and businesslike that I knew my clowning would never work. As far as he was concerned, it was "shape up or you're out of here!" I shaped up. How can you get attention if you're not even there?

That instructor probably never heard the term, but he was an expert in reality discipline, which is what I really wanted all the time, even more than the laughs and the attention. Last borns especially want and need reality discipline, which deals directly and swiftly with the student's problem and demands that he be accountable for his actions. We'll be looking more closely at reality discipline in chapter 13.

Miss Wilson Saw through My Facade

I should have been a much better student—I had the ability—but the schools I grew up in did not hold me accountable. They just pushed me through. They wanted to get rid of guys like Leman—and the sooner the better. Very few of my teachers saw through my last-born charade. I have mentioned the no-nonsense English instructor. There was also a math teacher who wasn't fooled. As I came down to my last semester in high school, Miss Wilson pulled me aside, looked me in the eyes, and asked, "Kevin, when are you going to stop playing your game?"[5]

"What game is that, Teach?" I asked. (Yes, I actually did call her "Teach." After all, this was 1961 and we were "cool.")

"The game that you play the best," she smiled. "Being the worst!"

I laughed and tried to act as if I didn't care, but she had me. Her words began to turn my life around and they are still with me today. Recently I talked with Miss Wilson and thanked her again for sounding the challenge that woke me up. She smiled and said "Oh, I did very little, Kevin.

You did it yourself. You were a challenge, all right, but I knew what you could do if you wanted to!"

What a beautiful, unselfish lady. And rather modest too. She didn't even mention how she had tutored me at her home during those final weeks when I was making a last desperate attempt to graduate!

"College? I Couldn't Get You into Reform School!"

When Miss Wilson "blew my cover," so to speak, I went to the high school counselor and said, "I've been doing some heavy thinking and I want to go to college."

The counselor, Mr. Masino, looked up at me over the top of his glasses and without hesitation replied, "Leman, with your record, I couldn't get you admitted to reform school!"[6]

His response was a bit discouraging, but I could sort of understand where he was coming from. I was ranked fourth in my class—fourth from the bottom—going into my final semester.

"Okay, I'll show you," I muttered. "I'll get into college on my own!"

In those days there weren't community colleges, so you either went to a four-year college or you went to work. I had a real aversion to the latter, so I chose school—*any* school. But because I didn't know quite how to begin, I turned to the College Admissions Center at Evanston, Illinois, a commercial firm that for twenty-five dollars would submit a student's "credentials" to 160 different institutions of higher learning.

My application went to schools of all kinds—ones with outrageous tuition fees and ones no one ever heard of. Somebody in the registrar's office at Upper Iowa University wrote back and told me he couldn't get me into U.I.U.

but he had a brother-in-law who ran a refrigerator repair school, and would I be interested?

The bottom line is that my counselor was right. All 160 colleges and universities turned me down, even the one connected to our church denomination, North Park College in Chicago.

But I wouldn't give up and I decided to focus in on North Park, hoping that church ties might overcome my puny grade point average. I kept writing back to North Park and called in reinforcements to bombard the school with their letters too. My brother, Jack, who had attended North Park for two years and later graduated from another college, sent a letter extolling my change of heart and determination to make it in college if given a chance. With my mother's help, I persuaded my pastor to write a letter, and then I added my own final argument: Scripture texts on the virtues of forgiving a wrongdoer seventy times seven (Matt. 18:21–22).

Nine days before the semester started, North Park relented and let me in on probation with the understanding that I carry a twelve-unit load. My dad cashed in some life insurance policies to pay for room, board, and tuition, and I was on my way to college!

During the first year the "fear factor" (fear of having to go to work) kept me going. Despite woefully weak preparation in high school, I eked out a C average. But then I ran out of gas. I guess I thought I didn't have anything left to prove. In my sophomore year I fell behind and started failing fast.

I also failed in areas other than academic. Reverting to my high school habits, I sought attention by teaming with my roommate to rip off the ice cream conscience fund (established because of a faulty machine in our dorm that dispensed free ice cream) and buy pizza for our entire floor. We saw our crime as more of a prank than anything else.

In fact we made sure we told everyone we had done it. How can you get attention if you don't advertise?

Two days later I attracted the kind of attention I didn't want. The dean called me in and asked if I knew anything about the theft of the conscience money. In true last-born fashion I manipulated things a bit and said, "Yes, sir, I have heard that unfortunately some inconsiderate person has stolen the conscience-fund box."

Well, the dean knew I was lying through my teeth, and he had no choice. He suggested that I had had a hard year and I needed a rest—permanently—from North Park. I thought about his offer and it seemed like an appropriate time to leave. Spring weather is always nasty in Chicago. My parents had just moved to Tucson, Arizona, where it was nice and warm. I was failing my courses and the dean had completely failed to see any humor in the conscience-fund caper.

I Struck Gold Selling Magazines—For a While

And so I left school and went home to Tucson, where I spent the summer trying to find a job, but to no avail. That fall I enrolled in a night course at the University of Arizona and continued trying to find work. Jobs remained scarce; the minimum wage was about $1.10 an hour, but then I saw the ad in the paper:

Earn $90 a Week, Guaranteed

I answered the ad and found myself applying for a job selling magazines door-to-door. I got the job, but selling magazines door-to-door was something I had never done, so the company gave me an "intensive" training course that lasted all of one afternoon. I learned a basic pitch that involved getting the customer to believe he was subscribing to three magazines and getting four additional ones free. The customer had to put seven dollars down and then pay $2.95 a month—for twenty-six months.

Even a Consumer Math flunk-out like me could figure out that this would amount to a final total of $83.70 (including the original seven dollars down). Obviously customers weren't paying for three magazines and "getting four free." They were paying what amounted to $12 a year for each of seven magazines. But my bosses taught me to count on the very basic human desire to "get a good deal" and buy on impulse.

Training completed, I reported back the next morning, was driven out to a middle-class Tucson neighborhood, dumped on a corner, and told, "Okay, see what you can do and be back right here at 1:00 P.M. sharp."

With real eagerness I started knocking on doors, giving the pitch, taking orders, and collecting the seven dollars up front. The morning flew by and I looked at my watch just in time to get back to my pickup corner by 1:00. Back at the office, I handed my sheaf of orders to my immediate supervisor. I thought I had done fairly well and was anxious to see what she'd say. Joyce looked at all the papers in her hand and said, "What are *these?*"

"Well, they're my orders . . . ," I stammered, thinking that somehow I had really blown it and that my sales career was over.

"You mean you got *all* these orders this morning?" she said with disbelief in her voice.

"Yep," I said with a sheepish smile.

"You better come with me," Joyce directed, and we walked back to the manager's office. She waved the orders in his face and said, "Larry, look! Look at what Calvin did!"

I was feeling so good I didn't even bother to correct her on my name. She was holding *twenty-seven orders* for magazines, a new one-morning record for Tucson, if not the entire nation, as far as that company was concerned.

And what was my big secret to magazine-selling success? Well, it didn't hurt to be wearing a University of Arizona T-shirt. And all those housewives felt sorry for me as I stood hot and sweaty on their doorstep. Occasionally I'd be invited in, handed a lemonade, and then my baby-of-the-family personality just took over. I never was pushy or hard sell. I used the soft sell approach, what I call "bringin' your dancin' shoes," and I usually left with an order.

With some money coming in, I continued my night course at the University of Arizona and sold magazines by day. While I had excellent intentions, the double load proved too much and I started falling behind in my schoolwork. That bothered me, but something bothered me even more. For a young kid, I was making really decent money selling magazines, but I kept having a gnawing feeling about what I was doing.

It wasn't really robbing people, but it was all just a little bit too slick. I talked to my supervisor, Joyce, about quitting and she couldn't believe it. "Why would you want to do that?" she asked. "You're the best salesman we've got. You're doing very well and you're just a kid."

I thanked Joyce for the compliment and said I still thought I'd better quit. Getting people to spend money on magazines they didn't necessarily need or want was starting to bother me.

"Sorry to lose you, Kevin," she said with a shrug. "You're a natural-born salesman if I ever saw one."

As I left the dingy apartment that served as the magazine sales office, I was glad that I had discovered that I was a "natural-born salesman" and that Joyce had even finally gotten my name right. At the same time, was I just going to waste my talent and never amount to anything? Where was I going to find a job that would pay as well as selling magazines?

Deep down, however, my conscience told me I had done the right thing. I had decided to use my abilities to serve people, not slicker them. I have never been sorry. Eventually I went on to get degrees that led me into my present very people-centered profession—counseling and teaching. I believe I didn't waste my God-given abilities at all. I just finally used them in a manner that gave me peace and total satisfaction.

Cleaning Urinals Put Me Nose-to-Nose with Reality

I knew quitting the magazine sales job was the right thing to do but I still had problems. I tried taking another night course at the U. of A. and also flunked that. My parents were impressed with my high ideals and ethics but they let me know that I still needed to earn some money so I could pull my weight while living at home. I eventually found employment—as a janitor at the Tucson Medical Center. I kept thinking about going back to school but I'd always put it off with one excuse or another.

After a few months of cleaning urinals, however, the realities of life sort of hit Baby Kevin right between the eyes. Yes, I had a year of college behind me and I knew I could do it if I wanted to. On the other hand, I had tried two courses at the "big school" and flunked them both. Now here I was, a janitor making $195 a month full-time. I knew that cleaning toilets wasn't really what I wanted to do with my life but I remained sort of stuck in limbo.

One day as I emptied the trash into my cart at the men's rest room door, I was mulling over the possibility of winding up being a janitor all my life. Then I looked up and around the corner of the hallway came my wife. Of course, she wasn't my wife yet but she was a very beautiful nurse's aide who was working in the building, and she looked like great wife material to me.

My first words were, "Pardon me. How would you like to go to the World's Fair with me?"

She laughed and said, "Excuse me?"

"Would you like to go to the World's Fair with me?"

She sort of laughed again and said, "Well, . . . I don't know about that."

Realizing I wasn't getting a flat no for an answer, I said, "Well, how about lunch then?"

Sande didn't quite know what to make of this weird fellow who was emptying trash, but being a nurse's aide, she thought I might need help, so she agreed to a lunch date. We wound up at McDonald's, where we split a twenty-cent cheeseburger.

We kept dating and soon we were going steady. Sande could tell that I was searching for something else in life and she shared with me her personal faith in God. It was through Sande that I made some spiritual commitments that at last turned me in the direction my math teacher had pointed way back in high school. I took another course at the University of Arizona, similar to the ones I had flunked, and I passed with a solid A, highest grade in the class of six hundred.

From there I went on to get my undergraduate degree in psychology, followed by master's and doctorate degrees. And I was on the dean's list most of the way through. A lot of things motivated me: memories of my English and math teachers, memories of getting a start at North Park and blowing it with stupid pranks, meeting Sande, and getting my life squared away by finding a real faith in God.

But there was also a remark made by Sande's supervisor in her nursing ward. This middle-aged lady pulled Sande aside one day and said, "Don't associate with that janitor— he'll never amount to anything." A comment like that is enough to spur any last born on to greater heights. From that day on, I was driven with one thought: "I'll show her!"

Long before now you've noticed I'm not bashful about using illustrations from my own family, not to mention my own life. But I turned this chapter into a miniautobiography for a reason. My antics as a kid and on up through high school are a classic demonstration of many typical last-born traits that can go to seed and become destructive. Frankly, before my math teacher nailed me that day in the hallway between classes, I was headed for real disaster. Miss Wilson made me realize that getting attention was not enough. Somehow it registered in my teenage brain: *The limelight is fun, Leman, but what do you do for an encore?* And that drove me on to a goal I had never even thought about—a college degree.

I like to describe myself as one of the few licensed psychologists I know who went through college and postgraduate work—thirteen years in all—without the benefit of a high school education. I literally did not learn much of anything in high school, a fact that hardly makes me proud. After earning a doctorate, I arranged to speak at a summer camp operated by our church denomination where I told the teenagers my story. I did this for several years, emphasizing that my behavior as a youth was hardly the kind they wanted to imitate. In fact I let them know, just as my math teacher had let me know, that being best at being worst is a stupid game for anyone to play.

Why Car Salesmen Are Often Last Borns

After confessing to using my sales skills to trick people into buying magazines, I need to clarify that there's nothing wrong with selling if you do it with the right motives. If I had stayed in the sales profession, I could have easily found myself selling cars. I have learned over the years that it's a line of work that attracts babies of the family in profusion.

Have you ever walked onto a used car lot to be greeted by a guy with a big smile, white shoes, matching white belt, dark blue pants, light blue shirt, and dark blue polka-dot tie? Maybe he wasn't quite that flashy, but he probably said, "*Well*, what would it take to put *you* in *that* car today?"

If you've ever had such an encounter, it's likely you were dealing with the baby of the family. You have to be careful with these guys—they'll sell you your own house and throw in a paint job by the owner to boot!

I jest a bit, but essentially it's true. Your good salespeople are often last borns. I do some consulting with businesses and one of my favorite stops is a car dealership. I was visiting a local car agency one day and started talking casually with one of the salesmen about birth order. It turned out he was a last born and so was just about every salesman in the agency!

And what about the manager? I went with the odds and guessed he was a first born. Right again. First borns often wind up in positions of leadership. This manager was an excellent salesman in his own right, but as a first born he had risen to what he really wanted to do: cross every *t*, dot every *i*, and enter those nice black numbers on the bottom line.

Not surprisingly this first-born manager was having trouble with some of his last-born salesmen. They just weren't attending to details, such as filling in reports on time, and so on. His superstar salesman was a last born and was in the most hot water with the manager. I sat down with the manager for a cup of coffee and had him consider: "What do you really want this guy to do—sell or do paperwork?"

The manager's answer boiled down to "both."

I recommended to the manager that he stop trying to turn a baby of the family into a paragon of well-organized efficiency. Why not alleviate the problem by arranging to have one of the secretaries or clerks do the paperwork and turn his salespeople loose to do what they do best—sell!

The manager took my advice and assigned a clerk to fill in the salesman's paperwork for him. Naturally enough, his sales went higher than ever, and it meant more money for the dealership.

Last Borns Live with Ambivalence

In *First Child, Second Child,* an excellent book I quoted earlier, the authors observe that growing up the youngest can turn you into a bundle of uncertain ambivalence. Last borns are on a seesaw of emotions and experiences that they find hard to explain or understand.[7] My own life as the last born bears this out. We babies of the family can be charming and endearing but then turn rebellious and hard to deal with. We can change from powerhouses of energy into basket cases who feel helpless. We can feel on top of the world on Monday and at the bottom of the pile on Tuesday.

I'm not sure about the exact reasons for this ambivalent streak that we babies of the family carry through life, but here are a few clues. Last borns are treated with ambivalence—coddled, cuddled, and spoiled one minute; put down and made fun of the next. In self-defense we babies of the family grow up with an independent cockiness that helps cover all our self-doubt and confusion. We say to ourselves, *They wrote me off when I was little. They wouldn't let me play. They chose me last. They didn't take me seriously. I'll show them!*

Donahue Turned Me Down Thirteen Times But . . .

Because we last borns want to show the world we can do it, one of our major traits is persistence. One hundred fifty-nine colleges turned me down but I persisted and finally got in the one hundred sixtieth. Quite a few years later, after I had written *The Birth Order Book* and was hoping to get it publicized on national TV, I wrote to the Phil Donahue program. I enclosed a copy of my book and asked if they would be interested in having a birth-order psychologist on their show. The first turn-down came as a form letter, telling me that they appreciated my suggestion but they had no use for my idea at that time.

Undaunted, I wrote again and, of course, sent another copy of *The Birth Order Book*. Again, the same kind of form letter came back, but I wouldn't give up. I kept trying. I tried thirteen times to get on the Donahue show, and somewhere along the line they quit sending me form letters. Instead, they went to postcards, a sample of which appears below:

```
Dear DONAHUE Correspondent:

Because of the great volume of mail received
in our office, we're sorry we cannot answer
your letter personally.

Your suggestion has been reviewed. However,
we do not plan to use your idea for a DON-
AHUE program.

Thank you for your interest in our show.

                        THE DONAHUE STAFF
```

But finally, almost miraculously, I was accepted. I'm not sure if they simply wanted to get me out of their hair or they felt sorry for me, but I did get to appear on Donahue, and it was one of the first really big talk shows that I had ever done. Just before I was scheduled to go on, the producer called and asked, "Will you be nervous? After all, you're it; there's nobody else who is scheduled to appear."

"No problem," I replied. "In fact if Phil ever has a day when he doesn't feel good, I'll be glad to sub for him."

Was that just last-born egomania talking? Partly. But there was also a lot of that last-born desire for attention that makes a last born bold enough to do things that might make other people quail or maybe even run for cover. Oh yes, the show went so well that it made the "Best of Donahue" list. Phil was impressed, and I was out of my last-born mind as sales on *The Birth Order Book* skyrocketed.

Last Borns "Just Do It!"

I wouldn't be surprised if a last born wrote that line for the well-known Nike commercial. Beneath our veneer of independence and persistence is that inner rebel who got away with murder. We last borns are impetuous and brash, vowing that we will get attention, we will make our mark. We will show our older brothers and sisters, our parents, and the world that we are to be reckoned with. We go ahead and *do it* and worry about repercussions later.

I'm sure that's what drove me to be such a little demon while growing up. I couldn't compete with a 10.0 sister and a 9.75 brother, but I could get their attention by driving them crazy.

Possibly my finest hour came when Sally got married. She was in her early twenties and I was a teenager. Sally couldn't figure out how to involve me in her wedding. She couldn't trust me to be an usher—who knows what I would pull right in the middle of the ceremony? So she assigned me to take care of the guest book.

The night before her wedding, we all attended the traditional rehearsal dinner at a fashionable downtown hotel. Even I showed up dressed to kill, in a suit and tie. As custom would have it, Sally gave everyone involved in the wedding a little gift. I opened mine and discovered a pair of bright plaid Bermuda shorts. Another fantasy formed and Leman the demon could not resist. I slipped out and did a quick Clark Kent change in a nearby rest room. Moments later I reappeared in the swank hotel dining room attired in suit coat, tie—and the shorts!

Sally's face turned bright red as her perfect evening dissolved into her guests' guffaws and menacing looks from the maître d'. But I was happy. Once again I was the center of attention. I would pay the price later when I faced Mom and Dad at home, but it was worth it. Once again I had struck a blow for all the last borns who have ever vowed, "I'll show them!"

Strengths and Weaknesses of Last Borns

Typical Traits	Strengths	Weaknesses
Charming	Likable, fun to be around, easy to talk to	Manipulative, even a little flaky; seeming to be too slick and a bit unbelievable
People oriented	Read others well and know how to relate and work well one on one or in small groups; social settings and events are their cup of tea	May come across as undisciplined, prone to talk too much and too long, the kind who talks a good game but can't always produce
Tenacious	Keep on coming with tireless persistence, not taking no for an answer	May push too hard because they see things only their way
Affectionate and engaging	Caring, lovable, wanting to help; like to get strokes and to give them	Can be gullible, easily taken advantage of; make decisions too much on feeling and not enough on thought
Uncomplicated	Appear relaxed, genuine, and trustworthy—no hidden agenda	May appear to be absent-minded, a little out of focus—like an airhead
Attention seeking	Entertaining and funny, know how to get noticed	May appear self-centered, unwilling to give others credit, having a big ego, temperamental, spoiled, and impatient

Assessing Last-Born Strengths and Weaknesses

Go over the chart above, which lists typical traits of last borns. Then consider each trait and decide if it's a strength or weakness as far as you are concerned. If it is a weakness, what changes could you make to improve in that area? If it's a strength, how could you capitalize on that strength or develop it even further?

Being Honest with Your Last-Born Self

1. Am I a mature adult, or are people still saying or thinking, "Why don't you grow up?"
2. Part of growing up is learning to pick up after yourself. Do I have trouble with this?
3. Do I enjoy working with people, data, or things? Do I need to consider changing my line of work?
4. If I have a love for the limelight (attention seeking), do I let it slip over into self-centeredness, when I'm always thinking about me and not about others? How do I know? What would my friends tell me?
5. Do I use my ability to make people laugh strictly to get attention, or do I do it to make others feel good and enjoy life?
6. Do I control my tenaciousness and persistence, not letting it get out of hand, when I become overbearing? Can I think of a recent example of when I have done this?
7. Would people say I am a good listener? Or do I just try to "read" people and not really listen to what they say? Do I need to improve my listening skills and take time to listen to others without thinking about what I am going to say next?

10

How to Let Your Birth Order Work for You in Business

Before we go on to look at how an understanding of birth order can help in marriage and parenting, I'd like to take a little detour and talk about how birth order can be of use in the rough-and-ready arena of the workplace. A little basic knowledge of birth order can be of great help in the business world, particularly in regard to sales.[1]

Can a basic knowledge of birth order literally increase a sales representative's effectiveness? I'll let Harvey Mackay, one of America's top CEOs and writer of many business best-sellers, answer: ". . . when you get right down to it, the salesperson who hits the top of the charts is the one who understands human nature the best."[2]

Early in my counseling career, I wouldn't have understood the wisdom of Harvey Mackay's words. For one thing, I didn't even realize that I too—a "distinguished psychologist"—was a salesman. Fortunately my father did.

My father had only an eighth-grade education but he was successful in raising a family and running his own small dry cleaning business. It's funny, but the older I got, the smarter Dad became. Unfortunately I had to get quite a bit older—well into my thirties—before I understood his message to be concerned about making sales.

In the early years of my counseling career, Dad would ask, "Kevin, did you have any customers today?"

"Dad," I would protest, "they're not customers; they're *clients!*"

"Do they pay you money?" he wanted to know.

"Yeah, of course they do."

"Then they're customers."

And of course he was right. My dad had a simple intuitive knowledge of human nature. Our practical little conversations eventually helped me realize that my clients were indeed my customers. And once I had that straight, it wasn't much of a stretch to see that what I had learned in my psychology courses, particularly about birth order, could be invaluable. As a counselor, I was basically selling people help—help with their problems, questions, and anxieties. But the more I counseled, the more I understood that you can't help people unless you really know them—particularly how they see life.

Fortunately because of the product I was trying to sell—counseling—I was forced into knowing my customers better and better in order to help them more and more. In fact I soon learned that after I obtained a client (i.e., customer), I wasn't through making my sale—I had only begun. The real job lay ahead—selling those I counseled on buying ideas and suggestions to make real changes in their lives.

So as a psychologist, I have constantly been in the business of sales. And that's why I can state the following with confidence: Know your customers, and selling your product will take care of itself.

> ✔ **Know your customers, and selling your product will take care of itself.**

Obviously I believe that a working knowledge of birth order is one of the most effective ways to know your customers. Am I saying that birth order will always work and guarantee you a sale? Of course not. No method *always* works. As I counsel, I don't always "make the sale" in trying to get people to change their dysfunctional and destructive ways. But that doesn't stop me from learning all I can about them—what I call getting behind their eyes to see the world as they see it. If I can do that, I can sell them the ideas I have to offer, which can make a difference in their behavior and their lives.

Part of learning about people includes their birth order. When a client sits down with me for the first time, I can ask about his or her birth order, as well as a lot of other "psychological" questions to gain insight into this individual's personality. The average person, however, doesn't have this luxury and, frankly, it's not advisable to ask customers direct questions about their birth order. For example, do not say something like: "You're always so well dressed and nicely groomed, tell me, are you the first born in your family, or at least the first-born male (or female)?"

This kind of question will make you sound like one of two things: a first-year psychology student doing research for a term paper or a mental case.

A much better approach is to engage the other person in conversation and ask casual questions such as, "Where did you grow up? Where's home for you?" As you get the customer talking about where he grew up, you have him talking about his family. From there you can ask what his family did—were they farmers? Was there a family business? Did he have any brothers or sisters? Was it a large or small family?

The other person may respond, "It was just me and my sisters and my kid brother."

To this you can comment, "I'll bet the kid brother got away with murder."

More than likely the other person will say, "Yeah, he did, as a matter of fact."

"So you had to do most of the work?" you say. "Tell me, who was oldest in the family—you or your sisters?"

With this kind of an approach, you always want to be casual, with your goal to form a relationship first and get birth-order specifics later. Keep making mental notes as you build a case for whatever birth order this person may be.

Another approach is to bring up something about your own family rather casually, for example, "I saw my older brother over the weekend. He and his family came down for the holidays. Do you have any siblings who descend on you at holiday time?"

As you engage in discovering a person's birth order, you will learn all kinds of other things: hobbies, favorite sports, favorite teams, favorite restaurants. The possibilities are almost endless.

The more personal knowledge you can gain about a customer (or someone you hope to make a customer), the better, because it will all help give you some clues about that person's "private logic." We all have our own unique and individual private logic—a very personal overview of how we see life, how we see others, and how we see ourselves. It's part of our total life-style.

Our private logic is more or less our personal agenda. Each of us views life differently. If you doubt this, call two or three of your siblings or close friends with whom you have shared a memorable experience in the past. Simply ask: "Do you remember the time . . .?" Describe the experience in a few words, then sit back and listen as you hear amazingly different views on what happened.

Always be aware of your customer's private logic. As you try to understand his or her point of view, you will really "get behind your customer's eyes." It is here you learn about the person's real biases, preferences, and desires. Mark it down.

> All of us have a private logic—our own unique and biased view of life from behind our own eyes.

As you call on your clients, keep making mental (and later written) notes about their birth-order characteristics. Soon you will have an invaluable little file right on the back of their Rolodex card that will remind you of how they think, what they like, and how they want to do business. This information can become a literal gold mine, but of course the bottom line is how you mine that gold—that is, how you use this information in actual sales situations.

Make the Sale Every Time—Well, Almost

I have used the following "secrets" for years as I've dealt with first borns, middle children, and last-born babies. Whether I'm selling myself as a speaker or counseling a client about how he can change if he chooses to do so, I use these tips almost automatically and instinctively.

So what follows aren't really secrets. They are simple, commonsense concepts that you can use when selling to anyone.

Secrets to Selling to First Borns

Selling to a first born (or the only child who is a super first born) is a little like clearing a minefield. You need to proceed with caution but you want to get in and out as quickly as possible.

Keep in mind that when talking to a first born, you're talking to Mr. Nuts and Bolts, Mr. Specifications Page. He is not likely to be overly impressed with flashy four-color brochures and lots of bold claims. The first born basically wants to know: What is your product or service going to do for me? and How much will it cost? So proceed with caution with first borns and watch out for red lights.

Getting in the Door and Off the Ground

All right, you have arrived a few minutes early (never even a minute late) for your appointment with Mr. Hennesey. The moment has come and you are being ushered into his office. To grab his first-born attention switch, you must be prepared. Remember that Mr. Hennesey is a very direct, no-nonsense, bottom-line kind of guy. If you don't get right to the point, he may just point you to the door.

So you have your sales pitch planned and you follow it to the letter. You don't ramble; you don't try to fake it; you say your piece—preferably in five minutes, three would be even better.

Why First Borns Hate the Question Why?

As you give your presentation to a first born, you may hear him asking questions like, Why? along with What? When? Where? and How much? Be ready to answer all those questions, of course, but whatever you do, try not to ask the first born any questions beginning with *why*. Naturally you're probably wondering, *Why not*? Because the question Why? is confrontive and puts the other person on the defensive, at least a little bit, but sometimes more than a little bit.

For the first born, especially, a question beginning with *why* is a threat to his or her being in control. Always remember that first borns like to be in control, and they are not at all pleased by surprises or questions that may put them on the defensive.

> First borns like to be in control, and they are not at all pleased by surprises or questions that may put them on the defensive.

It's also good not to press the first born for a decision. I'm not saying you shouldn't try to close a sale; we'll get to that in a moment. But remember that first borns like plenty of detail, so encourage questions as you proceed.

One other thing to remember is that first borns have substantial egos. When you have an opening, you may want to ask the first born what makes him or his company successful. Be cautious, however, about saying anything that sounds like insincere flattery. In fact if you really want to impress Mr. Hennesey, try to do some homework on his company before you arrive. If the company is listed on the stock exchange, you can call a broker and try to get updated on the latest action regarding that firm.

Closing the Sale with a First Born

As you wrap up your presentation, always keep in mind that first borns want to know the cons as well as the pros, the negatives as well as the positives. Don't try to fool them by claiming what you are selling is absolutely foolproof and flawless. You know better and so do they.

Instead, use the psychological principle of "oppositional attraction." It's the same thing that I've often used with small children in counseling situations. Way back in graduate school, we learned that if you move *toward* the average two year old, saying, "Come here; come to me," he will usually go the other way—as fast as his little feet will carry him. But if you want to get the average two year old to come to you, you *back up* and say, "Come, come to me." When I first heard this I didn't believe it would work, but in nine cases out of ten it actually does. There is something about backing up that leaves the child feeling in control and not as fearful.

And what does handling two year olds have to do with handling forty-five-year-old purchasing agents or CEOs? A great deal. The idea is that you don't just make your sales pitch saying, "Please sign with me and my company." Instead, as you move toward your close, you will want to let the first born know he is in control—he's the one who will make the decision. One of the best ways to do this is to state the obvious pluses and minuses. For example: "Now I know that you have been with this other company for seven or eight years and they've been giving you good service. I'd be lying if I said only we give good service— lots of companies give good service. But what I'm excited about is the new dimensions of what we offer. We are ahead of our competitors in several areas. We've not only broken ground, we've established ourselves and we have proven product (or service)."

Then leave it with the first born. You've made your pitch, and he will make his own decision. If things have gone well, you may hear him say something like: "I want to think this over. I know someone (across town, in the next state) who uses your product (or service). I think I'll give him a call and see what he thinks."

On the other hand, you may hear a polite, "Thank you very much. I appreciate your presentation and we'll be letting you know."

In many cases, especially with first borns, the latter comment is probably what you will get when making a first call. All you're really trying to do on this first call is get your toe in the door. Your foot can come later.

As a group, first borns are formidable but reachable. They're impressed by efficiency and a concern for their time and busy schedule. With first borns, remember: Don't try to get chummy, just get done and get out.

Secrets to Selling to the Middle Child

Probably no other birth order is more sensitive to the axiom, Sales are relational, than the middle child. Middle children are relational by nature because they have a hunger for it. As you will remember, they are the ones who go outside the family first to find friends and groups where they feel somewhat in control and not squeezed as they do at home.

As you prepare to call on a middle child, you want to remember that he is a good team player, reliable, steady, and loyal. And unlike the first born, he actually enjoys being asked questions—in fact the more questions, the better. Why is this? It's simple: He never got asked that many questions while growing up at home. He was simply ignored.

While most middle children tend to be more laid-back and relational than others, there are exceptions. You can run into a middle child who is something of a buzz saw—very competitive, even a scrappy aggressor type. And instead of seeming to like relationships, the middle child may be a loner, quiet, or shy. It has been my observation, however, over years of counseling that the typical middle child who winds up in some kind of middle management position where he is making decisions regarding purchasing supplies or services, is more inclined to be the relational negotiator and mediator.

Some Ideas on Approaching the Middle Child

When calling on relationship-hungry middle children, you may want to ask them if there is anybody else they would like to bring along—to sit in on the conversation or perhaps go to lunch. With a third party, it's often easier to keep conversation flowing and this may put the middle child at ease. But it is the middle child's call and not yours. Never bring along one of your own colleagues as a surprise, thinking that the relationship-hungry middle child believes "the more the merrier." Middle children like relationships, but on their terms. Otherwise you could easily wind up making the middle child feel overwhelmed.

Another good idea is to contact the middle child outside the office—at lunch, for example. Do everything you can to make your call less the sales call and more the social contact. The middle child usually responds best to a presentation that is slower than you would make to a first born and is given with sensitivity. If it's a first call, you may want to leave the impression that you're not there to sell something as much as you are just to make a contact and get to know each other.

Do everything you can to convince the middle child you are concerned about him and his particular interests. If he is a small businessman and your company usually sells to bigger firms, let him know that that doesn't make him any less important to you. For example, you may be able to say: "We've just opened a new division to accommodate small businesses, and I'd like to show you a package that will save you money."

Another effective approach to the middle child is to ask him what his biggest problem or hurdle is. What's the greatest difficulty he faces in business today? Learn how you can help with this and then move in to do just that. For example: "I'd like to invite you down to our plant. I'd like you to see what we can do for you."

A variation of this could be: "I'd like to invite you down to meet some of our people. I want to show you what we're doing for businesses like yours on a regular basis."

You'll probably have to make more calls on a middle child before you close the sale. Build your relationship slowly; cast out your lines and wait. As a rule, middle children may need more lines cast than the decisive first borns or the more impetuous babies. The middle child is more go-with-the-flow. He may take longer to sell, but in the end he may be a more loyal customer (if you give him good service).

Middle Children Like the Warm Fuzzies

Again, remember that middle children are more likely to appreciate the old proven ways. Their motto is definitely, If it ain't broke, why fix it? or, If I've been getting along fine with the product from XYZ Company, why should I switch to ABC Company? Obviously price can be a factor but it isn't always the main consideration. Middle children, in particular, will be looking for service, for relationships, for the warm fuzzy kind of thing that will help them feel more secure and more at home with you as a supplier.

Middle children are not as afraid of (or as disturbed by) change as first borns may be. First borns like the status quo because it helps them stay in control. But because the middle child never had that much control while growing up, he's a little more willing to roll with the punches.

And while middle children may not be as much the perfectionists as first borns, that doesn't mean that you can't find a middle child who isn't a perfectionist. Any birth order can succumb to perfectionism. It's just that first borns and only children are more likely do so because of the tremendous pressure they have been under ever since they can remember.

Closing the Sale with a Middle Child

While the money-back guarantee or no-obligation promises are always powerful tools with any birth order, they are particularly attractive to the middle child. Keep in mind that he is slightly insecure and still rebelling (maybe more than a little bit) against the childhood that had him in the middle, squeezed, left out, and sometimes ignored.

It never hurts to emphasize to middles how they can check with others about your claims and how you will specifically service them if they do buy anything from you. For example, you might say, "We both know there are many companies that do what we do, but I believe that the company I'm representing really focuses on fitting our product (or service) to a customer's needs. We will bend over backward to accommodate specifically what will enhance your production."

When dealing with middle children, you must always remember three things: Sales are relational. Sales are relational. Sales are relational.

Secrets to Selling to the Last-Born Babies

There is one more birth order that is, in some ways, more relational than the middle child. I speak, of course, of the babies of the family. When selling to last borns, I always like to say, "Bring your dancin' shoes and a weather vane." In other words, be as fun and as charming as you can and be aware that as the winds change the last born can change as well. Babies fly by the seat of their pants and they never stay put for very long.

Sell Them before They Sell You!

As you prepare to approach your last-born client or potential customer, the more entertaining you can be, the better. It doesn't mean that you come prancing in with party hat and horn. All I'm saying is that your typical baby of the family is looking for fun in life and, while he or she may appear quite businesslike on the surface, this fun-oriented attitude can be right there waiting to come out.

If a social environment is good for approaching a middle child, it's even better for the last born. Babies of the family like to work hard and play hard. Sometimes they like to do both at the same time.

As you're chatting with your last-born customer, be aware that he always loves hearing or telling a good story or joke. Ask, "Would you tell me some of your favorite stories—things that have happened in your business? I'd love to hear them."

When you tell stories, however, stay away from anything even remotely off-color. As much as I love humor, I always follow this rule, not because I think it's a safer way to do business, but because it's the best way to do business in any setting.

Time Counts, So Keep Things Moving

As I mentioned, you need to move fast with first borns because they are all business and have no time to waste. Last borns may want to waste a bit of time, but balanced against that is their short attention span. If your last-born client starts having fun with a story or two, you'd better be well aware of the time. It may be up sooner than you would have liked, and your baby may be gone or halfway out the door, headed for another appointment, before you've had an opportunity to sell your product.

As you make your presentation, be aware that the typical baby of the family is highly susceptible to being impressed by name-dropping. It won't hurt at all to mention highly visible people or firms who already use your product or service.

Closing the Sale with a Last Born

The typical last born is 180 degrees from the typical first born. You'll remember that first borns could care less about full-color photos and slick-looking layouts. They want the specs, the numbers, the graphs. Babies, on the other hand, could care less about specs, numbers, and graphs. They love those full-color pictures, the flash, and the glitter. That's how babies arrive at the bottom line.

In other words, the baby tends to ask first, "What does this whole thing really do for *me*? Does it make *me* feel good?" I'm not saying the baby can't make sound business decisions; I am saying that when it comes to weighing the business side of things against personal pluses and minuses, the baby will be giving the personal side significant weight.

Last Borns Are Often Risk Takers

Studies show that the later borns in the family, particularly babies, are far more likely to be risk takers than first borns. A professor of marketing from a major university in the South called me on one occasion to say she had just read *The Birth Order Book* and loved it. She speculated that because first borns are such leaders and the ones who move things forward in so many areas of life, it would make sense to know what first borns were thinking in order to predict the next trends in marketing.

I was impressed with how she was trying to use what she had been learning in *The Birth Order Book*, but I had to say, "You're absolutely right, first borns are the leaders of society, the evidence is overwhelming, but if you are looking for trends, you want to see what the later borns are doing. They're the ones who are far more likely to be willing to take a risk and to change things."

Knowing that last borns tend to be risk takers can help you as you move in to close your presentation. Because they want to act now, not later, babies are typically spontaneous and impetuous. You can be a little more confrontative and press a little harder for a decision. If the baby of the family is leaning at all in your direction, don't hesitate to ask for a commitment or to sign on the bottom line.

When I bought a Chrysler Sebring convertible recently, I went in and made the deal I wanted to make, true enough, but the sales manager—a first born, by the way, who was a very dapper dresser—also did a good job of recognizing how I was operating and he dealt with me accordingly. For example, he noticed I was in a hurry and impatient. Maybe he even remembered that I tend to be a bit impetuous because he had dealt with me before. At any rate, he didn't hem and haw. He made the deal, signed me up, and let me drive out the door in a very short time. In other words, while he'd never had any kind of course on selling to different birth orders, he sold me—a last born—pretty well.

Selling to babies can be fun, but don't get the idea they're airheads. Remember that there is that dark side to the baby—the side that says, "I want to *show them!*" Last borns remind us of a universal truth: All of us want respect, some of us more than others.

> ✔ All of us want respect, some of us more than others.

The Best-Kept Secret in Business

As I said, the above secrets to selling to different birth orders are all based pretty much on common sense. But maybe the best kept secret to making sales, working for an employer, or managing your employees is this: Take a personal interest.

As an author, I'm often out on the road pushing my latest book. My publisher sends me on a tour of several cities where I appear on TV and radio and then drop in at the local bookstores to greet and get to know people. I usually enjoy these bookstore stops a great deal. On rare occasions, however, I experience an author's worst nightmare: having a great TV or radio interview and then going downtown to stop at a bookstore and not finding my book anywhere!

I was in a large midwestern city not too long ago, being escorted about by a very classy lady who not only knows books, but she knows people, especially the managers of the bookstores. As she took me over to meet the manager of one bookstore that is part of a well-known national chain, she told me about how this manager's daughter had been in an accident. The damage had been so severe it had taken a year for the little girl to recover.

I told my escort I appreciated that information, and a few minutes later, when she introduced me to the bookstore manager, I said, "I hear you're quite a woman. I've heard some good things about you. I know it's been a rough year for you."

Immediately the bookstore manager perked up and the conversation jumped several levels above the usual perfunctory introduction. The reason was simple. With a couple of comments I had gone into a relationship kind of mode and let the lady know that I knew how it had been for her.

And then I added, "You know, I have four daughters myself."

That was all we really needed. The manager and I talked about her daughter's injuries and how her recovery had been slow and frustrating.

Later—quite a bit later, in fact—we got around to talking about why I was really supposed to be there—because I was in town on a book tour. It was as if a light went on and the store manager said, "Oh, my, what shows were you on today? Say, I don't think we have your book in stock. I'll order some right away!" In a few minutes, she put a sizable order for my book in the computer.

Later as my escort drove me to the airport, we talked about the conversation I had had with the manager and she mentioned how impressed she had been with the way I could build a relationship so quickly. I commented, "You know, if you call that lady two years from now and mention my name, she'll remember me. Why? Because I was interested in *her* and *her child*, not primarily in pushing my books."

And that's the point of this little story. Obviously I could go around being interested in bookstore managers (and everyone else) only to manipulate them to get what I want—more book sales. I want more book sales as badly as any author but I can honestly say that I build relationships because *I am truly interested in the people I deal with.* The benefits that come out of that are obvious and, to some extent, automatic.

As someone said, "What goes around, comes around." If you always try to treat people the way you'd like to be treated, your motives will be right, and what comes around will almost always be good.

That's not only true for business, it applies to all of life, including marriage, the most intimate relationship of all. To see how birth order can affect any marriage, including yours, turn to the next chapter.

11

Birth Order Marriages Aren't Made in Heaven

Before I started doing psychological counseling of couples and families, I used to think that marriages could be made in heaven. Now I know they are made on earth and my first question of any couple who comes for marital counseling is, "What is your birth order?"

The answer I get most often is, "I'm a first born and so is she," or "I'm an only child and so is she."

This is not to say I don't counsel couples who are middle children or last borns, but over the years, as I have counseled thousands of couples, the most competitive, most volatile, and most discouraged are combinations where both spouses are first borns, or worse, both are only children.

Their relationship is the opposite of the true concept of marriage, which is pulling together, sharing, melting into the unity of one. Instead, they are like mountain sheep, constantly butting heads, or they lock horns over something and neither one will back off.

And what do they disagree about? Everything. First borns and only children are by nature perfectionist flaw finders and nitpickers. There's a country song that goes, "You want things your way, and I want them mine." How true it is!

I Ejected One Couple for Fighting

One pair of first borns I counseled would spend the first ten or twenty minutes of every session fighting as I sat there and listened. Finally I got tired of it and threw them out of my office.

"No charge for today," I said. "I'm sick and tired of listening to you two run each other down. You go home and think it over. When you're both ready to take a run at making a marriage, come see me again."

Admittedly, ejecting this couple for fighting was a harsh counseling tactic but it is something I have done on rare occasions over the years when I felt the situation warranted it. I didn't hear from this couple for about a month and I began to think, *You blew that one, Leman. They won't be back.* But a few days later, they called and made an appointment. This time they didn't fight (at least in my presence).

What had happened? The couple had made a simple decision that had "unlocked their horns." They had decided to quit bumping heads. More precisely, they had decided to quit using their tongues as chisels to chip away at each other and their marriage. They had been at each other over the little things (a true sign of perfectionism). But it's the little things that drive first borns crazy: clothes in a heap, unentered checks, lights left on, and so on.

They often locked horns when they were going somewhere in the car. First-born husband would be driving, taking his familiar route to the freeway when his first-born wife would say: "Why did you turn here? We're taking the freeway, aren't we?"

"I always go this way," her husband would reply.

"Well, you should have turned back at Elm Street," the wife would respond matter-of-factly. "It's three blocks shorter."

We didn't really start getting anywhere until I asked them a simple question: "Who's winning this marriage? With all the lambasting that you've been doing to each other, who's coming out on top?"

They looked at each other and admitted, "Well, neither one of us wins . . ."

"Exactly," I said. And then I reminded them again that they had married within their own birth order. Once they understood how two first borns can be a volatile combination, they learned how to give in and accept each other.

They didn't really need any more sessions. I sent them on their way with some final advice: "Remember to never let the sun go down on your anger. Talk about things before you go to bed at night. When either of you gets picky over some little thing, learn to laugh about it and, above all else, take Elm Street to the freeway!"

Over the years I have counseled more discouraged-fast-becoming-destructive perfectionists than anyone else. But a marriage between two middle children can be destructive too, and so can a match with two babies. The first principle (not a rule) for a riskier kind of marriage is this: Marry someone in your own birth order. If you want better odds for a happier marriage, marry out of your birth order. We'll discuss that later in this chapter, but right now let's take a look at some examples of couples who married within their own birth orders and see what happened.

Perfectionists and Sex

Shirley, an attractive thirty-eight-year-old blonde, and George, a forty-one-year-old engineer, both first borns, came to see me with what George called "Shirley's sex problem." The oldest of four children, Shirley grew up in a family with an extremely domineering father, whom she described as intelligent and explosive. According to Shirley, her dad had always tried to run her life. And while still in her teens, she vowed she would "never marry anyone like Dad."

But, of course, Shirley had married someone just like Dad. Why? One explanation that usually hits the mark is that, as a rule, the parent of the opposite sex has the most influence on us. And in Shirley's case, domineering Dad had made his mark. Despite all her vows to never marry anyone like him, there was an even deeper drive telling her, *"I could never satisfy Dad so I'll find a man just like him and please him. I'll win yet!"*

While George wasn't as explosive as her father had been, he was very demanding and critical. He also wanted sex every day! But Shirley was a classic perfectionist who approached sex like everything else—as a carefully regimented performance. Shirley and George had intercourse with no deviation in technique, position, or lighting (none).

Shirley had tried to please George but the demands she had placed on herself to meet his sex drive had caused her to become uptight, unable to enjoy intercourse. She had grown unresponsive to George who was a perfectionist himself and was constantly nitpicking her about sex and everything else. The nitpicking only made Shirley more uptight and resentful and she saw George as just another domineering male like her father.

The one ray of hope was that Shirley and George wanted to save their marriage. This was greatly encouraging because my approach to every marriage counseling case is the same: If a couple has stood before God and man and said, "I do, for better or for worse," the couple should try everything possible to stay together. So we had two first-born perfectionists locking horns and banging heads with the bedroom as their main battlefield. The first step toward unlocking horns was to suggest a less rigid and demanding schedule regarding sex. This really wasn't too hard. Because of all the tension and fighting, they had already dropped down to "only" four times a week.

I gave Shirley and George several suggestions and techniques on how to relax and enjoy each other while they made sex a celebration instead of a performance (i.e., ordeal). Soon they started making good progress as a couple and I also gave Shirley assignments of her own that she carried out very well. First, I had Shirley admit to her perfectionism whenever she saw it popping up. This simple exercise started making her much more aware of the demands she was placing on herself as well as on others.

I also instructed Shirley to watch her expectations, to take smaller bites of life. That included learning to say no and refusing to take on more than she could handle. Like Kathleen (in chapter 7), Shirley was a classic pleaser, who worked outside the home, did all the housework herself, and also served on several volunteer committees in her community. She had been carrying a double load and then some as long as she and George had been married.

As Shirley learned to say no, she learned how to give herself space. She quit living under the tyranny of her "to-do" list, which she had been literally taping to the steering wheel of her car to constantly remind her of all she had to get done that day. She planned less and managed to accomplish it, rather than finishing each day irritated and frustrated because "she had not gotten everything done."

Just as predictably, the relationship between Shirley and George improved radically, particularly in bed. They started having sex less and enjoying it more!

Something else Shirley had to deal with was her image of George as a very dominating husband. Rather than playing a passive role to George, I encouraged her to take a certain amount of initiative in their relationship, especially when it came to sex. I suggested things like "kidnapping" her husband from work and getting out of town to a nearby resort for an overnight. Another idea was taking time for a picnic lunch in the middle of a workday.

Perfectionist that she was, Shirley really threw herself into her new assignments with enthusiasm. I remember the delight with which she told me of the time she picked up George after work for an evening that included a picnic supper, time in a hot tub, and staying at a hotel for the night. She had thought of everything, making the reservations and arranging for Grandma to stay with the kids.

While Shirley and George had problems, it was Shirley who was the key to getting this marriage back on the right track. As soon as she started dealing positively with her perfectionism, she was able to rearrange priorities. As she started controlling her own expectations and goal setting, the scene changed. By marrying a man much like her father—domineering and critical—she had set herself up for failure. It was like a train that had been roaring full speed toward a washed-out bridge. But Shirley stopped the train, threw a switch, and got herself and George on a track that led to safety and happiness.

Sylvia Plus Mark Equaled No Communication

Another birth order marriage that can run into trouble is that of two middle children. As we saw in chapter 8, the middle child shoots off in his own direction, depending on the strengths and weaknesses of the first born ahead of him. The middle child can go in a lot of directions but most middle children develop the ability to mediate, negotiate, and compromise.

In short, middle children are often diplomats, which sounds like a wonderful skill to carry into marriage, but ironically what often happens with two middle children is a tendency to desire peace at any price. They become avoiders—of their problems and eventually each other. Middle children prefer the oceans of life to be smooth. They don't want to make waves and the result can be a quiet surface, but underneath all kinds of storms are brewing because they are not communicating.

Such was the case with Sylvia, a quiet thirty-two-year-old brunette and third-born daughter in a family of five children. With two sisters above her and two boys below her, Sylvia got lost in the middle during her childhood and teenage years. She grew up shy, passive, and definitely an avoider of conflict. She tried to please her parents by taking over a lot of the care of her two younger brothers while their mother worked.

Mark was twenty-nine, the second of three children. His older brother had always been the best at everything, and his little sister got the typical "baby princess" treatment that often left Mark feeling as if he hadn't gotten a fair shake.

Mark went outside the family early to find his own friends and social life, another classic mark of the middle child. One of those friends was Sylvia, his high school sweetheart, whom he married soon after graduation. After eight years of marriage, Sylvia and Mark had two children, seven and four years of age.

Sylvia arranged for the counseling, acting on the urging of one of her older sisters, who was tired of hearing her complain of feeling trapped with little children and unable to communicate with her husband. Sylvia was also worried about another woman because during the last few months Mark had been insisting he had to work longer hours at his job.

I talked separately with Sylvia and Mark. It turned out there was no other woman. As you may recall, the middle child is the most monogamous of all birth orders, and this was true in Mark's case. It seemed one woman was all he could handle, especially when he felt she tried to run his life. Sylvia was still operating with Mark the way she had with her two younger brothers. She told him what to do, and Mark resented it, even when it came from a sweet, shy girl like his wife. But as a middle child, Mark didn't want to make waves. He wanted to avoid conflict whenever he could, so the simplest solution was, "Sorry, I have to work late tonight."

Sylvia, on the other hand, didn't know how to approach Mark and could only guess as to what was going on. Communication was at zero when Sylvia came to me for help. Sylvia and Mark made good progress when they committed themselves to spending time talking after the kids were in bed and they could concentrate on each other. Having Mark share his feelings really helped Sylvia because his silence and secretive devotion to work had bothered her a great deal. Mark learned that he could tell Sylvia how he felt and she would not reject him.

While Sylvia appreciated the talks with Mark, she admitted it was difficult to verbalize her own thoughts. I suggested that she supplement the talks by writing Mark positive notes now and then. Mark had to travel occasionally for his company, and Sylvia began slipping little notes and cards into his suitcase. Finding these little love notes and brief bits of encouragement between his shirts when he was unpacking in the hotel made the trips much easier for Mark.

Another plus that came out of the new effort to communicate was that Sylvia felt less trapped as the mother of two small children. Mark had his job as an outlet and he learned to come home and say, "What can I do to help?" Sylvia was thrilled and, as Mark became more willing to be helpful around the house, she learned to back off on her "motherly little ways of telling him what to do."

As middle children, Sylvia and Mark were really good candidates for marriage. The irony in their situation, however, is what faces any couple when both of them are middle born. They may not communicate because their urge to avoid conflict and make the oceans of life smooth wins out over their natural tendency to be mediators and negotiators. It sounds like a paradox, but that's how relationships often flounder.

Peter and Mary: Born Last, First in Debt

Marrying your own birth order is usually not a good idea for the babies in the family either. On the positive side, two last borns may have a ball during their courtship because they both have a fun-loving, go-for-broke nature. But once the two last borns are married, one of them better take responsibility for the family budget or they will "go for broke," indeed.

By the time they came to see me, Peter and Mary, babies of their families, were in serious difficulties with the bank and several other creditors. They were in their early thirties and had no children and they had a good income but they were hopelessly in debt. Every credit card balance was well over the maximum, several department store bills were overdue, and their car and ski boat were about to be repossessed. The only reason they weren't in trouble on a house payment was that they were renting an apartment. And the only reason they weren't behind in their rent was a no-nonsense landlord who threatened immediate eviction proceedings if the rent was even one day past the ten-day grace period.

All of this fiscal chaos led, of course, to marital warfare. Neither Peter nor Mary had been particularly overindulged as children but when they got out on their married own, they decided to live by the pleasure principle. If they saw something they wanted, they bought (that is, *charged*) it. They blamed each other for their overindulgence; ironically enough, both were also overweight. There was no control anywhere in sight.

My first step with Peter and Mary was putting them in touch with a financial counselor. He put them on a tight budget, consolidated all their debts, and arranged a payment program. He even had them cut up all their credit cards. As a rule, last borns cannot live on a tight budget. As a last born myself, I understand that perfectly. I leave it to my first-born wife, Sande, to keep us out of debt.

Peter and Mary saw me only a few more times. Their real problem was money, not their marriage. They loved each other and were committed to staying together. Once they committed themselves to not buying anything on credit for at least two years, and to selling a couple of their "toys," like the ski boat, they were well on their way to stability.

Peter and Mary are typical examples of how lack of order and stability are often weak links in the makeup of last borns. As we saw in chapter 9, the last-born child grows up spoiled, overindulged, coddled, and cuddled. This hardly helps him get basic training for running a budget. On the other side of the coin, last borns are often treated as if they don't know quite enough, are always behind, too young, too small, too weak, and "stupid." Last borns often develop an attitude that says, "Who cares anyway? I might as well have a little fun while I can." Once Peter and Mary realized they could control their spending and still have fun, they enjoyed life with each other a whole lot more.

Which Birth Orders Make the Best Matches?

As the above examples show, marrying in your own birth order can lead to problems, so the question is, What is the best combination for a happy marriage? From my own counseling experience, I draw this general guideline: For a happy marriage, find someone as opposite from your birth order as possible.

> **For a happy marriage, find someone as opposite from your birth order as possible.**

Opposites not only attract, they are usually good for one another in a marriage setting. Psychologists have done studies that prove this theory.[1] According to their research, only children and last borns supposedly make the best match, followed by first borns and last borns. Next come the middle children and last borns.

Following is a quick rundown on six birth-order combinations and why they tend to go wrong or right in a marriage, plus some practical tips for each combination. Keep in mind there are no guarantees that a certain birth order combination will lead automatically to a successful or miserable marriage. But the point is that there are *indicators* in birth-order information that can help a couple deal with any tensions they may have. For more information, see my book *Were You Born for Each Other?*[2]

First Born Plus First Born Equals Power Struggle

As we've already seen with George and Shirley, when two perfectionistic first borns get together, there is a bumping of heads (i.e., a power struggle). The issues usually focus on perfectionism and who has control. If you are a first-born or only child married to another first-born or only child, here are some tips for reducing tension and increasing harmony in your marriage:

1. *Stop "improving" on things your spouse does or says.* To a perfectionist, this may be a real trick, but bite your tongue and do it anyway. The New Testament compares the tongue to the bit in a horse's mouth or the rudder of a huge ship (see James 3:3–4). This vivid metaphor says it all. The bit and the rudder control everything, and the tongue can literally determine the direction of your marriage.

2. *Stop "shoulding" your mate.* For first-born perfectionists, criticism is second nature. If you are being hard on yourself and/or your mate, lower that high-jump bar of life. Once you quit trying to jump so high, you can stop asking your mate to do so as well.

3. *Define roles carefully to avoid arguments over control.* In other words, decide who does what. One spouse can do the shopping while the other pays the bills and balances the checking account. Help each other with assigned tasks and try to be considerate and aware of the other's responsibilities. Example: If one spouse does the shopping, the other should not complain about the high grocery bill. I counseled one couple where the perfectionist, critical husband complained incessantly until his wife told him, "Okay, *you* shop this week." He did and came home in "sticker shock," never to complain again!

4. *Get rid of the we've-got-to-do-it-my-way attitude.* The old cliché applies: There is more than one way to skin a cat (and your way is not necessarily best). One of the best sentences any first-born perfectionist can learn to say to his or her first-born spouse is: "You may be right. Let's try it your way."

First Borns Find Middle Borns a Paradox

The first born who marries a middle born should first take comfort in the fact that middles have the best track record for building a lasting marriage. At the same time, the middle child can be a vexing paradox. Middle children grow up having to learn to negotiate, mediate, and compromise, but they can also be secretive and play it close to the vest with their emotions. I have found that middle children typically will throw their first-born spouses a bone once in a while without letting them know how they really feel. Some practical suggestions for first borns married to middles include:

1. *Make it a point to have regular recaps and discuss feelings and what is happening.* Do not let your spouse toss you a bone by saying, "Everything's fine." Ask what your spouse means by "fine."

Daily recaps—at least a recap every few days—are valuable in any marriage, but are particularly useful if one mate tends to be less inclined to share feelings. I know of one couple who did their recapping while discussing the sermon they had heard at church. Discussing their spiritual beliefs and values was a way to open up about feelings that were bothering one or both of them.

2. *Make your spouse feel special.* Remember that the middle-child husband or wife very likely did not grow up feeling special, so anything you do—small gifts, love notes, saying *sincere* little things he or she likes to hear—will touch the heart and strengthen your marriage. While the following applies to every birth order, it's especially good for the first-born husband of the middle-child wife to remember: Every day women ask in one way or another, "Do you really love me?" Every day they need your affirming answer.

> Every day women ask in one way or another, "Do you really love me?" Every day they need your affirming answer.

3. *Work on drawing out your middle-child spouse.* Keep in mind that as a first born your natural inclination is to give the answer, solve the problem. Instead, back off and ask, "What do you think?" "Tell me how you really feel," or "Tell me more." First-born husbands of middle-born wives should always ask for their opinion, particularly on issues of people and feelings. Middle borns are not only more perceptive, but they like the problem-solving role and smoothing a way for everyone.

First Born Plus Last Born Equals Bliss (Usually)

According to one study of three thousand families, the odds for a happy marriage increase a great deal when the first born hooks up with the last born.[3] What is at work here is the opposites-attract-and-are-good-for-each-other factor. The first born teaches the last born little things that may be lacking, such as being organized and having goals, while the last born helps the first born lighten up and not take an overly serious approach to life.

According to the researchers, the best possible match you can find is the first-born female and the last-born male. I took no part in this research so I can't be accused of making this claim because that happens to be the match Sande, my first-born wife, and I have. I'm just *very* thankful it happened.

First-born females are often mothering types and last-born males often need mothering. I started out being fortunate to be the last-born brother of my first-born sister, Sally. Eight years older than I, she mothered me quite a bit and taught me a lot about women. For example, she taught me that girls don't like being approached by a bunch of boys who are show-offs—pushing each other, talking loudly, and doing stupid things that guys often do. Sally also told me girls want a guy who is tender, understanding, and a listener, who realizes manners have not gone out of style.

Most marriage counselors agree that men do not understand women very well. So *any* extra learning a boy can get while growing up is going to help him later when he has a wife and family of his own. Of course in my case, I certainly didn't come into our marriage a finished product. I still needed some work, and Mama Bear was happy to oblige.

How Mama Bear Reformed Cubby Bear

It may be a good rule of thumb to say any combination of first born and last born has a better chance for marital success than do other combinations, but success doesn't follow automatically. Good marriages are made, not born. Two people must work together on being considerate, caring, and mutually supportive. When I married Sande, it was a classic matchup of the pleaser Mama Bear taking on the playful Cub. Naturally the Cub took advantage of his new caregiver. Sande had to put up with my fussy eating habits and picking up my clothes after me wherever I dropped them.

This went on through the early years of our marriage. One day, while I was working on my doctorate, Sande heard me expostulating on how to discipline children and hold them accountable for their actions. The light dawned. *If holding children accountable for their actions is good, holding a husband accountable might be even better,* Sande thought. She went into action.

Soon I found my little piles of clothing where I had left them. In no time the apartment became covered with my piles. Then came the day when I could not open the door because Sande had shoved a giant stack of my clothes against it to make room for whatever she was doing. *That* got my attention. Sande and I had a long overdue talk and shared our feelings.

She said: "Look, I want to be your wife, not your mother. You learn to pick up your own clothes and put them where they belong. Also, I'm going to fix different things for dinner. I expect you to at least try some new dishes. You owe that much to yourself and to our children—if you want to be the good role model you keep talking about."

I said: "Okay, I'll try to do better, but you have to promise me that you'll serve only canned peas and corn—no frozen peas!"

Learning to pick up my clothes and eating different foods was just a start as Cubby Bear learned how to grow up and become Papa Bear.

Here are some tips for first-born/last-born couples:

1. *Don't let the last-born spouse take advantage of you.* Sande was gentle-spirited but firm. She started expecting me to be a leader in our home and take an active role in meeting responsibilities. At times, she reminded me of my high school English teacher—the one in whose class I *never* goofed off because I knew better. I even learned that changing diapers is not off-limits for a psychologist with a doctor's degree, and when our children started to arrive, I did my share of diapers, giving baths, and other baby care. In short, Mama Bear taught Papa Bear that *parenthood isn't woman's work.*

2. *First borns prone to faultfinding must back off.* If you want to find your last-born spouse's flaws, you certainly can because they are all over the place. Accept all the flaws you can or make gentle suggestions on how to correct them. And if you're the last born, remember not to flaunt your flaws in your first-born spouse's face.

3. *If you're a baby, remember others need the spotlight too.* Last borns are notorious carrot-seekers as in, "Look at me, I'm performing—toss me a carrot." First borns may act as if they don't need any attention or strokes, but they do, and their last-born mates should provide some.

4. *Last borns must remember they are not a one-man team.* Because they have that first-born spouse who is probably

keeping things organized and running smoothly, last borns may go off on their impetuous own now and then—to buy something, schedule something, or just do something without letting their spouse know.

One of the best bits of wisdom I ever received concerning marriage came from Dr. James Dobson, author of such best-sellers as *Dare to Discipline, The Strong-Willed Child,* and *Hide or Seek* and founder of Focus on the Family. An only child, Dr. Dobson is scholarly, organized, conscientious, and reliable. So one day while Sande and I were having lunch with him, I asked, "Jim, if there was one bit of advice you could give to me, what would it be?"

He glanced at Sande and then back at me and said without hesitating, "Kevin . . . before you do anything, *whatever it is,* run it by Sande first."

Obviously Dr. Dobson's advice applies to *any* birth-order marriage match, but it especially applied to the last-born Cub and Mama Bear! I said to myself, *If an only child with Jim Dobson's credentials thinks that's a good idea, then I do too!* I've tried to follow his advice ever since and it has *always* paid off.

Middle Plus Middle Can Equal a Muddle

As we have seen, two married middle children will probably not communicate well. They tend to feel it isn't worth the hassle to confront each other. They may also discount the value of their own opinions. These attitudes are typical of middle children.

One simple little device that I have used with great success when counseling a middle married to a middle is the suggestion bowl. Place a clear bowl or jar in a prominent place where both of you can see it and deposit in it your suggestions. Keep pads of paper and pencils or pens handy. The husband should use one color of paper; the wife another. When the husband wants to tell his wife something, he writes a suggestion on his pad and drops it into the bowl. And when the wife wants to give hubby a suggestion, she does the same.

Some spouses—particularly men—think the suggestion bowl is too much of a crutch, but I talk them into trying it anyway because, the fact is, some of us simply can't look our mate in the eye and tell him or her what is on our mind. Some other tips to keep the middle-child marriage healthy include:

1. *Build up each other's self-esteem.* Middle children often have a poor to only fair self-image, so let each other know you appreciate the other's strengths and abilities. Be sure to make sincere comments, not obvious pat-on-the-head remarks designed to flatter or manipulate.

2. *Provide plenty of space for outside friendships.* Remember that as middle children you both are probably big on having friends and social acquaintances. Encourage each other to make these kind of contacts, but only with the same sex. I know it's the '90s, but my files (and the files of thousands of other counselors) are full of examples of affairs that started because one spouse had a "special friend" of the opposite sex.

3. *Do special things for each other.* I've already mentioned this, but it bears repeating: Middle children usually don't grow up feeling very special because they are squeezed and ignored. You don't have to spend a lot of time and money. Love notes are always good. A single rose, a small bottle of cologne, a special dinner—it's definitely the thought, not the amount of money, that counts.

4. *Above all, show each other mutual respect.* You show respect when you telephone if you're running late; check with your spouse before making commitments; refrain from talking about your marriage in front of others; back each other up in front of the children, particularly on discipline matters; and never bad-mouth each other in the presence of others.

Middle Child Plus Baby—a Pretty Good Match

According to birth order studies, middle children and last borns rank right up there as potentially successful pairings for marriage. The middle child, typically strong in negotiating and compromising, pairs up well with a socially outgoing baby of the family.

And somewhat paradoxically, this kind of marriage has a high probability for good communication—sharing feelings and rolling with the punches. Yes, I know I said earlier that middle children tend to clam up and not share emotions, but the plus factor here is that middle children are not as threatened by babies of the family as they might be by meticulous exacting first borns. So, the odds—and remember, all of these birth order pairing observations go by the odds—are good for decent communication. Here are some tips for making a fairly good blend even better:

1. *Middle-child spouses should work things out, but guard against being condescending.* Last-born mates will smell that in a moment because people have been writing them off in a condescending way all their lives.

2. *Blend your social interests with your last-born spouse's desire to have fun.* If you're a typical middle child, friends are important and you enjoy having people over and other social outreach. If your last-born mate is typical, he or she will always be ready for adventure and trying something new. When daily connections and pressures make it impossible to get away, the middle-child spouse should grant in fantasy that which is impossible in reality by saying something like: "Honey, I'd love to go with you to that bed and breakfast, and we will as soon as the kids settle down a little" (or as soon as things settle down at work).

3. *Last-born spouses should realize they have a selfish streak and a desire to hold the spotlight.* Work at backing off from your demands for service or attention. Do everything you

can to make your middle-child mate feel pampered and special.

4. *Don't have fun at your spouse's expense.* This is good advice for any birth order, but it applies particularly to last borns who want to have fun, play practical jokes, and get in sarcastic little digs—all just to get a laugh. Keep in mind, however, that many middle children battle feelings of inferiority and it's easy to press the wrong button or push too hard. The general rule is always try to laugh *with* your mate, not *at* him or her.

Last Born Plus Last Born Equals Chaos

I have already touched on how last borns can get into financial trouble in a marriage. They have a big problem with answering the metaphorical question, "Who is running the asylum?" And before long their home has turned into a real one.

Two last borns must put their heads together and decide who will pay the bills, who will do the shopping, who will cook and clean up, who will take charge of the social calendar, who cleans house, and who is point guard on disciplining the kids. Notice I said "point guard" for discipline, which suggests that Mom and Dad are a team, but that one of them may have to take the lead while the other one is backup.

If last borns don't get a grip and make firm decisions on these practical matters, they can arrive in big-time trouble fast. Babies of the family have a tendency to forget or assume their spouse was going to do what needed doing. ("Was *I* supposed to gas up the car? I thought *you* were going to!")

Last borns have a built-in tendency to pass the buck and blame to someone else, and who is handier than one's spouse? But if your spouse is last born, guess who's catching the buck and throwing it right back in your face? Here are some other tips for the last-born/last-born couple:

1. *Beware of selective listening.* Remember that you're both manipulators. You may wind up playing games with one another and selectively hearing only what you want to hear. Then when you're finally called to account you'll come back with the old standby: "Oh, I didn't understand it that way at all . . . I never really agreed to do *that* . . . Why didn't you *tell me?* . . . I had no idea!"

2. *Learn to be active listeners.* The best cure for selective listening is active listening, which means you listen with more than your ears. Look directly at your partner and sense his or her feelings as well as trying to understand the facts being communicated.

A counseling device I often use with couples is to sit them in chairs facing each other with their knees practically touching. Then they hold hands and talk about their problems. They have one rule: While one person speaks, the other cannot interrupt; and before replying, the one who has been listening has to "feed back" to the speaker's satisfaction everything that the speaker said.

Yes, this is a ponderous way to have a discussion. But it does wonders for helping spouses learn how to hear each other and understand what each other is saying.

3. *Hold each other accountable.* I suggest trying a simple plan: Sit down once or twice a week and ask some pointed questions. "How are we doing on the budget?" "Is the checkbook under control?" "Are we both aware of our next important date or engagement?" "Do you think I'm really trying to listen to you?"

That last question might open up the door for practicing more active listening, as long as you avoid being defensive. And that brings us to the next tip:

4. *Stay loose and laid-back.* Those are your natural qualities anyway, so use them when things get a bit tense. Remember, as the baby of the family, you "earned a living" by looking up and learning how to get around all the older kids and

other insurmountable problems. You can get around marriage problems too, if you work together with your spouse. And that suggests one more tip:

5. *Keep your sense of humor and never give up.* But remember what I said to the last-born spouse of the middle child. It applies here as well. Don't make fun of each other. Laugh together, not at each other.

An Arrow, Not an Answer

Now that I've touched on the so-called "best" and the statistically "not so hot" birth-order combinations for marriage, have I left you encouraged or discouraged? Maybe you're a bit puzzled because you're supposed to have a dandy marriage but things aren't going that well. Maybe you're indignant because you aren't considered a good match and you get along just fine, thank you! So what does Leman know about anything?

All of these discussions of which birth-order combinations make strong or weak marriages follow the same principle that I have been repeating and will continue to repeat throughout this book: When talking about birth order, all general statements are indicators, not rules.

> When talking about birth order, all general statements are indicators, not rules.

In other words, all these general guidelines are arrows, pointing in a certain direction, but that hardly means that the fate of your marriage has been decided by your birth orders. And they aren't an excuse for saying, "Well, it's hopeless. We're both first borns and that means we're doomed to divorce."

I know plenty of marriages where two first borns get along very nicely. My own first-born sister, Sally, is an example. She married first-born, Wes, a meticulous perfectionist who is a dentist. You would think that by now Sally and Wes would have picked each other to pieces, but not so. They have built a great marriage around a common faith in God, a sense of balance, and plenty of hard work, and they have three super kids to show for it.

So the good news remains the same. Birth order is never a final determinant of anything, only an indicator of problems and tensions that you may discover or create for yourselves. No matter what your birth order and that of your spouse, what counts is how you use your particular strengths and how you modify or deal with your particular weaknesses.

There is no big mystery in making your marriage work, but it is always difficult. Knowing birth-order characteristics of you and your mate is just one step toward learning how to get along and have a happy life together.

Another important step is understanding each other's *life-style*. In the next chapter we'll talk about what happens when a man and a woman try to build a home and family by putting their individual (really unique) life-styles together.

A Quiz for All Spouses

1. Do I nitpick? Do I find fault with what my mate wears, says, or does? How often?
2. Do I take the time to encourage my mate?
3. Do we talk things out? Have we set aside time "just for us"?
4. When was the last time we took a weekend away from the children?
5. When was the last time I gave my mate a compliment?
6. When was the last time I gave my mate a special present for absolutely no particular reason except to say, "I love you"?

7. Speaking of "I love you," when was the last time I said those three little wonderful words to my mate?

8. What is the one thing I *know* my mate would love to have me do? Am I planning to do it this week?

9. Do we worship together? Or are we like too many couples who seem to have decided that God is like the Edsel, obsolete?

10. Do I take the time to find out what my mate is really interested in? Do I take the time to understand the "ins and outs" of his or her favorite pastime or activity?

11. When was the last time I "kidnapped" my mate from the office (or maybe from the ironing board), taking him or her away on an overnight?

12. When was the last time I came home early from work to take care of little Buford or Festus and let my mate go window shopping or run some errands?

13. When was the last time I said, "I am sorry. I was wrong. Will you forgive me?"

I Only Count
When . . .

TAKING A LOOK AT YOUR LIFE-STYLE

*t*hink about how you would complete the statement
that is the title of this chapter. The way you finish the
sentence says a lot about you—and your marriage.
When couples are having problems and have decided to "try
the psychologist," one of the first things I look for is the life-
style and life theme (or lifeline) of each spouse.[1] From a psychological standpoint, these terms mean the following:

> *Personal life-style*—a unique way of looking at oneself,
> other people, and the world. Every person sees life
> differently. For each of us, reality is what we see from
> behind our own eyes.
> *Personal life theme*—or lifeline, which is lived out every
> day—actually every moment. We may seldom state our

life theme in so many words, but it is there, directing our every move.

Life-style is a term coined by Alfred Adler, who founded the school of individual psychology in the early 1900s. Adler believed that from early infancy, all of us start forming an individual life plan that causes us to pursue certain life goals. According to Adler, we would not know what to do with ourselves if we were not oriented to some goal or objective. As he put it, "We cannot think, feel, will, or act without the perception of some goal."[2]

Adler believed that when a baby is born, he quickly sizes up what is going on around him (his environment) and starts forming his goals. Obviously he doesn't do this consciously, making notes in his appointment book, but the information is all being registered in his little brain, nonetheless. Adler wrote:

> The goal of each human being is probably formed in the first months of his life. Even at this time, certain sensations play a role which evoke a response of joy or comfort in this child. Here the first traces of a philosophy of life come to the surface, although expressed in the most primitive fashion.[3]

You may be wondering where genetics comes in. Does a child learn *everything* from his or her environment? Good question. Psychologists have long argued whether heredity or environment influences a human being the most. According to Rudolph Dreikurs, one of Alfred Adler's leading disciples, a growing child experiences both heredity *and* environment and draws his own conclusions. As he experiences his environment (mainly his family), he discovers where he is skilled and strong and where he is weak and lacking in ability. As the child sorts out all of his experiences, with their pluses and minuses, his personality takes shape.[4]

As an infant grows and pursues his primitive goals, he starts developing what Adler called a *style of life*—or *life-style*. Every child is born with the need for attention, and one of his or her primary goals is to gain attention in one way or another. When a child's attempt to gain attention, either positively or negatively, doesn't get the desired results, the child becomes discouraged and then turns his or her efforts toward another goal: gaining power. If his or her attempts to be powerful (to control the parents) fail, he or she becomes still more discouraged and the goal may become revenge.

Getting attention, power, or revenge are three basic motivations for a child's behavior. Most children concentrate on gaining attention or power; they seldom reach the revenge stage. Those who do, often end up in prison or other correctional institutions.

As a child develops his or her own unique life-style by pursuing his or her basic goal, the child also develops a *life theme*. The complete psychological definition of a life theme, or what some counselors call a *lifeline*, could get a bit too involved and time-consuming to wade through. For simplicity's sake, just think of a life theme as personal mottos or slogans, ideas that you subconsciously repeat to yourself daily and *believe with all your heart*. If you doubt that you have a life theme, look back over your behavior for a week, a month, or a year, and you can see this life theme exhibited again and again in your behavior.

A life theme always has to do with your self-image and your sense of self-worth. I like to describe anyone's life theme in terms of "I only count when . . ." The way you finish that sentence will tell me about your life-style and will give me some definite clues about your birth order.

> A life theme always has to do with your self-image and your sense of self-worth.

The problem, of course, is that your life theme is a lie or at least a partial lie. You are not *completely* what your life theme tells you that you are because you have the capacity to change, compensating for or conquering your weaknesses and capitalizing on your strengths.

Controllers and Pleasers

While everyone's life-style is different to some degree, there are broad categories into which most people fit. Because the two life-styles I counsel the most are controllers and pleasers, we will look at them at some length. Then we will also consider other broad life-styles such as martyr, victim, attention-getter, and driver.

Controllers

Controllers are powerful people who operate out of one of two motivations. Often they are first borns, who were expected to take care of their younger siblings. Their strong need for power motivates some to want to control everything and everyone. Nothing escapes their critical eye; no one they deal with is free from the strings they try to attach.

Another kind of controller, however, operates out of fear. This person is on the defensive and basically out to be sure no one takes control of him! Controllers are more comfortable with people at arm's length. They avoid intimacy because they fear losing control. Not surprisingly, controllers tend to fear death because, after all, death is the ultimate loss of control.

Another characteristic of controllers (and, remember, a controller doesn't necessarily have all the characteristics mentioned here) is a critical, perfectionistic approach. They're always trying to clear the high-jump bar of life and making those around them clear it as well. Naturally, controllers have a tremendous need to be right. They love to argue and they seldom lose an argument.

While it may sound as if controllers are aggressive, assertive people, they can also be temperamental, insecure, and shy. They may manipulate others, particularly their families, with tears or temper tantrums—or both. Whatever their weapons, they are always operating from a position of power.

Some controllers pound the table, shout, even scream. Others work quietly and may seem gentle, even loving on the surface. Underneath, however, it's a different story. A controlling mom can dominate her family by worrying about everyone. A controlling dad may keep everybody under his thumb with his silence, refusing to say what's on his mind. Fearing the unknown, the rest of the family walks on eggshells around him.

Typical life themes for controllers include the following:

"I only count when I'm in control of the situation."
"I only count when I'm in charge."
"I only count when I'm running the show, when what I say goes."

Pleasers

One hundred and eighty degrees from the controller is the pleaser, often a compliant first born. As you might guess, controllers are often married to pleasers, and we'll look at that more closely in a moment.

A driving force behind the pleaser is the need to be liked by everyone. Pleasers try to keep the oceans of life smooth so that they can gain everyone's approval—particularly in their families.

Pleasers typically have a poor self-image. That's why they're always trying to do everything they can to keep everyone else happy. They believe they're valued for what they do, not for who they are. They live behind masks, smiling and nodding agreement, but inside they may not agree at all; and often they're hating themselves because they don't have the courage to speak up.

Speaking up is something a pleaser seldom does because he or she knows that's the sure route to rejection. Pleasers much prefer to go along with the ideas of others. They become skilled socially, able to read signals that others send and know how to keep everyone happy.

Pleasers, by the way, can be perfectionists, but they work out their perfectionism differently from controllers. They are constantly worried about measuring up, being good enough, being perfect. You might say they are perfectionists out of fear of being anything else.

Life themes for pleasers can include the following:

"I only count when I keep everything smooth and on an even keel."
"I only count when everyone likes me."
"I only count when everyone approves of what I do."
"I only count when I put others first."

Among clients from the churchgoing community I often hear the life theme, "I only count when I please God and make him happy." Instead of having a healthy desire to please God, these men and women are such perfectionists, they see God as a harsh taskmaster who demands flawless perfection from them. Serving this kind of God is a perfect way to wind up perfectly depressed.

Controllers and Pleasers Often Marry

As I mentioned, the two life-styles I counsel most are controllers and pleasers, and there is a simple reason for this. Controllers often marry pleasers (the old opposites attract influence) and then the controllers, more often than not, give the pleasers a bad time. Typically, the husband is the controller and the wife is the pleaser, but there are some cases where the reverse is true. There are nine pleaser males in the continental United States. However, we're not releasing their names or addresses!

It's hard to get a controlling husband into my office for counseling because he is sure that his wife is the one with the problem; there's nothing wrong with *him*. But when the controller finally agrees to come in and talk to me, he lets his true colors show in a hurry. I hear statements that add up to life themes like these: "I only count when I'm in charge . . . when what I say goes . . . when I'm running things."

To help my clients recognize when the person they are dating or married to is a controller, I've developed the following quiz. Because most controllers are male, the following statements use the masculine pronoun.

Telltale Signs of a Controller

Read each statement and score 4 for always, 3 for often, 2 for sometimes, and 1 for seldom.

_____ 1. He tends to be critical—a faultfinding perfectionist with a high standard of excellence for himself and others.

_____ 2. He finds it difficult to laugh at himself, particularly when he may have done or said something awkward or wrong.

_____ 3. He puts down or degrades others with subtle or not-so-subtle humor.

_____ 4. He has a weak (or even poor) relationship with his mother (or other women who have been, or still are, part of his life, such as a sister or a supervisor).

_____ 5. He complains about authority figures who "don't know what they are doing" (employers, teachers, pastors, or the president).

_____ 6. He is a real competitor who always has to win at sports or table games.

_____ 7 He gets his way, subtly or not so subtly, about where the two of you will go or what you will do.

_____ 8. He prefers to run the show rather than be a team player—on the job, in committees, or in situations involving family or friends.

_____ 9. He has a hard time saying "I was wrong" or makes excuses that will make him look good in the face of adversity.

_____10. He loses his temper (raises his voice, screams, curses).

_____11. He can get physical—shoving or hitting you or smashing things.

_____12. He makes you account for every penny you spend but he spends rather freely.

_____13. Sex is something the two of you engage in for his pleasure and at his convenience.

_____14. When he drinks alcohol, even in modest quantities, he starts to become a different person.

_____15. He makes excuses for excessive drinking.

No quiz like this can be absolute proof of anything but it can give you some clues that may help you analyze your relationship to your spouse. If the ratings you gave your spouse add up to between 50 and 60, he is a super controller—whose only hope is a professional counselor—if he'll listen. If you are engaged and your fiancé scored between 50 and 60, my advice is to give back the ring and run.

If you scored your husband or fiancé somewhere between 40 and 49, he is a typical controller, who is probably open to being confronted and asked to change his behavior.

If you scored your husband or fiancé between 30 and 39, he should be a fairly balanced person who can be in control at times but flexible at others.

If you scored your husband or fiancé at 29 or less, first recheck your figures. If you haven't made a scoring error, you may have one of the few pleaser males in captivity. But take a second look to see if he scored higher than a 2 on any of the following questions: 10, 11, 12, 13, 14. All of these suggest a high degree of need to control, even dominate, with violence and abuse.

Telltale Signs of a Pleaser

The following statements use the feminine pronoun because most pleasers are female. Score 4 for always, 3 for often, 2 for sometimes, and 1 for seldom.

_____ 1. She walks on eggshells to keep everyone happy.

_____ 2. She wonders why she can't do things right.

_____ 3. She feels insecure, lacking confidence.

_____ 4. Her father was or is authoritarian.

_____ 5. She avoids confronting others because it "just isn't worth it."

_____ 6. She's often heard saying, "I should have . . ." or "I ought to . . ."

_____ 7. She feels overpowered by her spouse and even her children.

_____ 8. She gets little affection from others.

_____ 9. She feels like hiding or running away from life's hassles.

_____10. Her spouse and children know which buttons to push to make her feel guilty.

_____11. She feigns agreement or approval when she feels just the opposite on the inside.

_____12. She is easily persuaded by others and will go along with whoever talked to her last.

_____13. She is afraid to try new things or take new risks.

_____14. It embarrasses her to stand up for her rights or take the initiative.

_____15. She gets little respect from her spouse or her children.

The spouse scoring between 50 and 60 would be considered a super-suffering pleaser, who could easily be in the hands of a misogynist (a woman hater who needs a professional counselor).

Anyone scoring 40 to 49 is a discouraged or depressed pleaser for whom there is hope *if* she is willing to take action and confront her husband.

Anyone scoring 30 to 39 is a mildly discouraged pleaser. Her positives in life outweigh her negatives, but she still would like a little more respect, particularly from her family.

Those scoring 29 or below fall into the "positive pleaser" category. They are able to balance their very giving nature with being able to receive the love, support, and respect they want and need.

Counsel for the Controller/Pleaser Couple

My suggestions to a couple suffering controller/pleaser problems include:

1. *If you are married to a controller, realize you are not going to change your spouse.* I tell husbands and wives: "Don't try to use a Brillo pad on the leopard's spots. You'll only make the leopard angry." In other words, you can only change your own behavior and way of interacting and then allow your spouse to decide to change.

2. *Try being positive, but refuse to play your spouse's controlling games.* Pleasantly but firmly refuse to be controlled. If you can force the controller's hand, he must act differently, because the payoff is no longer there. The key is to

let the controller know that if he wants to control himself, he is welcome. But when he tries to control everyone else in the family, something has to give.

3. *If you are a particularly loud and blustery controller, try getting alone and ventilating feelings to yourself aloud.* People who have a hard time talking to others can really do much better by talking to themselves and learning to articulate their feelings in an acceptable way. Later they can try to communicate with their spouse in the same way. (Note: If your controllerism has reached any level of verbal or physical abusiveness, run, don't walk, to the nearest competent professional therapist and get some help.)

4. *If perfection is your goal, you'll always feel a void in your life.* You'll never get there. It is a hopeless, fruitless quest. You must have the courage to accept yourself and your spouse as you both are—imperfect people, still learning, growing, changing.

5. *My final counsel to controllers is that it is futile to try to control everyone and everything.* It simply doesn't work. In marriage it all comes back to what I said earlier about two being one: When two are one, *both* are in control, *both* are free to do their thing.

Beyond Pleasers and Controllers Are Martyrs and More

Each individual has his or her own unique life-style, but we can identify certain broad categories into which most men and women fit. Besides controllers and pleasers, there are many other broad descriptive labels for people, and many people can have more than one label. For example, a pleaser may also have a touch of the martyr or victim, both natural offshoots of wanting to please and always have the approval of others.

Martyrs are people who almost always have a poor self-image and they seek out others who will reinforce that poor self-image, primarily the people they marry.

Martyrs have an uncanny ability to find losers who will walk on them, use them, or abuse them in some way. Martyrs often wind up married to alcoholics and they tend to enable their alcoholic mates by making excuses for them out of "love."

Martyrs learn to be doormats while growing up, usually from fathers who were very strict, possessive, and controlling. Martyr wives often have husbands who wander, who have left them, or who are planning to leave them for other women. The reason is simple: A martyr isn't worth pursuing. A doormat finally gets tiresome and worn out.

Martyrs suffer for a cause. Often the cause is a husband who has failed her in some way. The martyr wife makes excuses for her husband, vowing to "stand by her man" to the bitter end—and the end usually is bitter. I often deal with martyr wives from the church community who have been taught to be submissive to their husbands. At best, their interpretation of this teaching enables their controlling (and often chauvinistic) spouse to take advantage of them. At worst, they become victims of disrespect, neglect, and abuse.

The life themes I often hear from martyrs include the following:

"I only count when I suffer."
"I only count when I'm taken advantage of."
"I only count when I'm hurt by others."

Close cousin to the martyr is the victim. The victim's life themes are very similar to the martyr's. Victims or martyrs could be called super pleasers, or pleasers who have gone to

seed. Victims, martyrs, and pleasers all have the same problem—low self-esteem. In victims and martyrs, the problem
is simply much worse.

Many victims frequently use words like *me, my,* and *I* as
they seek sympathy or pity while complaining about their
misfortunes, aches, and pains. They often feel taken advantage of, but through all their complaining, they get what
they really want—to be the center of attention.

Other martyrs or victims aren't primarily after attention
but they keep their life-style because it's "comfortable." Perhaps the best illustration of sticking with something because
it's comfortable, though less than desirable, is the way I cling
to my old pair of crummy, ragged, worn-out slippers. Sande
is always tossing them out because they're "gross." She
expects me to wear a new pair she gave me or one of the
pairs the kids have bought me for Christmas or Father's Day.

Of course, I immediately rescue my old slippers from
the trash can and she finds me wearing them once more,
as crummy and ugly as ever.

"Why?" she wonders, "do you insist on wearing those
old, cruddy, crummy slippers when you have so many nice
new pairs to choose from?"

All I can say in return is, "I wear them because they're
comfortable."

The way I return to my crummy, old slippers is similar to
the way martyrs and victims return to the same abusive relationship or continue to take the same guff they've been getting for years from family, friends, or coworkers. The abuse,
lack of respect, being made fun of—whatever—is "comfortable." This type of victim is sometimes called a disaster
waiting to happen.

The life themes of victims are often:

"I only count when I'm put down."
"I only count when I'm mistreated."

Another broad life-style category is attention-getter, which has some similarities to the controller. Whenever you're gaining attention, you are trying to take control to some extent. Last borns of the family often have this life-style because they are the powerful little buzzards in the family who are desperately seeking lots of attention, mainly because they see all those bigger buzzards (their siblings) circling above them in a rather intimidating way.

My own life-style is primarily attention-getter because when I was very young, I perceived that I could never outdo my super capable first-born sister or my big brother. Obviously I had to take a different route. Because it was easy and fun, I chose to become the family clown.

My life-style was pretty well set by the time I was five or six. (I'm not exactly sure because no psychologist dropped by to check on me.) After that, it was all downhill, so to speak, and whatever happened only confirmed my belief that I had to be funny and cute or a mischief maker. My life theme became: "I only count when I gain attention by being entertaining." Other life themes of attention-getters include the following or variations thereof:

"I only count when I'm in the spotlight."
"I only count when I'm the star."
"I only count when I make people laugh."

Meshing Life-Styles in Marriage

Life-styles and lifelines don't always have to cause tension in a marriage. Sometimes they can mesh nicely and be enjoyable, even when you put a manipulative last-born husband together with a pleasing, gullible first-born wife.

Just before we were to be married, I told Sande there was a tradition in the Leman family that said the wife had to buy the marriage license. As we've seen, one of the strong traits in many first borns is a willingness to please other people and, unlike later-born children, the pleasing first born is not so likely to be worldly wise and alert to the wiles of those trying to take advantage. In other words, my lovable wife is an easy mark.

So it was not surprising that she thought it was wonderful when I asked her to fork over five dollars for a wedding license. I took the five-dollar bill from her, laid it on the marriage license clerk's desk, and said: "You've just started a tradition."

She just laughed. I laughed too. We both knew I was trying to get through graduate school and was flat broke. She had the job, owned the car, and was our sole means of support. The whole thing was good for a laugh then, and we still chuckle about it today. At the time we both got a harmless payoff for the life-styles we followed. I got noticed and had some fun; Sande got to play the pleasing role she enjoys so much.

What's Your Life-Style?

I've discussed in this chapter only a few of the possible life-styles people choose. There are many others. A driver is a goal-oriented person who must reach his objective at any cost. His life theme reads, "I only count when I achieve," or "I only count when I get everything done."

Another life-style I see quite often is the rationalizer, the person who tries to avoid or deny responsibility by throwing up a smoke screen of theory, facts, and opinions. The rationalizer's life theme says, "I only count when I can find a good excuse or explanation," or "I only count when I can put on a front that makes me look good."

A goody-goody, first cousin to the pleaser, is another common life-style. The goody-goody's life theme may be "I only count when I follow the rules," or "I only count when I live a righteous life."

Now that you have some basic information regarding life-styles and life themes (or lines), it may be interesting to assess what your life-style and lifelines are, as well as those of your spouse. To do that, use the exercise below:

1. What words below would best describe your life-style? If you feel that you have characteristics that fit more than one description, check them both off but put a big "X" by the one that is predominant. Then write down your life-style, putting the dominant description first.

    ____ Controller
    ____ Perfectionist
    ____ Driver
    ____ Pleaser
    ____ Victim
    ____ Martyr
    ____ Goody-goody
    ____ Attention-getter
    ____ Rationalizer

2. My life theme is:
    "I only count when _____."

3. Using the life-styles listed above, give your own estimate of which ones apply to your spouse (remember, you can use more than one style, but write the predominant one first): _____.

4. From the descriptions that you have given of your spouse above, state what you believe is your spouse's life theme:
    "I only count when _____."

This exercise can be even more interesting if you let your spouse complete these very same questions. Then the two of you can compare your individual perceptions of each other's life-styles and life themes.

Lying Lifelines Shorten Marriages

Today's statistics tell us that the average marriage lasts seven years. No marriage will get very far if you and/or your spouse live out a lifeline that is so extreme and unhealthy it becomes destructive to both of you.

When counseling married couples, I proceed on the premise that every husband and wife counts simply because he or she is made in the image of God. I try to get both spouses to abandon lifelines that begin with, "I only count when . . ." and use terminology such as, "I count because . . ." If they insist on using a lifeline beginning with, "I only count when . . . ," I suggest, "Then tell yourself you can really count when you help your spouse grow and mature as another human being."

If you must live out a lifeline that says you only count when you control, are perfect, please everyone, get attention, or something else, be aware of the lie you are always telling yourself at a subconscious level and keep it under control with cognitive discipline. For example, the next time you are in a stressful situation of any kind—at work, at a party, wherever—stop and use cognitive discipline by asking yourself, "What did the old me usually do?" After identifying your usual lifeline and course of action, ask yourself, "What is the new me going to do *differently?*"

This isn't some kind of magic formula that causes instant change. But as you keep using this simple old me/new me approach, you will be able to change your lifeline and be able to say more often, "I count because I'm me!"

Your Favorite Lifeline

Have you come across your favorite lifeline yet? There are many more than the ones discussed in this chapter. Listed below are a few more variations of, or additions to, "I only count when I am perfect, avoid conflict, am noticed, or in control." With each lifeline is a brief analysis and suggestions for how to cope with it.

"I only count when I perform." This could be a lifeline for a perfectionist or someone who needs attention. It would depend on what you mean by "perform." Perfectionists have to realize they can never do it all and that their true worth lies in who they are as people, not in what they do as performers. As for people needing attention, they perform to be noticed, applauded, or given another carrot. This is selfish behavior and very frustrating because they can never get enough carrots!

"I only count when I win." This is a variation of, "I only count when I control." Another way to describe this lifestyle is "win-lose." There's no in-between. We hear a lot of talk today about succeeding and winning, but living by the win-lose code is a constant burden and hassle. I like to say that winning isn't everything—helping others win is everything.

"I only count when I'm cared for." This is a hybrid that relates back to, "I only count when I'm noticed," or "when people pay attention." It is a typical lifeline of a last born, especially a baby princess who is used to being spoiled, cared for, and having her older brothers protect her.

"I only count when I give of myself." This is a variation of the pleaser's line, a favorite of the compliant first-born perfectionist who grows up never failing to obey Mommy and Daddy. But in a marriage, a pleaser must always be wary of overdoing it, especially if he or she is married to a controller or a critical perfectionist. Marriage is a give-and-

take proposition. When one person has to do all the giving, it takes its toll on the relationship.

"I only count when I serve God." I often counsel church members who equate sincere belief with "being busy for the Lord." People with a natural tendency to feel they only count when they perform or when they please can quickly burn out in a church, because they wind up doing all the work!

13

Why Reality Discipline Works with Any Birth Order

*t*he proud owner of the brand-new twenty-one-foot day cruiser hadn't sailed the waters around Buffalo and Grand Island that much before, but Lake Erie was choppy so he decided to head down the Niagara River and show his lady friend some of his navigating skills.

The west branch of the Niagara provided some idyllic views, and then, as they headed on north past Navy Island, he decided to cut the engine and just drift with the current so that they could enjoy the scenery. As they came around a bend, he wasn't sure but he thought he saw rapids up ahead—and was that *mist* in the distance?

Just then a siren shrieked to the starboard, and he looked up to see a Coast Guard patrol boat bearing down on him at high speed. As the long arm of the law came alongside, a bullhorn bellowed, "DO YOU HAVE ENGINE TROUBLE?"

"No, not really," the weekend admiral shouted back. "We were just drifting for a ways to enjoy the scenery."

"MAN, DO YOU KNOW WHERE YOU ARE?"

"Not exactly. I think we just came out of the West Niagara River."

"THAT'S RIGHT, AND ABOUT A MILE FROM HERE YOU WOULD HAVE GONE RIGHT OVER NIAGARA FALLS."

"Thhhaanks for the warning," the day cruiser owner managed. "We're outta here!" He hit the throttle and was out of sight in seconds, no doubt a shaken but wiser man.

I know this scene may sound a little farfetched, but, unfortunately, it's reenacted many times each year when unknowing boaters wander too close to the danger zone above Niagara Falls.[1] As I grew up in the Buffalo area, I often heard about boats that had wandered too far down the river and gotten into real trouble.

Are You Drifting toward the Falls?

As I have counseled hundreds of families, original and blended, I've sometimes thought of those boats drifting downstream, headed unknowingly for Niagara Falls. Parents often come to me because their children are totally out of control and they are at the end of their rope.

One of my first questions is: "Do you love your children enough to discipline them?"

I usually get an answer along the lines of, "Well, of course, I do," or maybe, "I guess so. What do you mean by discipline?"

I hasten to explain that by *discipline* I do not mean *punish*. Over the years I have counseled hundreds (if not thousands) of kids and their parents. I speak to thousands of parents, teachers, and workers with children at seminars and conventions. I talk about a lot of things, including birth order, but I have only one basic theme: Love your kids enough to train them with an effective system of discipline.

Love your kids enough to train them with an effective system of discipline.

If anything is missing in today's families, it is a system or a strategy for applying consistent, loving discipline to the children. I see the fruits of inconsistency and lack of discipline almost daily in my office.

Parents come to me and ask questions like these:

"What can I do to motivate Richard? He has so much potential but he just doesn't seem to care."

"We're scared. Lisa is drinking an awful lot and running with the wrong crowd. What can we do?"

"What shall we do with Billy? He just doesn't listen to us anymore. He's downright rebellious and his language is abusive."

"Our Sherry is smoking pot and is brazen about it. She sees nothing wrong. How can we get her to stop?"

When I inquire about what system of discipline parents with these problems use to cope with their children, I often get the feeling they are adrift with no real plan in mind. The approach they are using is obviously not working, and unless somebody sounds the siren, they are headed for real disaster.

You have probably heard some child-rearing expert comment: "People are required to take a course to learn how to drive; they are required to take a course to learn how to give CPR; but *anyone* can become a parent with no credentials whatsoever."

Authoritarian and Permissive Discipline

Without training or input, most people tend to parent the way they were parented. When they marry—or remarry— they bring the same parenting style they grew up with, which in most cases means either authoritarianism or permissiveness or a mixture of both.

Authoritarians Are Too Strong on Limits

Authoritarianism is based on a warped idea of limits— the more limits the better: "As long as you live under *our* roof, you had better toe the mark, *or else.*"

Authoritarian parents are those who believe they know what is best for their children. Many parents of my generation grew up in authoritarian homes. If that was your experience, you remember quite clearly that you didn't have a lot of input. You did as you were told and you kept quiet. And if you didn't obey orders and keep quiet, you got the switch.

I can recall chatting with a TV personality when I was "resident psychologist" on her talk-variety show. We were talking about birth order and, as a first born, she remembered well the many pressures that were on her to perform and "be perfect." And when she wasn't perfect, she was given the assignment to go out and cut her own switches from the limbs of trees or bushes, bring them back to her father, and submit to a good tanning. Needless to say, this lady grew up in an authoritarian home.

Permissiveness Is Really Warped Love

Permissiveness is based on a warped idea of love: "All we have to do is *love* little Buford and everything will be just fine." In homes where parents are permissive, we see the child doing just about what he likes:

"Oh, Johnny, honey, it's 8:00 P.M. Have you chosen to go to bed yet?"

"Oh, that's all right, dear. Let little Jennifer play with the Hummel—she likes it." Permissive parents use an interesting form of logic that says, "If I let little Festus do his own thing, he will love me and always act like a nice little boy."

Of course, the opposite is true. Permissive parenting produces little tyrants who run the house. Permissive parenting *causes* rebellion, rather than preventing it, because the children feel anger and even hatred toward their parents for lack of guidelines and setting of limits.

How to Raise a Yo-Yo

In many homes, however, there is still another problem called inconsistency. It's not uncommon for one parent to be basically permissive while the other's style is authoritarian. In other cases, one parent may use both styles, depending on how the parent feels at the moment. Usually the parent tries to be "nice" and is permissive to a point. Then, when little Festus builds a fire in the living room without the benefit of a fireplace, the parent goes ballistic and cracks down with authoritarian wrath.

Swinging back and forth—from permissiveness to authoritarianism and back again—is an inconsistent approach that treats the child like a yo-yo. It's no wonder that so many children grow up to become "yo-yos" who have a terrible self-concept and practically zero self-esteem. When they marry and become parents themselves, they may be aware that what they're doing isn't working, but it's not easy to do it differently, since the only mode of discipline they've seen is what their parents used.

An Answer to the Problem

But there is another parenting style that I believe is the answer to the problem. We can stop the inconsistent swing between authoritarianism and permissiveness by standing on the middle ground that I call *authoritative* parenting. It's unfortunate that authoritative sounds so much like *authoritarian,* because people get them mixed up. There is, however, a world of difference in the two approaches. Authoritative parents don't dominate their children and make all decisions for them. And they certainly don't let the children dominate them and make all the decisions for the family.

Instead, authoritative parents guide their children with the action-oriented techniques of reality discipline, a system that is tailor-made to help them give their children loving correction and training. And what exactly is reality discipline? I spent one entire book describing it: *Making Children Mind without Losing Yours.* In the foreword I describe reality discipline this way:

Action-oriented discipline is based on the reality that there are times—sometimes several per day—when you have to pull the rug out and let the little "buzzards" tumble. I don't mean that literally, of course, but when I talk about pulling the rug out, I mean disciplining a child in such a way that he accepts responsibility and learns accountability for his actions.[2]

Some moms cringe a little when I talk about "pulling the rug out and letting the little buzzards tumble." I mean no offense. Here in Arizona we think "little buzzards" are cute—especially the ones who roost on backyard swing sets. And pulling the rug out is not supposed to suggest mayhem. It means confronting the child with reality about what he's done and having him learn that he has to pay some kind of consequence.

How Authoritative Parenting Works

In *Making Children Mind* I illustrate how authoritative parenting works with the example of the seven year old who breaks a toy belonging to another child. What should the parent do? An obvious choice would be a good swat or two, if this has been a regular pattern of behavior. Another obvious choice might be sending the child to his room or grounding him for a week. I don't believe any of those choices is the best one. I think the kind of discipline needed in this situation is one based on reality, and reality says if you break someone else's property, you pay for it.

How can a seven-year-old child pay for a toy? Out of his allowance or piggy bank. Allowances, by the way, are one of the best techniques any parent has for teaching reality discipline. It is absolutely amazing how early in life children become financial experts. Even the youngest child soon understands the concept of "the bottom line." When the consequences of his actions start coming out of his own pocket, he immediately starts to really think about what he is doing and why.[3]

Reality Discipline Can Save Your Day

There is a great deal more to reality discipline, and if you want the full story, you will have to get a copy of *Making Children Mind without Losing Yours*. I give you this blatant commercial without apology, because I believe it is truly a sound and sensible solution to making children mind. The book goes into many areas that parents are interested in:

> It talks about why reward and punishment don't really work and why love and encouragement do.
> It explains the difference between discipline and punishment.
> It gives practical steps any parent can take to teach children how to be accountable and responsible.
> It shows you how to "pull the rug out and let the little buzzards tumble"—that is, move in and apply reality discipline where it is really needed.

In short, *Making Children Mind without Losing Yours* gives you a game plan for parenting that is simple, sensible, and biblical. The apostle Paul was not a specialist in family counseling, but he was right on when he said: "And now a word to you parents. Don't keep on scolding and nagging your children, making them angry and resentful. Rather, bring them up with the loving discipline the Lord himself approves, with suggestions and godly advice" (Eph. 6:4 LB).

Consistency is always the way to go. Over the years I've been the guest on some premier television and radio programs, including *Focus on the Family* with Dr. James Dobson. Occasionally *Focus on the Family* replays certain programs they feel were of real value, and they were gracious enough to include some of mine. But what is interesting to me is when they replay these programs from ten to fifteen years ago—done in the '80s when my older children were small—I am happy about two things: (1) that Holly, Krissy, and Kevin have grown up to be responsible, well-adjusted people; (2) possibly even more significant, that there is a consistency in what I was saying as a younger parent and what I say today. Reality discipline has worked, is working, and will always work, because it deals with the real needs of children.[4]

I Believe in Spanking, If . . .

Reality discipline is not a "boot camp" approach to kids but it does involve "pulling the rug out," which may mean using a swat. When I say "swat," I mean one to three firm pats on the bum-bum, with the open hand. You are trying to get the child's attention by inflicting a limited amount of pain. When I say I believe in spanking, I mean using the swat as I've just described it. I never, *never* advocate beating a child with a stick, a strap, a belt, or anything else. That is not discipline; that is child abuse.

There are those times when a good swat is by far the best discipline at the moment, but the trick is to know when to use the swat and when to use some other approach. In *Making Children Mind* I discuss the right and wrong way to spank. If you do spank, be under control, not in a rage, and be absolutely sure there is "follow-up time." When you spank a child, you have the obligation to tell the child exactly why he was spanked. And the most important thing during follow-up time is physical contact. Hold your child and talk to him or her about your feelings. Explain why you were upset. Explain what made you angry and why it was necessary to spank. And explain what you expect from your child in the future by way of behavior.

You have the further obligation to listen and, if your child wishes, allow him or her to talk about his or her feelings. What made your child angry? What made your child say what was said or do what was done? Your child may want to apologize or show remorse. If he or she apologizes, be encouraging, warm, and loving. You may want to say you're sorry too but you had a responsibility to spank to teach your child the right way.[5]

I get calls all the time on our radio show, challenging me about my view on spanking. Callers will claim it doesn't work and they may even cite a recent government-sponsored study showing how horrific children who are spanked act. Of course, the subjects in this study were children who were spanked *at least twice a week*. I don't have any data on exactly what "spanking" meant for each child, but I have a fairly good idea.

Imagine someone calling in and saying: "Yes, Dr. Leman, my husband and I have been married for just two years and now we're pregnant. We are planning on spanking our child 104 times a year. What do you think?"

What would I think? If you want horrific children, treat them in that horrific kind of way.

A colleague whom I greatly admire is John Rosemond, whose parenting column appears in one hundred newspapers. He has also written many best-selling books, including: *To Spank or Not to Spank: A Parent's Handbook.* In it he comments that our culture seems hung up on two extremes. One side believes that any swat to a child's bumbum is psychologically and physically abusing. The other side spanks at will, justifying beatings by quoting the Bible: "Spare the rod and spoil the child." Rosemond says, however, "The more you spank, the less effective any given spanking is."[6]

I totally agree. The other day Sande and I counted on our fingers how many times we had ever spanked any of our children. We could come up with no more than a total of eight spankings for all five kids.

One other important question I often receive in seminars is "How old should a child be before I start spanking—or stop?" I believe that no child under two years should be spanked. They don't have the conceptual ability to understand exactly what you're doing. Above age two, however, they can start to conceptualize.[7] A good reason to spank is when the child's safety is involved—when he repeatedly insists on doing something dangerous, like running out into the street.

As for when to stop spanking, it is my opinion that spanking is not very effective beyond the age of six or seven (it could depend on the child, but this is a general estimate). Frankly, after six or seven there are usually more useful and effective means of disciplining the child, which are discussed at length in *Making Children Mind.*

One more important point: If you were physically abused yourself as a child with severe whippings or beatings, *do not use spanking as a discipline.* There is just too much chance that you will go out of control. And, if you're spanking all the time, you have to realize that there is something wrong with your relationship to your child. As Josh McDowell puts it: Rules without relationship lead to rebellion.[8]

Rules without relationship lead to rebellion.

Why Reality Discipline Works

Making Children Mind without Losing Yours contains countless ideas for dealing with kids—everything from temper tantrums to battles over bedtime, from dealing with lying and fighting to getting them to do their homework and getting up in the morning. It works with all birth orders because it employs basic principles and distinctives that all children need as they grow up:

1. *Reality discipline is the best system I know to avoid inconsistent meandering between authoritarianism and permissiveness.* Most parents know instinctively that they should be authoritative—in charge but reasonable and fair. Staying with the authoritative happy medium is best done through reality discipline.

2. *With reality discipline parents never seek to punish; they always seek to discipline, train, and teach.* In the long run, discipline will be more effective than punishment.

3. *Reality disciplinarians use guidance rather than force but they are action-oriented, not satisfied to use just words.* If "punishment," pain, or some kind of consequence is involved, the parent is not doing it or causing it—reality is. Your child is learning how the real world works.

4. *Reality disciplinarians hold their children accountable for their actions, whatever those actions are, to help their children learn from experience.* That experience may include failure *or success,* but *in all cases the children are responsible and accountable for what they do.*

5. *Above all, reality discipline is your best bet for avoiding what I call the super parent syndrome.* Super parents are powerful role models who teach their children that they dare not fail. And, of course, when parenting the child who

has tendencies toward perfectionism (as we will see in the next chapter on parenting the first-born and only child), this can cause real problems.[9]

Never Treat Them All the Same

I firmly believe that parents should never treat all their children exactly the same. I get a lot of questions on this from Moms and Dads who call in to *Parent Talk* or who hear me speak at seminars. Why in the world, they ask, wouldn't you treat your children exactly the same? Don't you want to be fair? I realize that my statement sounds contradictory and the problem is that in the minds of most people being fair means doing the same thing with each child.

But I believe that being truly fair *does not* mean treating each child in exactly the same way. It means treating each child differently as that child's individual needs and differences at certain times in that child's life and development demand. Each birth order is different. You have to treat individuals at each birth order with certain distinctive techniques and understandings.

I'm not suggesting you baby anyone or indulge one child and not another. In fact when you use reality discipline and treat each child differently according to his or her needs, it is the only way you can be sure you are being entirely fair!

For example, I'm a firm believer that children need different responsibilities in the home that are age appropriate. What usually happens, however, in most families is that the oldest child or possibly the two older children who may be close together are assigned more than their fair share of work while the younger ones "get off the hook" because "they aren't big enough" or "can't be trusted."

When children hit fourteen or fifteen and get into high school and have to cope with rigorous homework assignments and numerous extracurricular activities, it's a good time to make sure chores are adjusted and younger ones get to step in and take up the slack. I actually recommend easing up on teenagers and assigning things like garbage detail to the younger siblings. The first born, in particular, should be given fewer time-consuming chores around the house.

When Holly and Krissy were sixteen and fourteen, they no longer pulled garbage detail. That went to their little brother, Kevin, who was ten at the time. Now I can hear you saying, "But I can't assign chores to the young ones, they just aren't responsible and trustworthy. My first born is the only dependable one in the house!"

That's probably all very true, but how are your younger children ever going to *learn* responsibility if you don't give them a shot?

One task Sande and I have given each of the children as they have grown up is writing the checks to pay all the family bills for a given period of time. We usually let our children do it for a year, but there would be nothing wrong with assigning it to a child for six weeks or six months, or whatever period you decide. The point is, it is a great way to introduce the child to the realities of economics, what things cost, and how things have to be paid for on time. And it's a good task to give an older child when younger ones inherit trash detail, doing dishes, or the like.

Other jobs for older children include maintaining the car or helping plan and prepare meals. Washing or ironing is another possibility—at least require the first born to do his or her own clothes.

Reality Discipline Builds Healthy Self-Esteem

In the next few chapters we will clearly examine the proposition that parents need to back off and stop doing for their children and instead help their children do for themselves. Parents must stop accepting excuses—that only makes the weak weaker. They must start making children accountable and helping them be the best they can be.

I heard recently of a school in a western state where Ds or Fs will no longer be given to any student. Instead, a note goes home saying that the child is "emerging" in math, history, or chemistry. Apparently this new strategy is designed to avoid labeling a child a failure—better to let him emerge than fail and destroy his delicate self-esteem.

Bull crumble. If you want to help build a child's self-esteem, it's better to be honest with the child. Tell him he bombed it on that test and urge him to work up to his capabilities. If he needs tutorial help, provide it, but don't cripple the child by letting him get by with poor work and then passing him on to another grade.

Most parents think it's what we *do* for children that increases their self-esteem. No, it's what they *do for themselves* in conjunction and cooperation with those whom they love—their parents and others in their families—that makes the big difference in having really healthy self-esteem.

When a child does something that contributes to the family, he walks away with the message, "I'm somebody. I can help. I can contribute. I'm important around here." This is how a child becomes a giver instead of a taker. And this is what separates—in my mind, at least—healthy self-esteem from all of the loosey, goosey, gooey jargon that passes for an intelligent discussion of building a child's self-image. The very bedrock of a good self-image is the realization that you are a child (creation) of God, who loves you just the way you are. The child who has a good relationship with her parents and with God is well on her way to establishing a good self-image and healthy self-esteem.

Don't Turn Your Kids over to Strangers

What I constantly tell parents is that reality discipline takes time, a lot of time invested by the parent. Too many parents simply want to get on with other things and hope their kids will behave themselves in the meantime. It doesn't work that way.

Some parents naively believe they can buy off their kids by giving them the things they didn't have when they were children. Your children do not need the material things you didn't have when growing up. They need *you*.

One of the biggest faults I find with parents is that they hand their children over to strangers instead of spending time with them themselves. If a stranger knocked on your door and said, "Can I take your car?" would you give it to him? Of course not. You'd say, "Pardon me, I don't even know you." Then why do we hand our kids over to strangers? If you think about it, that's what we're doing in our American society today.

By age five we have kids playing soccer; by age six, T-ball. We have them enrolled in clubs and dance classes. Why? Because we think it's good for them. There is no empirical evidence, however, that I am aware of showing that it's good for a young child to be involved in all these activities. Based on my practice over the years, I find it amazing when I have to give psychological service to seven- and eight-year-old kids who are stressed out on life. This tells me there is something wrong with our society. What parents need to consider is, just who is being served when a child plays soccer, T-ball, or some other sport while he's very young? Some children just aren't ready to get all that intense about it as the following story illustrates.

I was out for a walk one day when I came by a Little League field where a T-ball game was just getting under-way. I decided to watch a couple of innings, just for the sheer fun of it. If you have been to a T-ball game, you'll know what I mean.

The first two batters got on base in the usual comedy of errors fashion that is typical of T-ball. Then, with runners on first and second, the third batter hit a sharp ground ball through the box and into center field. As I watched the ball roll at high speed, I thought that this could easily be a ground-ball-inside-the-park home run if somebody didn't cut it off.

Just then I spotted the center fielder, that is, I spotted his little bum-bum. He was down on all fours, facing away from the field, apparently looking for something. Suddenly the air was pierced with shrieks from this little guy's parents who were screaming, "Logan, Logan, get the ball!"

Oblivious to the ball as it sped by him headed for the fence, Logan cupped his hands to his mouth and yelled back, "I'm looking for a four-leaf clover!"

Later when Logan's side finally came to bat, he and his fellow outfielders ran in and went right up to their coach, saying, "We want to sit."

The coach didn't quite understand, and thinking they were asking if they could hit, he told them that they had to wait their turn according to the batting order posted over there on the tree.

"No, no," one of the kids said. "We don't want to *hit*, we want to *sit!*"

The coach was incredulous and muttered something like, "You mean . . . you don't want to play?"

That was exactly what the kids meant!

This true story says several things: (1) Little Logan and his buddies were playing T-ball because Mom and Dad thought it would be good for them to participate in athletics; (2) Logan was too young to have his "head in the game," as my old baseball coach used to put it. His mind was somewhere else, which is a severe handicap when a baseball is moving toward you at high speed; (3) Maybe parents should seriously consider slowing everything down. Don't put kids out there on the fast track so early in life.

I love sports; I played Little League baseball as a kid myself (so did my son, Kevin), but there is no sense in having children involved in three or four activities at the same time of the year. Not only is it stressful on them, but it is stressful on you, the parent. As any soccer mom might put it, "Help, I'm a cabby and my minivan isn't even yellow!" But that's the kind of life-style you will live if you get sucked into the thinking that you've got to get kids involved in everything or they're somehow going to "get behind everyone else."

My advice is to let the child choose one activity per semester. Slow things down and take time for the family. If you're a single parent and going it alone, you may feel it makes sense to keep the kids busy in activities. As one parent reminded me, "It's better than smoking crack cocaine at the mall, isn't it, doctor?" To answer the question, "Yes, it is, but in the long run, overinvolvement isn't the best thing for kids."

Busy hands, arms, and legs don't necessarily make happy minds and hearts. We need time to bond with our children in our own home. Nobody can teach your kids better than you can. *Take time with your kids.*

Take time with your kids.

How to Be Your Child's Best Friend

Here are nine ways you can be your child's best friend— and make him or her mind at the same time.

1. Discipline should fit the infraction. For example, the child misuses his allowance. When he asks for something extra before the week is out, you simply say, "Sorry, you will have to use your allowance and if you haven't any left, you will have to wait until Saturday."
2. Never beat or bully your child into submission. Remember, the shepherd's rod was used to guide the sheep, not to beat them.

3. Use action-oriented methods whenever possible.
4. Always try to be consistent.
5. Emphasize the need for order. Work comes before play, chores come before breakfast, and so on. This concept reinforces obedience and emphasizes that in all of God's kingdom, there is a need for order. Order is important.
6. Always require your child to be accountable and responsible for his or her own actions.
7. Always communicate to your child that he or she is good, even though the behavior may have been irresponsible.
8. Always give your child choices that reinforce cooperation but not competition.
9. If spanking is necessary, it should be done when you're in control of your emotions. It should *always* be followed up with explanations for why the spanking was necessary, and those all-powerful words, "I love you and I care about you."[10]

14

Flaunt Your Imperfections

PARENTING FIRST BORNS AND ONLY CHILDREN

*t*he scene is a preschool class and the teacher has just handed little Marilou a pair of scissors (rounded tips, of course) and a sheet of bright red construction paper. Marilou's assignment is to cut out a nice big circle. She labors away and is doing a fairly nice job when all of a sudden she crumples up the paper and throws her half-completed circle on the floor.

The teacher comes over and asks, "Marilou, what's wrong?"

"I can't do this!"

"I'll help you . . . here, let me . . ."

"No! I'm not going to do it. It's dumb!"

And teacher sighs and wonders, *What's gotten into Marilou?*

It's really no mystery. Marilou is a first-born child and her parents are both very capable, confident people. Already at the tender age of five, Marilou is exhibiting a major characteristic she shares with almost all other first borns and only children—a burden she will carry throughout life: perfectionism.

Perfectionism

Yes, I know you may disagree with my assertion that almost all first borns and only children are perfectionists. Parents tell me about their first-born Harlan, who is seventeen and has yet to make a conscientious move. In fact he hasn't moved to make his bed for the last six months.

Or perhaps they'll mention first-born daughter, Drucilla, who is so laid-back they have to put a mirror in front of her nose to be sure she's alive. She's getting C- in history and math and an A+ in MTV.

But even though Harlan and Drucilla seem to act like anything but perfectionist first borns, I stick to my guns for two very good reasons—the same two reasons that have made Marilou into a little discouraged perfectionist while still in preschool—Mom and Dad.

When you are little—very little—and try to imitate someone much older and bigger, you soon get the idea you have to be "perfect." To show you what I mean, let's observe Marilou at home with Mom. Marilou has made her own bed and for a five year old she's done a very good job of it. Mom comes in to check and says, "Oh, Marilou, honey, what a beautiful job you did on your bed!" Marilou beams—until Mom proceeds to "straighten out a few wrinkles."

The message for Marilou? "Your bed doesn't measure up. Your bed isn't perfect." No wonder Marilou goes a little ballistic when she cuts a less-than-perfect circle at preschool. If she can't be perfect, she won't be anything at all. Marilou is a budding discouraged perfectionist, and unless Mom stops nitpicking her to death in a very "positive" way, she will be in full bloom by the time she is a teenager. I counsel many young children who are budding discouraged perfectionists. They are not hard to spot:

> Budding discouraged perfectionists are children who don't pass in school assignments, even though they are completed. Their problem is they're not sure it's done *exactly* right.
> Budding discouraged perfectionists are children who start lots of projects or activities but don't finish them.
> Budding discouraged perfectionists are children who fear the enormity of a task and, therefore, don't even start!
> Budding discouraged perfectionists are children who are described by their teachers as "having *so much* potential."
> Budding discouraged perfectionists are children who have controlling, critical, or pushy parents.

Discouraged Perfectionism Can Get Serious

Two vivid examples of discouraged perfectionists that stand out in my mind are young men we'll call Frank and John. Frank was twelve when his only-child father (a surgeon) and his first-born mother (a registered nurse) brought him to me because of his extreme "temper problem." It seems Frank would blow his cool when his "plans for the day" didn't go right. While most twelve year olds can't plan the next fifteen minutes, Frank knew exactly what he wanted to do from morning until night, something he picked up from his highly exacting, tightly scheduled, surgeon father.

Frank, by the way, was a "functional first born" in that he was the second of two children, born seven years after his older brother. With that much of a gap and with such high-powered professionals for parents, Frank couldn't help but have a lot of first-born traits.

In fact Frank could have easily passed for an only child because he had a very difficult time getting along with children his own age, which is typical of only children. But it seems Frank wasn't getting along with anyone. His friends could care less about his "to-do" list, and when Frank's day didn't go well (which was often), he would blow his top and get in fights. At home, if someone messed up his plans, Frank started kicking things, throwing things, putting holes in the walls—once he tried to put holes in the family dog.

A very conscientious boy, Frank felt terrible about his behavior but he was trapped in his prison of perfectionism. I was finally able to help Frank by pointing out that everybody makes mistakes and fails—even Babe Ruth, who hit 714 home runs but also struck out 1,330 times. But the real key was Frank's dad who had the courage and the sense to start admitting his own faults and imperfections, which he had been keeping carefully hidden.

Frank remained a perfectionist in many ways, but at least he got control of his temper by learning that he couldn't control *everything* and, above all, he didn't have to be perfect to win his father's approval and love.

Oh yes, John? I didn't counsel John; in fact I never got to meet him when I was assistant dean of students at the University of Arizona. But I had access to his records. Throughout his academic career, John never got less than an A and he was about to graduate from the U. of A. summa cum laude. His suicide note said: "I just couldn't measure up to the standards of this world, perhaps in the next world I can do better."

Wanting to Be Just Like Mom and Dad

Yes, perfectionism can get serious, even deadly. Most people don't wind up like John, but it's always a possibility. Meanwhile, many struggle with perfectionism because in one way or another they just can't measure up to Mom and Dad who may or may not have been perfectionists themselves. Keep in mind that it doesn't take a surgeon and a nurse to turn out a discouraged perfectionist. It only takes an adult who is simply trying to be a capable, loving parent. Coming back to Harlan and Drucilla for a moment, it's doubtful that their parents sat down just after the children were born and discussed how they could produce discouraged perfectionists. But they each produced one anyway simply by trying to be capable, loving parents. How? It's very simple.

Very early during his first year of life, the first born starts to pick up on his adult role models—Mommy and Daddy—and starts setting his sights on being "just like them." That includes being just as capable as they are, which is obviously impossible for a tiny child. That's why when first borns like Harlan and Drucilla get older, they may not look like perfectionists or act like perfectionists, but they are discouraged perfectionists. Slobs and poor students are usually discouraged perfectionists who have given up trying because it hurts too much to fail.

> Slobs and poor students are usually discouraged perfectionists who have given up trying because it hurts too much to fail.

The first born's desire to follow in Mommy's and Daddy's footsteps usually increases as the parents give the first born a lot of extra attention—or overparenting. They tend to be overprotective and, of course, they unconsciously push the child to accomplish everything he or she can (and some things he or she can't). It's no wonder first borns walk and talk earlier than any other birth order and they have a larger vocabulary. First borns, along with their perfectionist cousins, the only children, grow up being "little adults."

I often apply the adjective "precocious" to first borns and especially only children. According to the dictionary, *precocious* means "characterized by unusually early development or maturity, especially in mental aptitude." And that often describes first borns and only children. They become very adult in a hurry because of all this imitating of Mom and Dad that they are trying to do. Part of their adult behavior is that they become very obedient to authority, another holdover from trying to please the two key authority figures in life—Mother and Father.

Every First Born Feels the Sting of Dethronement

Not only do all first borns struggle with perfectionism, they all undergo "dethronement" with the arrival of the second born in the family. First borns are the center of attention for a relatively long time, as time is measured in a young child's life. In chapter 12 I mentioned the life-style every child develops by age five or so. If Mommy and Daddy don't have a second child until the first born is three years old, three-fifths—*60 percent*—of the first born's life-style has already been formed before the intruder comes home from the hospital. A great part of that life-style has taught the first born that he or she is kingpin. One of the most challenging tasks of parenting is preparing the first-born child for the intrusion of the second.

My advice to parents awaiting the arrival of number two is to have their first born put away some of his special toys in a safe place so "the baby can't get them." At the same time, let number-one child choose some toys he's willing to give to his new little brother or sister. And, finally, be sure to reassure your first born that when his little brother or sister arrives, there will be plenty of kisses from Mommy and Daddy for both of them.

When the second-born child comes home from the hospital, it will soon dawn on the first born that the "thing" is not temporary, that it is going to stay. At this point it's excellent strategy to get the first born involved in caring for the new baby. If the first born is big enough, he or she can help feed it, even diaper it, if possible. Yes, the diaper may look a bit askew, but bite your tongue and fight off that urge to redo it "perfectly."

The second strategy is to talk with your first born about what the newborn *can't do*. "[Baby's name] can't catch a ball, can't walk, can't talk, can't do anything." And then there is bedtime. Tell your three year old that he won't have to go to bed so early; he gets to stay up later with Mommy and Daddy.

Dethronement Is Never a Minor Problem

In the 1990s I have seen more parents who better understand the problem of dethronement and they try to take steps to do something about it. But a word of caution. No matter how much you try to help the first born with the adjustment, keep in mind that it is a *profound* intrusion. He can't help wondering, "Why? Wasn't I good enough?" There is a natural rivalry that starts between the first born and the second born. It may not be overt and in plain sight at first but it is always there and it always comes out sooner or later.

Sande and I are still amazed when we watch some old super eight movies my mother took of the two of us plus Holly and newborn Krissy. When we took the movie, no one—not even my mother—saw eighteen-month-old Holly slip into the picture and smile broadly as she dug her elbow into Krissy's midsection.

When we got the film back, our reaction was ambivalent. Yes, Holly's little elbow toss was cute, but it also graphically demonstrated how first borns feel dethroned and how they make perfectly natural (selfish) moves to regain their "fair share" of attention from parents.

This natural inclination toward selfishness (really a matter of self-preservation and survival as far as the child is concerned) is why you have to be careful about giving your first born "special treatment to balance things" when the new little intruder arrives. Guard against having your first born manipulate you to get special advantages or spoiling. Never give in to a temper tantrum or outburst of tears. If necessary, isolate the first born briefly and then go in and talk about it.

If you must discipline your first born, always follow up with lots of hugging, touching, and talking when you emphasize the first born's "superiority" over the new baby because he or she can do so many more things. Always enumerate the things the first born can do that baby can't. This way you will lay groundwork for a cooperative first-born child who will get through the dethronement crisis more easily, knowing that he is more capable, bigger, stronger, etc.

But while you assure your first born that she is bigger, stronger, and smarter, don't confuse that with "being perfect." For probably two to three or more years, your first born has been learning to be a perfectionist by watching you. But when you tell her she's bigger or stronger, be sure to let her know that everyone makes mistakes; nobody does everything absolutely perfectly.

Keep in mind also that when your first born does get dethroned by your second born, issues like power and authority become very important. No, he doesn't come to breakfast and say, "More power to the first borns, pass the Corn Pops." But inside his little head he understands plenty about power and authority and how precious it is. Dr. Alfred Adler emphasized the importance of the power struggle that goes on when a first born loses the exclusive small kingdom that had belonged to him before the second-born brother or sister arrived. Consequently, as the first born continues to grow up into adulthood, he or she may exaggerate the importance of rules and laws. In other words, first borns "go by the book" and don't want any deviations.

What better example than the Prodigal Son, who undoubtedly was a baby of the family. He split with his share of the inheritance and promptly lost it all. The elder son— the first born—stayed home and worked hard in the fields. When the Prodigal finally wised up and came back, his father threw a big bash, complete with fatted calf and gold ring (today, he would probably buy the boy a nice little Mustang GT convertible).

The elder son—who was out in the fields, naturally— heard all the commotion and when he saw what was going on, he got irate. Here his father was throwing a big bash for his ne'er-do-well younger brother and what had he ever gotten? Not even one little party!

Where is the fairness in *that*? But as we see, the father was being fair by treating his children differently. He pointed out to the older boy that he had always been with him and everything he had was his. But the younger boy, who needed love and understanding, had been lost and was now found; so why not celebrate? (See Luke 15:11–32.)

Also be aware that it's typical—almost inevitable—for new parents to be more strict and lay down more rules and regulations for their first born than they do with later-born children. After all, they must "do it right" with this first child, so part of that is keeping a tight rein on him or her.

Wherever I speak and teach, I emphasize the need to be an authoritative parent who is loving and fair but also consistent and firm. As we saw in the last chapter, the authoritative parent is the happy medium between the permissive parent and authoritarian, who overdoes it on rules and limits and simply cracks down too hard.

If I Had It to Do All Over Again

Even psychologists with doctorates know there is a big difference between correct theory and right practice. People sometimes ask me: "As you look back on rearing your children, do you have any regrets or things you'd do differently?" Good question. If there is anything I would have done differently, it would be in the way I handled Holly, our aggressive, go-by-the-book, perfectionist first born.

In an earlier chapter I mentioned how a parent of one birth order can overidentify with a child of another birth order in different ways. I tend to overidentify in an indulging way with later borns in our family, particularly our son, Kevin. In fact when the only children we had were Holly and Krissy, I overidentified with Krissy, who was the younger, because she was constantly getting teased and pressured by her older sister who was still smarting from dethronement and wanted to compete with her little sister in every way she could. I became protective of Krissy and cracked down too hard on Holly.

Of course, I had good reason to crack down, or so I told myself as a young father with two daughters who were in constant competition. Actually much of the competitiveness came from Holly's side (we're back to dethronement again, of course). When Holly "threw that elbow" at Krissy during the movie, it was just for starters. She proceeded to make a career out of running Krissy's life.

We have on tape an occasion when Holly snatched a certain toy from Krissy and said, "You don't want that—here play with this." Of course, the "this" was an old beat-up rubber frog.

And when it came to money, Holly would constantly try to tell Krissy, "Those big nickels are worth more than these little dimes."

To give Krissy her due, as she got a little older, she didn't take all this manipulation and direction by big sister lying down. There were many times when I would arrive on the scene after hearing a squall of protest from Krissy and would reprimand Holly because she was older and "should know better." Now I'm sure that in many of those instances Krissy had set up her big sister with the skill that only younger children possess.

But I confess that Krissy usually faked me out (after all, she was later born and how could *she* be guilty?). So I would correct Holly rather severely: "Holly, that's Krissy's. You have your own! Now stop it."

Occasionally, however, when Holly was being really unfair (in my opinion) I would send her to her room, or even give her a swat. Did I do this out of authoritarian perfectionism? Hardly. I did it out of last-born frustration with an older child taking advantage of a younger one, something that had happened to me on numerous occasions while I was growing up when my big brother, Jack (and even at rare times, my loving big sister, Sally), would give me a bad time.

In retrospect, I realize that I should have followed my own reality discipline advice and disciplined both of them when I found them fighting and arguing. Fighting and arguing, after all, are acts of cooperation and it takes two to cooperate.

Authoritarians Grow Discouraged Perfectionists

People often ask me which style of parenting is more harmful, the authoritarian or the permissive? I really can't

give the nod to one or the other but I will say that authoritarian parenting is more likely to produce the discouraged
perfectionist who can't measure up to the demands the
parents place on him.

Nicole, fourteen when her parents brought her in for
counseling, is a good example. She had been suspended
from school for cutting class and smoking pot, and what
could I do to cure her "rebellion"?

I talked with Nicole alone and quickly learned she had
little freedom and she made very few choices of her own,
even at fourteen. Her parents controlled everything—
clothes, going out, coming in, bedtime. To hear Nicole
tell it, she lived in a home with about as much freedom as
juvenile hall. To find opportunities to slip away with her
peer group, she would lie and sneak and that's how she
had begun using drugs and alcohol, as well as being promis-
cuous with boys at school. Nicole had a plan—turn eighteen, get out of the house, buy a car, and split.

Nicole was the first-born child, who had a younger sister, eleven, and a younger brother, eight. She also had an
ultraperfectionist mother who kept the home impeccably
neat. Interestingly enough, Nicole kept her room immaculate at all times, but it was actually a cover—part of her
I'll-tell-them-what-they-want-to-hear strategy.

I didn't make much progress with Nicole until I got her
parents to see how they were being too authoritarian and
why Nicole was afraid to tell them what was really going
on—she feared retribution big time and maybe even being
kicked out of the house completely.

Fortunately Nicole's parents listened and learned, and
we did make some progress. At the end of six weeks Nicole
wrote a summary of the positive things that had come out
of counseling. Among the things Nicole said: "Mom and
Dad are giving me more leeway and I am not lying to them.
I am being honest with them and it makes me feel good . . ."

Nicole is a classic example of a first-born child who grows up watching Mom and Dad and wanting to imitate them. But this lasts only to a certain age. As she became a teenager, the authoritarian treatment proved to be too much. She became a discouraged perfectionist and turned to wild behavior as a way of crying for help.

Nicole is convincing evidence for why I believe no parent should ever think a first-born child is not a perfectionist simply because the child isn't toeing the mark and obeying all the rules. The child may be breaking a lot of rules because he or she is a perfectionist who can't handle the cards life has dealt.

Super Parents Often Have the Critical Eye

Let's face it. There is a lot of concern about how to raise children. For any parent who wants to take advantage of them, there are literally tons of books, articles, pamphlets, tapes, CDs, films, and videocassettes available to teach you how to be super parent. And I'm well aware that at times I can sound just like the rest of the experts:

Be sure you don't do this . . . be sure you do that.
Be faster than a speeding bullet as you use actions, not words.
Be more powerful than a locomotive as you enforce the rules of reality discipline.
Leap tall problems with a single bound, to be loving, caring, and aware of your child's feelings.[1]

If I have given that impression, I apologize. Actually I believe that we don't need super parents, and that goes double or maybe triple for parents of all those little first borns and only children. They have enough problems trying to be perfect and fail-safe as they imitate Moms or Dads who, in their little minds, at least, are giants and never make mistakes. I don't believe there is a parent alive who has never made a mistake. There are, however, a lot of them who refuse to *admit* their mistakes!

The Deception of Perfection

Because I often conduct weekend seminars in churches, I get invited to speak on Sunday mornings. Sometimes I give just a short word and sometimes I wind up giving the sermon, not exactly what I'm trained to do but I let fly in true Billy Graham style. My most frequently used message is entitled, "The Deception of Perfection." I cover many areas but I zero in on three basic sins that parents with the critical eye of perfectionism can so easily commit.

First, the critical parent can be guilty of Pharisaism (or legalism). The Pharisees, as you may know, were the legal beagles of Jesus' day, and he had many an exchange with them in which he pointed out that they had it all back-wards. They were busy cleaning the outside of their cups while what was on the inside (in their hearts) was corrupt and dirty. Many of the Pharisees were hypocrites.

While making this point, I start by asking the parents in the congregation: "Have any of you yelled at your kids today?" Slowly hands start going up all over the room (after all, most of us aren't really into public confession).

"Isn't it amazing," I continue, "how on Sunday morning, you're trying to get to church on time? You finally get everyone out to the car and then you count the kids. Whoops, you are one short. You walk back into the house and there's your little four year old, his underwear in his back pocket. That's obviously not a good sign. So you yell at him, 'We *are* going to worship the Lord *together* today. GET IN THE CAR NOW!'"

So you drive the seven miles down to church, lecturing everyone all the way on the merits of obeying parents and being on time. You walk in and see someone you know—

the pastor, perhaps—and you say in your best Sunday-morning manner: "Oh, hello, how *are* you? Isn't it a *lovely* day to worship?" And your kids—especially your four year old—look at you and mutter to themselves, "What a bunch of baloney!"

You see, the point is that we have become a society of flaw pickers. Just listen to the newscasts or pick up your newspapers. A child brings home a report card with four As and a B. Dad gives it the critical eye and says, "Not bad, too bad about the B." The bottom line is that it's so easy to be critical, even while trying to be positive. Remember Marilou's mother? She didn't shout at her child. She just nicely remade Marilou's bed after Marilou had done the best she could at the job. There are many ways to be a Pharisee.

Point number two of my sermon talks about pride. If Jesus taught us anything, it's that God doesn't love men more than women, adults more than children, or white more than nonwhite. He sees us all on a horizontal plane where we struggle with our carnality and our humanity. In Romans 7 Paul says he doesn't understand himself. He tells himself he's not going to do certain things and what happens? He does them. He tells himself he is going to do certain good things and what happens? He doesn't do them. Paul winds up by saying, "What a wretched man I am, who shall deliver me from this body of death?" The answer, of course, is to turn yourself completely over to God living within your life, letting him fill you with the desire to be an excellent parent—but not a perfect one.

My third major point concerns forgiveness. Jesus told Peter that he should forgive seventy times seven (meaning indefinitely). No one needs to learn about forgiveness more than the critical-eyed parent who pursues perfection. You may do it politely and sweetly but, as you enforce your perfectionistic will on your children, are you showing them forgiveness for their mistakes or are you judging them (all in the name of trying to help them, of course)?

> No one needs to learn about forgiveness more than the critical-eyed parent who pursues perfection.

I conclude by pointing out that the best way to learn to forgive is to ask for forgiveness yourself. Has your three-year-old first-born or only child ever heard you say, "I blew it! I was wrong! I forgot! I'm sorry"? Has your thirteen year old ever heard you say any of those things freely and openly? A lot of parents choke on those words, particularly the ones who are first-born or only-child perfectionists themselves.

If any of the above "preaching" has you thinking that you might be a perfectionist with a critical eye, at least to some degree, what should you do? The last thing I want you to do is to try to confess all these sins, *once and for all,* and go forth to sin no more. You will sin again—and again—because this is something that's in the grain of your wood (your personality). When you do slip into perfectionistic overdrive, stop, shift gears, ask God for forgiveness, and ask your child for forgiveness as well. Then pray for God's help in modifying and changing your personality. To do that, there is no better place to start than by learning to seek excellence instead of pursuing perfection (review chapter 6).

It also helps to remember that all children need encouragement more than prodding. Learn to simply hold your child when he or she is having problems. Just say, "Everything's going to be okay. What's the problem? Do you say this isn't working out right? Would you like me to help?"

Remember little Marilou—the five-year-old discouraged perfectionist who went ballistic when she couldn't cut out the perfect circle? Marilou, by the way, grew up to be a perfectionist career woman who went ballistic when her husband didn't do his share of the housework. She had to do it all after a long day of working herself. Marilou and her husband wound up in my office where I tried to explain what had happened to her and how much better it would have been if Mom or Dad could have helped her learn to cut less-than-perfect circles. They could have said, "It's hard; I don't always cut perfect ones myself. I remember how hard it was when I was small."

The point is that teaching kids to seek excellence instead of pursuing perfectionism can start when they're very young. Picture this classic scene: Mom is tired of the four year old's messy toy box and messy room and sends him in there to clean it all up. There is one problem. The task looks gigantic to the four year old. Toys and books and crayons and puzzles are scattered from one end of the room to the other. How can he possibly do this?

He never will do it unless you, the parent, follow him into the room, sit down, and say something like, "There's a lot to do here, isn't there? While you pick up your toys, I'll talk to you about what we're going to do tonight after dinner." Chances are, the kid will get on with the job and at least get part of the room cleaned up. If getting certain items in good order is extremely difficult, you can give him limited help. But the last thing you should do is wind up doing most of it yourself.

The idea is to get the child to do the job as you encourage him and show him how to organize the crayons, puzzles, and toy pieces. If he doesn't get everything just right, don't berate him or come along behind him and straighten everything up for him. The key is: *Be satisfied with a less than perfect job* (the room is going to look less than perfect soon anyway).

The great temptation for the perfectionist, critical-eyed parent is to send messages to the child that say, "You've got to measure up, kid. You've got to do an absolutely flawless job, or I won't approve."

Please be assured I am *not* saying you should let a child get away with goofing off or not doing the job at all. With true reality discipline in mind, hold him accountable for his responsibilities. But that doesn't mean that you have to demand that he be perfect. Relax your perfectionistic rules a bit. Maybe part of cleaning up the room is making the bed. Since four is a bit young to make beds, you may have the child help you, but be sure he does as much as he can, and if it's wrinkled in spots, congratulate him but *don't do it over for him*. So what if some of it looks like a toy truck got left under the covers? You can shut the door and no one needs to see it.

As you learn to be flexible, steer away from giving orders and move toward helping your child do things. Remember, you are the child's role model, not his sergeant or supervisor. Few parents completely understand what I mean when I talk about being a role model. I'm not just suggesting that you set a good example for the child. You should, but there is much more to being a role model than that, especially for the first-born or only child. He or she has no brother or sister to look to or pattern after. *You* are what he or she has to pattern after and you are an awesome act to follow! So look for ways to show your child that you are human, that you understand, that you are not perfect, and that mistakes are not the end of the world. In other words:

FLAUNT YOUR IMPERFECTIONS!

Every time you do this, you help your first-born or only child become less of a perfectionist who grows up to whip and drive himself with expectations that are far beyond human capacity.

One way to show your child you're not perfect is to ask him or her for help now and then. I don't mean simply helping with the baby or doing simple chores, good as those things are. I'm talking about a deeper level where you ask your young child questions like, "Will you help me decide what to have for dinner tonight?" "Where do you think is the best place to put these flowers so we can all enjoy them?" "Do you think your little sister is old enough to play this game?"

Coming back to deciding about dinner, it might be wise to give the child a choice and ask if he would prefer chicken or hamburger; otherwise you may wind up with a request for peanut butter sandwiches, Oreo cookies, and lots of ice cream. You can give him some choices for dessert, but, again, they should be choices that you know everyone will like.

Tips for Parenting First Borns and Only Children

At the end of chapter 13 I gave you nine tips for being "your child's best friend." But you will note that none of them talk about becoming a kid yourself, being buddy-buddy with your child and abdicating your parental responsibilities. All nine tips deal with how to use the principles of reality discipline with your child. When you do that, you will indeed be the best friend your child will ever have.

I especially advise new parents of first borns to review these tips often. Also be sure to go over the tips given below. Keep in mind that you are new at all this, and all children make mistakes—just as their parents do. So go easy on trying to turn out the world's first perfectly behaved child. I can assure you it isn't going to happen anyway—none of mine even made it!

Here are some additional tips, especially for parents of first borns.

1. When disciplining the first-born child, beware of reinforcing his ingrained perfectionism by "shoulding"

him all the time. Actually it's not wise to "should" anybody in your family, but when the first born hears "should," it's like waving a red flag in front of a bull. The first born is already "shoulding" himself, and when you chime in, it's a double whammy: First, he resents it; and, second, in private he is all the harder on himself, which will only keep lowering his self-esteem and probably make him harder to deal with.

2. Don't be an "improver" on everything your first-born or only child says or does. It's just one more deadly way to reinforce his or her already ingrained perfectionism. Accept the slightly wrinkled bed, the not-quite-cleaned-up room, whatever your child has done. When you do it over, you only send a message that your child is not measuring up.

3. Realize first borns have a particular need to know exactly what the rules are. Be patient and take time to lay things out for your first born from A to Z.

4. Recognize the first born's first place in the family. As the oldest, the first born should get some special privileges to go along with the additional responsibilities that always seem to come his way.

5. Take "two on one" time—both parents out with the oldest child alone. First borns respond better to adult company than children of any other birth order. First borns often feel that parents don't pay much attention to them because they're always concentrating on the younger ones in the family. Make a special effort to have the first born join you and your spouse in going out alone for a treat, or to run some kind of special errand.

6. Stay away from making your first born your "instant baby-sitter." At least try to check with your first born to see if his or her schedule would allow for some baby-sitting later in the day or that evening.

7. As your first born grows older, be sure you don't pile on more responsibilities. Give some of the responsibilities to the younger children as soon as they are capable of taking on these jobs. One first born told me at a seminar, "I'm the garbage person." By that he meant that he had to do everything at home while his brother and sister got off much easier.

8. When your first born is reading to you and has trouble with a word, don't be so quick to jump in with a correction. First borns are extremely sensitive to criticism and being corrected. Give the child time to sound out the word. Give help only when he or she asks for it.

15

Two May Be Company . . . or a Crowd

PARENTING THE TWO-CHILD FAMILY

A few months ago, Sande and I took Holly, our then twenty-five-year-old daughter, to dinner. After ordering, we all settled back in our chairs and Holly said with a big smile, "This is how it was supposed to be!"

Sande and I laughed as hard as Holly because we both knew what she meant. At age twenty-five she was still good-naturedly acknowledging that having siblings—particularly her arch rival, second-born sister, Krissy—had not been all sweetness, light, and roses. She bore a few scars from dethronement, but here—for one night at least—she would enjoy a moment of triumph and have Mom and Dad all to herself!

When Number Two Arrives, Rivalry Often Begins

If parenting first borns means preventing discouraged perfectionists, parenting second borns means watching out for rivalries.

It all begins when that first born is dethroned and suddenly has to share the summit of the mountain with little second born. These days, more and more families get only that far—a first and a second—so it's well worth our time to devote a chapter to parenting the two-child family.

It's a lot like Hertz and Avis, the two car rental companies. While the analogy isn't perfect, in a way Avis came along and tried to "dethrone" Hertz. And how did they do it? By trying harder, of course, which is exactly what the second born may do when he or she looks up and sees that first born at the top of the family. In fact I wouldn't be surprised if the copywriter who thought up that famous tag line that Avis used for years—"When you're number two, you have to try harder"—was a second-born child!

Whenever a second-born child arrives, some key principles are always at work, including: Second-born children develop their own life-style, according to the perceptions they have about themselves and the key persons in their lives.

> Second-born children develop their own life-style, according to the perceptions they have about themselves and the key persons in their lives.

Needless to say, that older sibling is a key person in the second born's life. We've already touched on the fact that for every child in the family, it's always that "one next up on the ladder" who influences him or her the most—the second born by the first born, the third born by the second born, and so on.

Second borns may compete with an older brother or sister in various ways. Some do it quite openly, others are a bit more clever—even a bit sneaky—in trying to reach their goal. One of the classic examples of a "sneaky" second born who put it over on his big brother is the biblical story of Jacob and Esau in the Old Testament.

I sometimes wonder if Isaac and Rebekah didn't make some kind of self-fulfilling prophecy when they named their twin boys. They called their first born Esau (meaning "hairy," which he was). The second born they named Jacob (meaning "supplanter"—someone who usurps the position of another, which he did).

Esau, the powerful older brother, was a rough macho type who spent a lot of time outdoors. Jacob was smoother—in a lot of ways. He hung around the house and was something of a "gentleman of the manor" as well as a gourmet of sorts. He was also his mother's favorite. When Esau came home famished from one of his hunting trips, Jacob saw his chance. Esau asked for some stew that Jacob had just prepared. With the savory smells filling the room, Jacob decided to put a rather high price on Esau's snack time: "How about the birthright in exchange for the stew?" he suggested.

Down through history the first-born son of the family would be given privileges above those of his younger brothers. This practice is called primogeniture and still goes on today. For example, in countries with monarchies, the oldest succeeds to the throne. In biblical times, the birthright meant the first-born son received a double portion of the inheritance, so when Jacob suggested to Esau that he trade his birthright for a helping of stew, he was obviously offering his brother an outrageously unfair deal.

For a first born, Esau wasn't exactly strong on thinking things through. To be blunt, he was a bit dense. All he could think of at the moment was his very empty stomach, so he said, "Why not? What good is a birthright if I starve to death?"

Esau was "starving" only in the sense that he had been outdoors burning lots of calories chasing game and he was *very* hungry. So Jacob ladled him out a bowl of stew and took the birthright in exchange. Later, he completed his role reversal with his not-too-bright big brother when he tricked his blind father, Isaac, into giving him the patriarchal blessing as well (for the story of Jacob and Esau, see Gen. 25:19–34; 27:1–40).

In the typical American family, we don't have role reversal occurring with the second born cheating the first born out of a birthright. Instead, the younger child can "take over" from the older in areas such as achievement, prestige, assuming responsibility, and pleasing the parents.

Parenting Two Boys Can Mean Fireworks

Rivalry is most intense when you have a two-child family with two boys. Something else to consider, however, is that while two brothers have no trouble learning how to interact with peers of their own sex, they tend to have little preparation for interaction with the opposite sex. The relationship between Mom and her two sons is critical. She is the one who has to do all of the teaching and modeling as to what women are really all about.

It's critical for the mother of two boys to use reality discipline—firmly and consistently. She should never—and I mean *never*—take any garbage from them. She should never get into power struggles or put herself in a position where the boys can walk on her or be disrespectful to her. Why? Because she not only is representing parenthood and motherhood, but she's also representing all of womanhood to her two sons. If her two sons learn to walk on her, they'll learn to walk on their wives later. The recent increase in battered wives is really no surprise, and a lot of it can be traced to how the husband learned to relate to women when he was young.

But let's look at the two brothers and examine especially the older brother. Typically our older brother is going to identify very much with the establishment (Mom and Dad). He is going to be the standard-bearer, the one who picks up on family values and practices them faithfully. He will probably be the leader, and also the family "sheriff" or "policeman" as far as keeping the younger brother in line. Older brother often finds himself being the protector of baby brother.

Older brother usually gets a kick out of having younger brother follow him, and in this very basic way the older boy learns a lot of practical leadership skills. This is a very basic reason you find more first borns in leadership positions in adult life.

At the other end of the family, the younger brother is eyeing older brother and deciding which way he will go. Another key principle that seems to apply in most cases is this: The second-born child will be the opposite of the first born, particularly if they are less than five years apart and of the same sex.

> The second-born child will be the opposite of the first born, particularly if they are less than five years apart and of the same sex.

The younger child looks the situation over and usually branches off in a different direction. That different direction may still put him in direct rivalry with his older brother. If he is determined to catch up with him and surpass him as far as leadership and achievement are concerned, this can get sticky. For the first-born boy it can get downright devastating, if a true role reversal happens.

Rivalries are most likely to be heated if the boys are close in age. If there is a three- or four-year spread, the rivalry usually will be less intense and there will be some good leadership on the part of the first-born male. Put them eleven months apart, however, and Mom and Dad may really have their hands full.

When two brothers are born close together, there is less chance for the older brother to establish a clear superiority. This can be particularly true when physical size comes into play. Younger brother can pull a complete role reversal on older brother due to a sheer height-and-weight advantage.

Helping Little Jimmy Deal with Big Mike

One of the most graphic examples of role reversal I ever worked with was fifteen-year-old Jimmy and his younger brother, Mike, who at age fourteen was six and one-half inches taller and forty-five pounds heavier than his "big" brother. Mike had always been bigger, stronger, even faster than Jimmy. All this left Jimmy feeling life had dealt him a very low blow. And it didn't help any when Jimmy's parents cracked down on him much harder than Mike with all kinds of authoritarian rules. At fifteen he had a bedtime of nine o'clock. He received no allowance because he "wasn't responsible." His parents claimed they couldn't trust him and gave him no freedom. Jimmy retaliated by becoming a liar, thief, and possessor of a volatile temper.

When Jimmy was sent to see me, he had been putting holes in the wall, smashing windows, and "borrowing" the family car, even though he wasn't old enough to drive. When I got the whole story, my first suggestion to the parents was to loosen the tight reins on Jimmy. Bedtime was made more reasonable for a fifteen year old, and he was given an allowance. I also got the parents to modify their ironclad rule on "no driving until you're eighteen." Telling the average youngster about to turn sixteen that he can't drive for two more years is sort of like pulling the pin in a grenade and hoping it won't go off. No wonder Jimmy had been having trouble with authority figures.

I also helped Jimmy make some progress in dealing with the role-reversal problem by suggesting he stop making so many comparisons between himself and his much larger brother. One thing that also helped was that Mike was a congenial kid who generally liked his older brother and wanted to be like him in some respects. He didn't try to reverse their roles; it simply happened.

Jimmy tried to take my advice on not making so many comparisons, and while he didn't completely rid himself of the sting of the role reversal, he made good progress. His bursts of temper subsided. The lying and cheating stopped, and his grades rose from Cs and Ds to As and Bs. The parents were so pleased that not long after he turned sixteen, he got his driver's license and particularly enjoyed giving rides to Mike, who was still too young to drive.

Parenting Two Girls Is No Cakewalk

What happens when both children in the two-child family are girls? The basic same-sex rivalry is there but it probably isn't as intense.

In a two-girl family, I believe the father is a key figure. Realize, Dad, the girls are vying for your individual attention. Try to give each daughter as much one-on-one time as you can. In recent years a lot has been made out of "family time"—those times when everyone goes out together for ice cream or to see a movie. While family times are a great idea, they will never replace times when a daughter can have Mom or Dad to herself.

Parents sometimes wonder if granting their children lots of one-on-one time actually caters to their selfishness. I say absolutely not. In most families, one-on-one time just isn't that plentiful and when you do spend it, you build the child's self-esteem and sense of individual worth.

That's why Holly's remark while we were out to dinner, ("*This* is how it was supposed to be!") was significant as well as amusing. While growing up, Holly always wanted more times when she could have Sande or me to herself, and so did Krissy, for that matter. I can clearly remember trying to work on the first edition of this book or some other manuscript through the evening and getting invitations from my first- and second-born daughters such as:

From Holly: "Please come to my room to talk."
From Krissy: "Can I sleep on the floor in your bedroom tonight?"

Whenever these invites came, I did my best to honor them and spend one-on-one time with each child. My little girls, in particular, often vied for my attention, and I wish I had given them even more—particularly Holly, who may be able to joke about having Mom and Dad all to herself at age twenty-five but who has always kept a strong rivalry going with her younger sister, Krissy. In the last chapter, I mentioned how fervently Holly competed with Krissy as they grew up, trying her best to maintain her first-born position of superiority, even when she really wasn't that superior.

While Holly has many talents and abilities, one of them is not singing. Monotone would not quite describe her voice. Nonetheless, when Holly was about nine, Krissy seven and a half, and Kevin four, they loved to put on shows for us, and one of their favorites was their own Tucson production of *Annie*. Following Holly's explicit instructions,

Krissy introduced Holly with great fanfare—"Here she is, our one and only Annie!"

And then Holly would dance onto the stage (the front of our living room) and sing "Tomorrow." Oh yes, Kevin's part? He crawled around on the floor playing Sandy, the dog.

My wife and I always marveled that while playing a dog, Kevin didn't howl a bit as Holly sang. Holly's rendition of "Tomorrow" always made you wish it was *yesterday!*

Krissy, of course, could sing like a bird and still does but she never got to play the part of Annie. Her big sister saw to that because she didn't want that little intruder who dethroned her in the first place to get the starring role. It was hard enough having a little sister breathing down her neck and threatening her place as first born.

And so the competition went on all through the girls' childhood. They would play "Marco Polo!" in our pool, and I would constantly catch Holly "stretching the rules." There would be Krissy dutifully keeping her eyes shut while she hollered, "Marco!" When it was Holly's turn, she'd yell "Marco!" then peek and easily find Krissy when she answered with "Polo!"

Now you may wonder why Holly—the first-born stickler for rules, regulations, and integrity, whose favorite TV star was Judge Wapner on *People's Court*—would lower herself to cheating. The answer is simple. Eighteen months behind her came these footsteps and she always felt Krissy breathing down her neck, so she had to win. If that meant stretching the rules, so be it.

Of course Krissy had not just fallen off the turnip truck. She knew she had been had and she'd retreat to the side of the pool and sit there with her little jaw jutting out, eyes narrowed, and arms akimbo—a pose well calculated to bring Daddy over and have him sit next to her and ask, "What's the matter?"

"Holly cheated!" she would say vehemently.

Back then I'd respond with sympathy for Krissy and admonitions for Holly. Now, in retrospect, I can see that Krissy was no pansy. She was as stubborn as a mule and as strong and quick as one of the little mustangs we have here in the Arizona desert. She wasn't the "poor little girl" who constantly had to take abuse from her big sister. She could give as good as she got, and now when I catch the two of them arguing over who is wearing whose sweater, I just smile and say, "You deserve each other."

A Boy for You, a Girl for Me

Rivalry between a boy and a girl is usually much less intense if it exists at all. Let's look, for example, at an older brother/younger sister combination, who are three years apart. Three-year-old Horace had to go through a mild dethronement crisis when little Hortense came home from the hospital, but he soon realized Hortense was a girl and not a serious threat to taking over his turf.

Little guys like Horace seem to have a natural instinct about this. They are also very aware that they get different toys, different clothes, and so on. In most cases, the competition between a boy and a younger sister is not that strong. In fact a first-born boy and second-born girl can often develop a close emotional bond.

In this kind of combination, little sister usually grows up to be super feminine. She has Mommy and Daddy and also her big brother all waiting on her, interceding for her, caring for her.

This can make for a fairly peaceful family while the two children are growing up, but it can cause trouble for younger sister later, if she becomes too helpless and dependent on men. When this kind of woman gets married, she often winds up disillusioned and an excellent candidate for the classic seven-year marriage.

The helpless dependent woman runs the risk of marrying a controller. I haven't had many wives come for counseling over the years—in fact, the exact count is zero—who have said, "You know what I love about my husband the most? It's his controlling nature."

When the sister is the older child, the typical picture is that the little boy has a second mother. This can work out fine, unless the little guy feels that "two mothers" are too much.

Why Shane Ran Away

I recall working with a boy of fifteen who ran away from home because his mother and older sister "ganged up on me to nitpick." In this case Mom was the chief culprit, but older sister didn't help when she told Shane, "You're *so* immature!"

Shane finally came home, after spending a week or so at a friend's house across town. When the family came to me for counseling I learned that Shane resented how his mom "wore the pants in the family" and dominated him, as well as his quiet, passive father. Fortunately the mother was wise enough to be willing to learn. After counseling sessions, in which I encouraged the father to do the talking and leading for a change, we got it worked out. Shane didn't pull any more runaway capers and eventually wound up helping teach younger kids in his church.

Granted, Shane's story is something of an extreme case. A more typical scenario finds the older sister and younger brother going in their own directions in a much less radical way. If given equal treatment and opportunity, they both take on first-born traits as first-born girl and first-born boy.

That was exactly what happened with my older sister, Sally, and my second-born brother, Jack. I have already extolled Sally's A+ qualities at great length. Jack wasn't quite in Sally's A+ league but he held his own nicely with a B+ average in high school, making the dean's list in college and going on for a Ph.D. He also became an excellent football quarterback in high school and played on his college team as well. Jack always had lots of friends—especially among the young women!

Jack never really competed with Sally that much, and she treated him with a lot of respect—even leading cheers for his football exploits. When they were small, Sally tried "mothering" her little brother (three years younger) on occasion but he never bought into it much. She had a lot better luck when bear cub Kevin came along five years later.

Beware Labeling One Child "Good," the Other "Bad"

Whatever combination you come up with, the two-child family is an excellent laboratory for practicing a basic parenting principle: *Accept their differences.*

Of course, we should accept differences no matter how many children are in the family, but there is something about having only two that focuses the challenge more sharply. We soon see that we can accept some things more easily than others. For example, when one child is six inches taller than the other, we can accept that. But suppose one child tends to challenge the rules or has a completely different set of attitudes and emotions? One child is easy to handle or what a lot of parents like to call "good." The other child is a handful and naturally his behavior gets labeled "bad."

The challenge for parents in families like this is to remember they must love each child but relate to each child differently. They must maintain some kind of order and consistency in the family and yet always be aware of the individual differences.

I can recall Olivia, a nineteen-year-old second born, telling me in a counseling session, "I wish you'd tell my mother I'm not like my older sister."

I had a good hunch what Olivia meant, but I asked her to explain a bit more. Out tumbled her burden: Her mother was always telling her she had to measure up to the standard-bearer in the family: big sister, Rebekah. Because Olivia wasn't making it, she didn't feel accepted in life. I counseled the parents to realize that, even though Olivia was an adult, they needed to go out of their way to tell her what they appreciated about her and to look for the positive points in her life.

Also they needed to do all they could to separate the girls at that point in life. Olivia had graduated from high school but had spent the past year working in menial part-time jobs while her sister, two years older, was about to start her junior year in a college, which the parents approved of a great deal. They had wanted Olivia to go to the same school, but I urged them to enroll Olivia somewhere else where she could make her own life and not be in the shadow of her older sister. If there is anything you can and must do as a parent, it's this: Give your children unqualified love that is not determined by how good their grades are, how well they perform at home, or anything else.

> Give your children unqualified love that is not determined by how good their grades are, how well they perform at home, or anything else.

The challenge is to just love each child for who he or she is. If you can pull that off, the two-child family can really be a breeze. Think of all the advantages: The whole family fits better in the average car. When you all go out to a restaurant, you don't have to wait as long—most restaurant booths are made for four. And, if Mom and Dad are still up to it, they can ride with the kids on the roller coaster, two and two!

The Night I Blew It Big Time

It's easy enough to hand out all this advice on reality discipline. I believe in it and have tried to practice it with all five of our children, but as I have already admitted, my first-born daughter, Holly, and I knocked heads constantly as she grew up. Holly never stopped competing with her sister as she fought for her first-born birthrights as the oldest. She had the constitution of a salmon who could leap tall rapids with a single bound. No matter how much I disciplined her for arguing and fighting with Krissy, she just kept coming. Whenever I thought I knew how to handle Holly, I discovered that I still had a lot to learn.

One of my most memorable lessons happened when Holly was ten and I had just finished writing *Making Children Mind without Losing Yours.* Because I was leaving the next day for a sales conference at Fleming H. Revell, my publisher, I thought I'd better brush up on some of the tips I gave in the book about how to be a loving, responsible parent. So I asked Holly if she could spend some time with me that evening.

"Without *them?*" she asked incredulously.

"Just the two of us."

"ALL RIGHT!" she said, and we took off on what was, indeed, a great evening. At 10:30 P.M. we pulled into the driveway. It was well past Holly's bedtime on a school night and I was eager to get to bed myself because I had to be up at 5:00 to catch a 7:00 A.M. flight to New Jersey.

"Daddy," said Holly, "for a special treat, can I pull my sleeping bag into your room and sleep on the floor next to your bed?"

As usual, my assertive little first born had really enjoyed her evening without *them* and now she wanted a little icing on her cake—just for general principles. Faster than any expert on reality discipline should, I replied, "Holly, no.

Listen, it's late; it's a school night. You need to get to bed and get a *good night's sleep.*"

My snap answer contained excellent logic and adult wisdom, but in giving it I violated one of my own key principles: Don't always give an immediate response to a child's request. Think about it for a few seconds or a minute and then try to answer with understanding and reason.

But I was in a hurry. Five A.M. was going to come all too soon and I was due in New Jersey where I would extol the wisdom of *Making Children Mind without Losing Yours.*

Holly was not impressed with my fatherly wisdom about a good night's sleep. I was being unreasonable and the tears began to flow.

"But, Daddy, I just want to sleep by your bed . . ."

"Holly, no, the floor is hard; you won't sleep all that well. C'mon—we've had a great evening together. Don't spoil it!"

But for Holly everything was already spoiled. "You never let me do *anything!*" she wailed, as our wonderful evening blew up in my face. As I got Holly into bed, she was still sobbing, "You never let me do anything," over and over.

Feeling frustrated, angry, and guilty, I tried to finish packing and be ready to go at dawn's early light. Sande had washed the slacks and shirt I wanted to wear on the plane, but my loving Mama Bear had forgotten to iron them and had gone on to bed. So there I stood at the ironing board. I could have probably worn something else, but I liked these clothes. Besides, when I spoke at the sales conference in the morning I could use ironing my clothes as an illustration of what a loving and sacrificial husband I am!

As I ironed, I could still hear Holly. She hadn't stopped her wailing. In fact it was getting louder. *She's being a powerful little buzzard, Leman,* I told myself. *Time to pull the rug!*

In this case pulling the rug meant firmly telling Holly to quiet down. But "firmly" turned into "loudly irate": "Listen up, Holly! I've had enough of this. Do you *understand* me? We had a wonderful evening—*wonderful*. Now it's time for you to be in bed and asleep. And do you know *why* I'm upset, Holly? I just found my clothes that your mother was supposed to have ready for me in a wrinkled mess, and I'M NOT IN A REAL GOOD MOOD!"

I capped my screaming and yelling by telling her she was going to SLEEP and that was FINAL!

Coming out of Holly's room, I slammed the door so hard it shook the whole house, waking everybody but Sande who sort of rolled over. To calm down I turned on the late news but then "the guilties" got to me. I knew I was wrong. In fact I had lost it. Holly's cries had stopped but I had to do something to make up. Maybe she was asleep by now but I still wanted to give her a kiss.

Feeling terrible, I gently opened Holly's door. She wasn't in her bed! I tore through the house looking for what I thought was a disobedient child. What had I just written in *Making Children Mind*—about using spanking sparingly? This time I had a few good swats to spare, all right.

I tried our bedroom where I thought Holly had carried out her original plan, but her sleeping bag wasn't there and neither was she. I checked Kevey's room, but no Holly. Then Krissy's, still no Holly.

Had she run away—at 11:00 at night?

Now I was really anxious and did what any trained therapist does to pull himself together. I headed for the refrigerator. As I walked by the sewing room, there was Holly, ironing one of my shirts!

Her first words were sort of cute, coming from a first-born perfectionist: "Daddy, I don't iron real good."

My ten year old was trying her best, using the old-fashioned method of sprinkling the shirt—with her tears. I just said, "Oh, Holly, will you forgive me?"

"I've ruined the whole evening!" Holly cried. "I've ruined the whole evening!"

"No, Holly, Daddy ruined the whole evening. I was wrong. Will you forgive me?"

One thing about Holly, she loves emphasis: "I've ruined the whole evening! I've ruined the whole evening!"

I tried again, "Holly, will you hush up and let me apologize?"

Holly put down the iron then burrowed her head into my chest. She squeezed me, hugged me, held me, and told me she loved me. I did the same. Two minutes later, Holly was in her bed, fast asleep.

Somehow I got the ironing done and caught the plane the next morning with only a few hours sleep. I presented my new book on parenting to the Revell sales staff. I chose not to mention my bumbling and stumbling the night before, but the easiest part of my presentation were the following words, which are useful if you're parenting two children or ten: I believe the time we really look big in a child's eyes is when we go to them to apologize for our mistakes and we say, "I was wrong. Will you forgive me?"

> I believe the time we really look big in a child's eyes is when we go to them to apologize for our mistakes and we say, "I was wrong. Will you forgive me?"

Tips for Parenting the Two-Child Family

As with all birth orders, you should first review the principles of reality discipline in chapter 13. What is particularly important with a two-child family is to put emphasis on consistency and fairness. For example:

1. Are bedtimes different for the two children? Even if the difference is as little as half an hour, it's important that that difference be enforced. Your first born is watching.
2. Are responsibilities and allowances also different? The rule is this: Oldest child gets the most allowance and the most responsibility, but as I said earlier, don't pour it on the older child. Be sure the younger one does his or her share.
3. Avoid comparisons. That is easy for a psychologist to advise, hard to do in day-to-day living. Be aware of the dangers of those famous words, "Why aren't you like your brother (or sister)?" Obviously one child is *not* like his brother or sister and your remark is not only damaging, it is a foolish waste of breath.
4. Don't feel compelled to do for one what you did for the other. In other words, treating each child differently may mean that sometimes one child gets a little more than the other. It all evens out in the end.
5. Do things with one child at a time. In other words, give both children plenty of one-on-one opportunities. How can you find time in your busy schedule to do this? You don't *find* it; you *make* it. Take one child alone on a shopping trip or even a business trip. If possible, leave half an hour early in the morning and stop for a quiet breakfast before dropping him or her off at school. Dozens of ways to spend one-on-one time will occur to you, if you really *want to do it*. Just remember the cardinal rule: If you do something with one child, be sure to do something with another, always gearing the activity to the need of each child.

16

Taking Off the Squeeze

PARENTING THE MIDDLE CHILD

*t*he only true "middle child" in the Leman family is Krissy, currently a friendly, outgoing, very together, twenty-four year old who is carving out a promising career in education. Krissy has been very friendly and outgoing almost since the day she discovered her older sister, Holly, and the reality that she would never have Mom and Dad all to herself.

Krissy is a graphic example of how the second born can play off the first born and take off in another direction. Holly has always been a perfectionist and exacting but she is still well liked by her teaching peers and identified as someone who will go far in her profession. Underneath her Judge Wapner–like exterior is a friendly, gracious young woman who overcomes her perfectionism through her warm compassion.

You would get the impression, from looking at Krissy's room, that she is a very orderly person, but she is certainly not a perfectionist. She has always had a hang-loose, relaxed approach to life. Her first day at kindergarten was a day my wife will never forget. With some trepidation, Sande put Krissy on a morning bus, said a "Thank you for taking care of her" prayer, and went back home to try to keep her mind on the morning's tasks.

Meanwhile, Krissy went to kindergarten and apparently had a great day. At 11:45 A.M. the kindergarten bus stopped in front of the house and two other little tykes who lived in the neighborhood got off. Krissy did not.

To her credit, Sande waited almost forty-five minutes before she hit the panic button. Surely, she thought, another bus would be along soon. When none appeared, she called the school. The principal informed her that Krissy had gotten on the bus and he couldn't understand why she hadn't gotten off at her house.

At this point, Sande forgot all about keeping up appearances and looking as if she had child rearing under control. She went a little crazy. Failing to reach me at the office because I was out somewhere, she started calling everyone she could think of to ask if they had seen Krissy. Between calls, the phone rang:

"Hi, Mom, this is Krissy."

"Krissy! Where *are* you?"

"I'm at my best friend's house."

"Honey, *where are you? Whose* house are you at?"

Krissy put down the phone. "What's your name again?" Sande could hear her saying.

It turned out that "what's her name" was Jennifer—a little girl Krissy had met for the very first time that very first day in kindergarten. Jennifer's house was on the way home, and Krissy had decided to get off the bus and visit with her new friend. It had never occurred to her that Mom might be worried when she didn't get off the bus at our stop. She wasn't trying to be disrespectful, she was simply being her easygoing, sociable self.

Krissy Started Floating at Eighteen Months

Actually Krissy was laid-back and easygoing even earlier than kindergarten. I can recall an eighteen-month-old Krissy swimming with the aid of "floaties" attached to her shoulders. Older kids were all over the pool, diving, splashing, making waves, and Krissy was out in the middle of it, just enjoying life. It seems Krissy has always gone along with whatever comes her way.

Holly, her older sister, has always taken the much more serious approach to things, which is typical of perfectionists. Holly *never* got off the kindergarten bus or any other bus before her stop. She always came straight home because rules are rules. Today, at age twenty-five, Holly lives by the code or life-style she developed while growing up and which all conscientious people know instinctively—rules are rules. Holly is thoughtful and analytical; she was always an excellent student and voracious reader. Today she is a gifted teacher and still a voracious reader. Holly has lots of friends, but some of her closest friends are books.

Krissy is like her father. It always was an effort to read anything and it still is. There's too much of life out there waiting to be tasted and enjoyed. Krissy would rather read people than books. She is a good example of hard work paying off. Schoolwork did not come as easily for Krissy as it did for her older sister, but she still did exceptionally well and graduated in four years flat from college, for which her father and his accountant give her heartfelt thanks!

So all this makes Krissy a typical middle child, right? Well, partly right. If you review the list of characteristics of middle children in chapter 8, you will see it is riddled with contradictions. One column tells us middle children are sociable, friendly, and outgoing. Krissy certainly fits all three of those. But another column says middle children are also characterized as loners, quiet, and shy.

The chart also describes middle children as taking life in stride with a laid-back attitude. That's Krissy most of the time. Underneath that blithe countenance, however, is a sensitive woman who can be stubborn and very hard to deal with if you get her riled (just ask her younger brother, Kevin, who used to flee before Krissy's wrath before he grew up to be 6′3″).

So Krissy presents her share of paradoxes and contradictions and illustrates nicely the idea that it's harder to get a handle on the middle child than on anyone else in the family. The only child, the first-born child, and the baby all stick out rather prominently, but the middle child sort of blends in like a quail in the desert.

Keying on Big Sister or Brother

The same principles that apply to the second born are usually equally applicable to the middle born. Like second borns, middle children follow their own version of Murphy's Law: I'm going to live according to what I see just above me in the family. I'll size up the situation and then take the route that looks the best. The key to this middle-child principle is "what I see just above me in the family." The second child looks above to the first born, and in a family of four, the third born looks above to that second born to get a clue on which route to take. For example, let's consider this family of four children:

The same principles that apply to the second born are usually equally applicable to the middle born.

Family K

Girl—16, first-born female
Boy—14, first-born male
Girl—12, middle child
Girl—10, baby

In this family the twelve year old is the true middle child, squeezed from above by an older brother (and an older sister, for that matter) and squeezed from below by her baby sister. For the most part, she will cue on her older brother to choose her life-style, but her first-born sister will also have some influence.

Let's take one more example to see how spacing in the family may eliminate a true middle child altogether:

Family L

Boy—18, first-born male
Girl—17, first-born female
Girl—15, middle child?
Boy—8, baby

In this family the third born—a girl—appears to be the middle child, but is she really? She looks above to her first-born brother and sister to get clues on which route to take to form her personal life goal and theme, but what about below? Her baby brother did not appear on the scene until she was seven years old and by then, her personality and life-style were already determined. For the first seven life-forming years, she was baby of the family and the odds are excellent that she will have many last-born characteristics and few middle-child traits because she never felt that squeeze when it really counted—during those all-important early years.

Feeling Squeezed

While Family L above doesn't have a true middle child, many other families do. And if there is one generalization you can make about middle children, it is that they feel squeezed and/or dominated. It's important for parents to be extra aware that the middle child often feels as if "everyone is running my life." Not only does the middle child have a set of parents in authority over him, but he has an older sibling right there also.

If the older sibling is close in age (within two or three years), he or she is almost sure to tell the middle child what to do. And of course just below the middle child is the baby of the family, who seems to be getting away with murder. The middle child feels trapped. He is too young for the privileges received by his older brother or sister and he's too old to get away with the shenanigans of the baby in the family.

With these pressures from above and below, middle children wind up feeling like fifth wheels, misfits who have no say and no control. Everyone else seems to be making the decisions, while they are asked to sit, watch, and obey.

While only eight years old, Krissy gave Sande and me a taste of how sensitive the middle child can be when parents make decisions for her. With her little lip jutting out and tears trickling down her cheeks, Krissy confronted her mother about a class in creative dramatics that Sande had enrolled her in a few days before. Our sensitive middle child let her mother know in no uncertain terms how unfair it was to be signed up for creative dramatics and to not even know about it! I happened to walk in on the conversation and I asked, "But, Krissy, don't you enjoy dramatics?"

"I love it!" (sob)

I laughed and said, "Then why are you getting on Mom's case?"

"You might think it's funny but I don't think it's so funny. How would you like me to sign Mommy up for swimming lessons?"

Krissy's extremely perceptive remark stopped me short. We have a backyard pool and Sande gets in it about twice a year to get wet. If Krissy or her dad tried to sign Sande up for swimming lessons, either one of us would wind up in the pool without benefit of a bathing suit. I got Krissy's point and then some. She wanted to do her *own* enrolling in creative dramatics. She didn't need Mommy's help!

When telling seminar audiences this story, I hasten to point out that it's important to ask the opinions of *all* your children, not just the middle borns. Giving any child of any birth order a chance to choose and decide for herself or himself is a critical part of developing self-esteem and a sense of responsibility and accountability. But for parents of extra sensitive middle children, the moral is clear: Always ask middle children for their opinion and let them make their own decisions whenever possible.

> Always ask middle children for their opinion and let them make their own decisions whenever possible.

Help the Middle Child Feel Special

So far this chapter sounds as if we should throw a big pity party for all middle children. What hope is there for poor little middle-born Mildred or Milford who wander off to find friends because they are fifth wheels at home? What can parents do for these kids who are such sensitive bundles of contradiction, who supposedly feel squeezed and dominated as adults ignore their opinions and make all their decisions for them?

One of the ways I have always tried to make Krissy feel special is by taking her out to breakfast on her birthday. When she was growing up, May 16 on my calendar was completely cleared of appointments. The reason was simple: May 16 is Krissy's birthday and we went out to breakfast together. If it was a school day, I'd take her to breakfast and then later I'd pick her up for lunch and take her to one of the classy places she enjoyed, like McDonald's.

Naturally there were two more inviolate dates on my calendar each year, November 14 and February 8. After all, Holly and Kevin also enjoyed choosing where they would eat and what kind of cake they would have, and so on. We have always been especially big on cakes at our house—rainbow cakes, space cakes, Charlie Brown cakes—*anything is possible on your birthday!* And now that Hannah and Lauren have joined the Leman band, you can be sure that two other dates are equally important, June 30 and August 22. (You may be observing that if Leman would have had more kids, there would be very little time left in the year to work.)

But I have to say that of all our children, Krissy was (and still is, for that matter) the most sensitive about having Daddy to herself on her birthday. In fact on Krissy's ninth birthday when we were having breakfast together, a local pastor walked by, recognized me, and said, "Aren't you Dr. Leman?"

I said I was, and he went on, "I'm so glad I caught you. Today is when I'm supposed to be writing you a note inviting you to talk to our pastor's conference *next year* on May 16." The moment he said "May 16," I knew we had a problem. I was waiting for an opening to let him know that May 16 was my daughter's birthday and I simply wasn't available, but he was going on in grand style, describing the beautiful resort where the conference would be held and how everyone would love to have me come and share, that I found it hard to interrupt. Krissy, on the other hand, did not find it as difficult, and as my pastor friend went on, she became more and more agitated. Finally, she poked me in the ribs and said, "My daddy can't come!"

This wasn't very good behavior for the daughter of someone supposedly skilled in reality discipline, so I said, "Now wait a minute, Krissy. Daddy and this man are talking . . ."

The pastor went on with more of his glorious plans for the conference on May 16 of next year as I kept hesitating to tell him I simply wasn't available on that day. Finally, Krissy could stand it no longer and said in an even louder voice, "HE CAN'T COME!"

While Krissy may have appeared to be a bit outspoken (i.e., rude) to my pastor friend, I couldn't reprimand her too severely. The problem was mine because I hadn't wanted to interrupt the pastor as he waxed eloquent about his conference a full year ahead (undoubtedly, he was a first born). Finally I had to explain that May 16 was Krissy's birthday and that was, indeed, why we were there in the restaurant having breakfast. If May 16 was the day he needed me, I was not available.

My pastor friend then admitted he wasn't positive it was May 16; he would check. Later he called and told me he was wrong about the date. It turned out he needed me on May 18, so I was able to keep both dates and my integrity with Krissy. If May 16 had been the date, however, too bad!

At our house, May 16 has always been off-limits to the outside world and always will be. Today, even with both of the older girls in their mid-twenties and Kevin twenty-one, we still make a big deal out of their birthdays. Now it is more of a family affair because the two younger girls love to take part and help blow out the birthday candles for their big brother and big sisters. So we all go out to dinner at a restaurant of the birthday person's choice and have a great time as a family. The younger girls, however, still get the same treatment that I gave their three older siblings when they were small—a special day devoted to them.

Give Middle Children Room to Share Feelings

In the birthday story, Krissy showed one of those contradictions that are typical of the middle child. She spoke up about her special birthday appointment, even when it was a year off. A lot of middle children would have been too shy, easygoing, or unwilling to confront and would not have spoken up. These middle children are the ones who neglect to tell you how they really feel. They are classic avoiders of conflict or confrontation.

But Krissy is sensitive, and in many middle children sensitivity bubbles over into anger. Krissy was so upset that she finally spoke up, and I am glad she did, even though it looked as if she was being a disobedient child.

In my counseling I find that people with anger or hostilities are usually first borns or middle borns. It takes a while to flush some of them out because they are pleasers and they may be denying their anger. With Krissy we always know when she's not happy with something. But with your middle child you may have to dig and probe a bit.

Give your middle child plenty of opportunities to share feelings with you. If you have two middle children, for example, the second and third between a first and a last, keep a close watch on number three, who can really get lost in the shuffle. Don't just make an occasional "How's it going?" remark. Schedule time for a walk or take the child along on an errand and talk in the car. (Talking in a car is a good idea—it's easier to look out the window than right at Mom or Dad when you're trying to share feelings.)

The Squeeze Builds Psychological Muscles

I've made a big point of how social and outgoing middle children may be. Feeling rejected, squeezed, or at least misunderstood at home, they are quicker to go outside the family to make friends.

Parents watch their middle borns come and go and wonder what it is that is so much more attractive about other people's houses. Meanwhile, without realizing it, the middle child is getting invaluable training for life. In making new friends, middle children get practice in committing to relationships and working at keeping them going. They sharpen and refine their social skills as they learn how to deal with their peer group and other people outside the family. When the time to leave home really comes, they are far more ready to deal with the realities of marriage, making a living, and functioning in society than other children may be.

So don't despair over your middle child who always seems to be running off somewhere. In fact you will be wise to let your middle child know that you understand friends are important. I realize that in some cases the peer group can be a problem, but don't automatically look on the friends as rivals who may lead your child astray. Try to invite your middle child's friends to your house for an overnight or even a weekend. It's another way to let your middle child know that you think he—and his friends—are very special.

And be aware of one other paradox at work in the middle child's search for friends. While the middle child may feel a little like a fifth wheel at home, his home should still remain a lot more safe and forgiving place than the outside world. While the middle child may feel good about all his friends, he can also foul things up with his peer group. When he does, his friends can melt faster than a fudgesicle on the fourth of July in Tucson. That's when he can learn that a squeeze or hug from Mom and Dad isn't so bad after all.

The World Needs More Unspoiled Middle Borns

Not all middle children are social lions, of course. Many factors may keep them from having a lot of friends: physical size and appearance, shyness, fears, the need or desire to work or study long hours. But even if the middle child stays home, so to speak, he or she still gets automatic training that helps make a better-adjusted person. That training comes in the form of negotiation and compromise.

Middle children can't have it all their own way. The oldest always seems to be getting more, staying up later, staying out later, and so on. The youngest is getting away with murder and receiving a lot more attention along with it. All this may seem very unfair at the time but it's great discipline. Middle children are far less likely to be spoiled and therefore they tend to be less frustrated and demanding of life. The typical hassles, irritations, and disappointments of being a middle child are often blessings in disguise.

On more than one occasion I have talked with mothers or fathers who are so very proud of their first-born teenage sons or daughters because these kids don't give their parents any flak about anything. They are always willing to help, always obey the rules, and so on. I smile and wish these parents continued success but I can't help wondering if their obedient first borns may be headed for big trouble. Could they be bottling up their feelings? Could they be classic pleasers who would never think of crossing their parents? And what will happen in a few years when the family umbilical cord is cut and they are out on their own? Will they have the psychological muscles to deal with life?

Now I am not saying that all obedient, ready-to-please teenagers are too weak to face life after they leave home. What I am saying is that I have counseled a lot of first borns and only children who were obedient pleasers of Mom and Dad as they grew up, but as adults they wound up having trouble coping with life, spouses, or neighbors they couldn't handle. And that's why they came to see me. The more I counsel, the more I realize that being squeezed a little while you are growing up isn't necessarily all bad. It can be excellent basic training for the real campaign that starts when you leave home and strike out on your own.

So don't despair if you have a middle child who seems caught in the squeeze right now. Do your best to take off that squeeze or at least help him or her through it. Keep your middle child's candle lit and in the end he or she may shine brighter than all the rest.

Tips for Parenting the Middle Child

Review the principles of reality discipline in chapter 13 and use them in combination with the following suggestions designed especially for use with middle children.

1. Recognize that many middle children avoid sharing how they really feel about things. If your middle child is an avoider, set aside times for just the two of you to talk. It's important to give this kind of time to every child, but a middle child is least likely to insist on his fair share. Be sure he or she gets it.
2. Take extra care to make your middle child feel special. Typically the middle child feels squeezed by the brothers or sisters above and below. The middle child needs those moments when you ask for his opinion or allow her to make choices. One night I took all three of our kids bowling. As we sat down to start our score sheet, there was an intense discussion over who would bowl first. While Holly and Kevey clamored for the honor, I noticed Krissy was not saying a word. I said, "Krissy, you get to choose." So she put down her daddy's name first, then Holly, then Kevey, finally herself.

3. Along with being sure your middle child feels special, set up some regular privileges he or she can count on having or doing every day or every week. Perhaps it is something as simple as watching a certain TV program with no interference from others in the family. Maybe it's going to a certain restaurant. The point is, this is the middle child's *exclusive* territory.

4. When was the last time you made a special effort to give your child a new item of clothing rather than a hand-me-down? In some families, income is sufficient so that this is not a problem, but in other homes economics make hand-me-downs a regular part of growing up. An occasional hand-me-down is fine, but your middle child may be particularly appreciative of something new, especially a key item, like a coat or jacket.

5. Listen carefully to your middle child's answers or explanations for what is going on or what he or she thinks of certain situations. His or her desire to avoid conflict and not make waves may get in the way of the real facts. You may have to say, "C'mon now, let's have the whole story. You aren't going to get in trouble. I want to know how you really feel."

6. Above all, be sure the family photo album has its share of pictures of your middle child. Don't let him or her fall victim to the stereotyped fate of seeing thousands of pictures of the older brother or sister and only a few of him or her! And be sure you take some of your middle born alone, not always with big brother or little sister.

17

Helping the Family "Cub" Grow Up

PARENTING THE LAST BORN

My first four words of advice for parents of the last born are: Beware of being manipulated! When the last born arrives, the real enemy is not that cute little buzzard who marks the end of the family line. He can't help being so darling. She can't help it if she charms everyone with one toothless smile. The real culprit parents have to battle is well known to Pogo fans, who have met the enemy and realize "he is us."

Remember the three styles of parenting discussed in chapter 13?

Authoritarian parents say, "Do it my way, or else!"

Authoritative parents say, "I'd like to have you do it this way because . . ."

But permissive parents tell their little last born: "Ahh, you do it your way, you cute little guy."

Getting Away with Murder

Why is it that parents can run a pretty tight ship with their older kids, but the last born seems to have some mysterious power that lets him "get away with murder"? I'm not sure there is a definitive answer. Maybe the parents get tired or maybe they get careless because now they think they "know the ropes" and can loosen up. Whatever it is, parents often look the other way when the last born skips chores and drives his older brothers and sisters crazy with pestering, or what I call "setups." (The setup is a particular skill of the last born and involves bugging an older sibling until he or she lashes out in anger; then the baby of the family runs screaming to Mommy for protection.)

I was an expert in setting up my big brother, Jack, whom I loved to call "God" because he was so big, strong, and superior to me, the little Cub of the family. When I heard him come home from school I'd say within his hearing but not necessarily my mother's, "God's home!"

Jack didn't appreciate being called "God" and he would often belt me one. Then I'd run to Mom, who always took my side, and Jack would wind up in trouble. If he'd belt me extra hard, he might wind up in trouble with my dad when he got home.

Recently Charles Swindoll, president of Dallas Theological Seminary, whose books have sold in the gazillions, appeared on *Parent Talk* and he shared at one point his own birth-order adventures. As baby of the family with an older brother and sister, he often felt put-upon and put down. "I usually called my older brother 'Hitler,'" he confided.

"Is that right?" I interjected. "Perhaps he knew my older brother, 'God.'"

For a second or two, one of America's great spiritual leaders looked at me in what seemed to be shock, and then we both burst into hearty laughter. Two babies of the family had found a common bond—memories of a big brother who made life a little miserable at times.

Calling my older brother by the unlikely name of "God" to set him up was just one way I got away with murder—there were many others. If last borns aren't getting away with murder, they are at least trying to manipulate, clown, or entertain, and are often likely to be found disturbing somebody's peace.

Now I realize that not all parents fall for the last born's charms and antics. Not all last borns get away with murder. Nonetheless, many of them still are able to manipulate parents with that famous line: "Mommy, I can't do it!" A plaintive cry for help is a great tool last borns use to get parents (as well as older siblings) to snowplow the roads of life for them.

Babies are particularly adept at getting help with schoolwork. I have counseled several children whose seeming helplessness turned their homes into a tutoring establishment right after dishes were done each evening. It's one thing to encourage children with their homework and get them started; it's another to do it for them. A lot of parents get suckered into doing the child's work, all the while believing they are helping the child. Of course, they are only hindering the child because it prohibits him from learning to do his own thinking.

For example, I worked with one seventh grader whose older brother was in his final year of high school. The parents sent this little redhead to me in the spring of his seventh grade year because he was doing so poorly in school. The boy was the last born of two children.

At first we didn't make much progress. The boy was in all kinds of trouble at school, and the parents were going to more conferences than they really wanted to be bothered with. He managed to pass seventh grade, but not by much. I continued working with him throughout the summer, and in the fall big brother went away to college. This seemed to be the breakthrough that was needed. As the boy started into his eighth grade year, he began responding to some reality discipline principles that I had set up, and the parents finally saw some positive results.

The reality discipline I asked his parents to use was rather basic:

1. Make the boy stand on his own two feet and do not help him with any more of his homework than absolutely necessary.
2. After dinner, no going out to play, no watching television, no doing anything of that nature until responsibilities were taken care of. Responsibilities included chores and certainly schoolwork.
3. No making Mom and Dad tutors for several hours each night. (This went back to making the boy stand on his own two feet.)

The last-born son made an excellent turnaround in the fall of his eighth grade year. The misbehavior stopped at school and his grades came up nicely without a lot of tutoring by Mom and Dad. The youngster had lived in the shadow of his older brother for so long that he had been completely cowed and discouraged. As I often put it, "His candle had been blown out." The older brother was so confident and competent and so much bigger and stronger that it just left the younger boy wiped out. Once elder brother physically left the house, the younger child began to bloom.

And Mom and Dad were relieved when they didn't have to spend three or four hours a night tutoring their last born to keep his grades barely above water. Once the son understood that he had the ability and could do it himself, everything changed.

Weekend Indigestion and Religious Fever

I have also counseled last-born children who just don't care for school. I understand where they are coming from because I felt the same way when I was growing up. Sometimes a child has learning problems or disabilities, but in many cases the true issue is attitude.

I'm convinced my disastrous school record could have been greatly improved with one simple step on the part of my parents. My mother should have stopped running down to the school to talk to the counselors. She should have stopped trying to find the cause of little Kevin's problems. If she had simply said, "Hey, kid, no Little League unless you cut it in school," I probably would have turned around by the sixth or seventh grade.

But Mom and Dad never called my bluff. They never drew the line. In a word, they were permissive, and I played it for all I could. For example, I had a strange ailment called Monday and Friday stomachaches. I would wake up on Friday feeling terrible, and, of course, I couldn't go to school. But strangely enough, by mid-afternoon a miracle had happened. I was instantly healed when the clock struck three! I remained well throughout Saturday and Sunday, but then on Monday morning back would come that stomachache.

There are other names for my illness. One might be: "Making the weekend longer by faking a stomachache on Fridays and Mondays." But somehow my mom never really caught on. I guess she just couldn't believe her little Cub could lie and be in such "pain" at the same time.

Another trick I mastered was catching "religious fever," particularly on Wednesday or Sunday night when there was work to be done. The dishes would be looming mountainously in the sink and the garbage cans and wastebaskets would be overflowing, but I let none of these mundane temptations keep me from the house of the Lord. "Mom, I've got to get to youth meeting! See you later!" And Mom stepped in and did all the work while I faithfully did all I could to drive the youth leaders crazy.

What or who spoils the last born? The obvious answer is, "Why, the parents do the spoiling, of course." And that's correct to a point, but sometimes parents can get a lot of help from the other children in the family. How spoiled a last born gets can depend on when and where he or she arrives in the family constellation. For example, let's diagram a family consisting of three girls and a last-born boy:

Family M
Female—11
Female—9
Female—6
Male—3

In this family it looks as if the little guy is totally outnumbered by females. But what can usually occur here is a strong relationship between the mother and the son. After three girls, little Harold will be very precious, especially to Mom, and she is likely to give him the benefit of the doubt when older sisters come and complain about his pestering.

Actually this family has two last borns, a last-born boy and a last-born girl. This almost guarantees friction between the six year old and the three year old. In this kind of family, it is very common for "alliances" to form. The way this usually happens in this particular sequence is that the eleven year old will form an alliance with the six year old and the nine year old with the three year old.

In many cases the third-born child in this family could find herself in an unfavorable position. This would be especially true if both of the older girls decided to really mother the little boy and take his side in all of the various arguments and incidents that occur in a family of four. On the other hand, all three of the older girls may decide that the little guy is a pest and be particularly irritated if Mom asks them to do a lot of baby-sitting.

Let's take another look at a family where the last born becomes very special. In this case we have a first-born girl, followed by two boys, and finally along comes "baby princess." The diagram looks like this:

Family N

Female—13
Male—12
Male—10
Female—4

On the positive side, the last-born girl is in good shape in that she has two older brothers who are likely to wind up becoming her champions, unless she is a total little brat. With two attentive older brothers, she can grow up learning that men are caring and loving. And with the older sister, she also gets the benefit of more mothering and cuddling, something that first-born girls love to do.

The bad news is that the baby princess can get the idea that the world revolves around her. She may become the apple of Daddy's eye and be able to wrap him around her little finger to get just about anything she wants. If this is carried too far, she can grow up believing she can do this with any man, and be a risky candidate for a happy marriage.

If parents are overly permissive, baby princess could be spoiled rotten. She could grow up to be an obnoxious adult who makes unreasonable demands on everyone.

How to Grow a Total Weakling

One of the most damaging effects of parental permissiveness is making things too easy for a child. Later, when the last born has grown to adulthood, he or she may not be prepared for real life. Adversities will be just too much.

I once worked with a family that consisted of a mother (a widow) and five children. There were two older sisters, followed by two older brothers, and then the youngest daughter, who was seven years behind the youngest brother. The father had died when the youngest daughter was thirteen. At the time I counseled the family, the youngest daughter was twenty-six and totally dependent on the mother. For thirteen years the mother and the youngest daughter had virtually lived alone together because the rest of the children had moved out of the house by the time the father had died.

The daughter had been totally protected and "smothered" by her mother to the point that when I saw her, she was uneducated and her confidence was at zero. The most challenging tasks she could attempt were housecleaning and baby-sitting.

I realize this is an extreme case of the parent needing the child so badly she didn't allow the child to grow up. But the same thing happens to lesser degrees every time the parent acts permissively and does too much snow-plowing of life's roads for a child. When you baby a child too much, you actually render that child useless, or at least cripple him or her in one way or another.

The Other Side of the Last-Born Coin

One thing I've tried to emphasize throughout this book is that no birth order fits only one mold. The same characteristics are not always true in every last-born child. Those ever present variables can throw in a lot of curve balls for last borns, as well as any other birth order. In fact Sande and I have seen the variable of spacing working overtime in our "second family"—Hannah, born nine and a half years after Kevin II, and Lauren, born five and a half years after Hannah.

Hannah's official description is "first born in the second family," but I describe her as a compliant first born who acts more like a baby of the family than anything else. It's important to remember that for the first five years of her life—that period when her life-style was really formed—Hannah was the last born in the total Leman family. She was also the beneficiary of a lot of loving care from what amounted to five "parents"—Sande and myself, of course, and her older siblings, all of whom came across to her as very big, very capable, and very loving.

We doted on Hannah more than a little bit, and it took all of our determination and experience to apply reality discipline to balance things up and not let her become spoiled. When we'd go to University of Arizona basketball games or other public events, we would sometimes take Hannah along, and all our friends would hold her and cuddle her. Today Hannah is a very balanced, well-adjusted, fun-loving eleven year old, who is extremely well liked, loves school, and loves her teachers.

In fact Hannah wants to be a teacher herself some day but, ironically enough, she struggles with certain subjects, particularly math. Now that I think about it, perhaps birth order has to go out the window on that one. Hannah's math weakness must be in the genes. As you will recall, I failed bonehead arithmetic and my final score in elementary algebra was 22, well below the absolute bottom line for an F.

As for Lauren, she definitely is the "caboose" of the Leman family(ies). But while she's the ordinal baby of them all, she really acts more like a first born or only child than anything else. Lauren is extremely thoughtful, analytical—and cautious—a sure sign of an only child or first born. I'm not sure why she's so cautious—maybe she just had too much adult influence with all those "big people" above her. Keep in mind that if Hannah has had five parents, Lauren has had *six*. She was born when Hannah's life-style had been thoroughly formed and even at the age of five she came across to her baby sister as very capable, strong, and all-knowing.

Earlier I mentioned that Lauren amazed her last-born father at the age of two with the way she would line up her little tape cassettes on the floor in nice neat rows, and then play them one at a time. But perhaps the most significant incident of them all happened one day when I found Lauren down on the floor with one of seven-year-old Hannah's computer toys, which was designed to help her learn to spell, do math, and learn to read. At the age of two and a half, Lauren had figured out how to turn it on, and the computer toy said, "Hello! Please select a category now."

The toy, appropriately named "Whiz Kid Plus," was designed with a time delay. If no command was given, the voice would repeat the instruction. Lauren hadn't seen me come in, so I watched my little daughter as she sat there listening to the toy continuing to tell her, "Hello! Please select a category now."

What's she going to do? I wondered. Finally, after this was repeated several times, Lauren leaned down to the machine, cupped her hands, and said loudly, "Lady, I can't! I'm only two years old!"

At that moment I realized that my little girl was two going on twenty-two and we had a quasi-only child, or at least a functional first born on our hands.

Last Borns "Get Set Straight" a Lot

These Leman second-family exploits are inserted here only to illustrate that last borns can turn out in a lot of different kinds of packages. You may be a last born who wasn't spoiled that much at all. Or maybe your youngest child is hardly what you would call a manipulator. If anything, your last born is the one being manipulated by the rest of the family. Ironically enough, while youngest children are often coddled and cuddled, they can get more than their share of being cuffed and clobbered, especially by older brothers and sisters.

Birth-order specialists claim youngest children have difficulty with "information processing."[1] In other words, they seem to have trouble getting things straight. The older kids always seem to be so smart—so authoritative and knowing. No matter that the older kids are often totally incorrect in their dogmatic pronouncements to the baby of the family—the baby *perceives* they are right because they are so much bigger, stronger, and "smarter."

As a last born, I can remember feeling plenty stupid when Sally or Jack set me straight on anything from the facts of life to the time of day. My big brother, Jack—five years older—had a very direct approach for setting me straight. He'd belt me one.

Of course, I often had it coming. As I have already mentioned, I was a pro at setting Jack up by goading and pestering him until he'd lose his cool and hit me. Then I'd scream bloody murder and Mom or Dad would get on his case. It was great fun, but there was a high price tag. Sooner or later Jack would get me alone where I couldn't frame him or convince my parents that it was all his fault. Of course he never really killed me. It just felt like it as he pounded on me a little for the sake of general principles.

In one case, however, he had a different approach to setting me straight. He became informer and turned me in for smoking cigarettes at age eight behind the chicken coop. That one really cost me. I had to go straight to bed with no dinner, pretty tough treatment for the baby Cub, who usually got away with everything.

As for Sally, I set her up much less often than Jack, but in all fairness to the memory of my checkered past, there were times when I could get to her just as easily as I got to him. I remember her screaming, "Mother, would you get him *out* of here?" And she also complained, "He gets away with murder—you never let me do that when I was his age."

But those were rare occasions and most of the time big sister Sally set little Kevin straight in another way. As my "second mother," she often became distressed when I was too coarse, too loud, or just plain too smart-mouthed. But she had a way of making me want to do better. She wouldn't say, "Don't behave like that," or "What's the matter with you? Why don't you shape up?"

Whenever anyone—parents, teachers—told me not to do something with that tone of voice, it was just like pouring gasoline on a fire. It only goaded me on to do more things to get attention by bucking the establishment.

But Sally's approach had a much different effect. Actually she was something of a master amateur psychologist. When I acted up, she would often say things such as, "Do you really want to act like that?"

I'd try to be cute and respond, "Sure I do—that's what makes it fun." But deep inside I knew differently. Sally was already planting seeds to be watered by my math teacher when I was in high school and carefully cultivated by a beautiful nurse's aide whom I would meet while doing janitor duties in the Tucson Medical Center.

North Park: A Good Place to Get Smashed

I was a lucky last born in many ways. I was reminded of this in vivid fashion not too long ago when I received a telephone call from North Park College and was asked to come to their annual alumni banquet where I was to receive their "Distinguished Alumnus Award" and be the featured speaker as well. To be honest, I was bowled over but I didn't let the caller know it. I haven't done much research on this, but I doubt there are many students who get tossed out of a college for stealing the conscience-fund money, and then are asked to return more than thirty years later to be named "distinguished alumnus"!

I told North Park I believed I could work them into my schedule, and traveled back to my old "alma mater," received my award, and spoke to all the alums who had made it, as well as the assembled faculty.

Some of the professors still remembered me and they sat there amazed at how I had turned out after leaving their midst unofficially voted "most likely to do time" in some penal institution. As I looked out over the audience, I saw Carroll Peterson, who had been head resident of our dorm when I attended North Park. Very late one night, well past curfew, C. P., as we called him, found me and my roommate, Beagle, lying on a landing between the first and second floors, slightly wasted because we had spent the evening discovering for the first (and definitely last) time what port wine tasted like.

We were fast asleep and would have spent the night on the landing, but C. P. awakened us and asked which room was ours. In our somewhat indisposed condition, we couldn't remember, so I got out my key and he got the number from that. Somehow he got both of us up to the third floor, to our room, and he put us to bed.

The bottom line to this story is that Carroll Peterson did not report us for our lack of good judgment, which would have undoubtedly resulted in immediate expulsion. This really good and godly man had gone on to become dean of students, well liked by everyone on campus.

C. P. probably enjoyed my talk that day more than any-one else present. He laughed especially hard as I shared how lucky I had been as a young man to have a place like North Park to come to. Yes, I added, North Park was even a great place to get drunk at, particularly when the head resident was so forgiving! C. P. understood college students and he knew the difference between a little bump in the road and a really big pothole.

Oh yes, one other minor detail: Without the twenty-four units I earned at North Park, I could have never transferred to the University of Arizona and gone on to get bachelor's, master's, and doctorate degrees after I finally woke up in life.

Last Borns: Bed of Roses or Bed of Thorns?

With all of their legendary "easy street" existence and their reputation for "getting away with murder," last borns face several bumps in life that belie the claim that they have it made. We've already looked at two major ones. First, last borns may become too dependent and stay babies if they are coddled and cuddled too much.

A second major problem is that last borns can take a lot of abuse, pressure, resentment, and teasing from older brothers and sisters. Parents may sometimes think they need a crystal ball—or maybe a new piece of wonder software for the computer—to help them figure out when the baby of the family is really getting it in the neck or when he is just working his manipulative wiles. When counseling parents of last borns, I usually tell them if they must err, let it be on the side of helping the baby of the family stand on his own two feet and cope, even it if means getting teased or intimidated on occasion.

One other hurdle for last borns is well worth underlining. Because they are last, nothing they do is really original. Their older brothers or sisters have already learned to talk, read, tie shoes, and ride a bike. And, let's face it. It *is* hard for Mom or Dad to get excited about the third or fourth lopsided pencil holder or paperweight to be brought home from school art class in the last five or ten years.

Family specialist Edith Neisser catches the spirit of frustration last borns often feel because nothing they do seems to be very big news. She quotes an eighth grader who had this to say about having older brothers and sisters:

> No matter what I ever do, it won't be important. When I graduate from high school, they'll be graduating from college or getting married; then if I ever do get through with college, Sis will probably be having a baby. Why, even when I die it won't be anything new to my family; nobody will even be here to pay any attention.[2]

If you have a junior high student in your home, you may have heard the same kind of exaggerated dramatics, but there is a kernel of real truth in what this girl said. The key phrase is "Nobody will even be here to pay attention." That is something every parent can be aware of with the last born: *Am I paying enough attention to little Harold's "firsts" in life? Yes, it's my third or fourth paperweight but it's only his first. I should make as big a deal out of his firsts as anyone else's.*

At least be assured that your last born is well aware of his special slot in the family. It's not likely he wants to trade. All of this was brought home to me in living color as I was driving alone with seven-year-old Kevey. Just for fun I asked him, "How about it? Would you mind if Mommy had another baby?"

There was a long pause as Kevey gave the question serious thought. Finally, he said, "I guess it's okay just as long as she's a girl!"

It was a *purely* hypothetical question, of course. When I asked it, Sande and I had no intentions of having any more babies, but, as all of us know, the road to additional parenthood is paved with good intentions. But I'll talk more about that in the epilogue.

Tips for Parenting the Last-Born Child

Using reality discipline is especially critical with the family baby because of the natural tendency of parents to ease up and slack off. Be sure to review chapter 13, especially the principles regarding accountability and responsibility. In addition, try the suggestions below.

1. Be sure your last born has her fair share of responsibilities around the house. Last borns often wind up with very little to do for two reasons: (a) They are masters at ducking out of the work that needs to be done; (b) they are so little and "helpless" that the rest of the family members decide it's easier to do it themselves.

2. Along the same lines, be sure your last born does not get away with murder in regard to family rules and regulations. Statistics show the last born is least likely to be disciplined and the least likely to have to toe the mark the way the older children did. It wouldn't hurt to make notes on how you held the older kids responsible and enforce the same bedtime and other rules on your last born.

3. While you're making sure you don't coddle your youngest child, don't let him get clobbered or lost in the shuffle, either. Last borns are well known for feeling that "nothing I do is important." Make a big deal out of your last born's accomplishments and be sure he or she gets a fair share of "marquee time" on the refrigerator door with his school papers, drawings, and awards.

4. Introduce your youngest child to reading very early. Six months is not too young to start reading to your child with brightly colored illustrated books. When your child starts reading, don't do the work for him.

Last borns tend to "like to be read to" and will let you do most of the work if they can get away with it. This may be one of the reasons last borns are well known for being the poorest readers in their family.

5. Whenever necessary, call baby's bluff. I have always felt my parents should have cracked down on me regarding school when I was young. But they never really put on the pressure. They never gave me choices like, "Shape up at school or drop baseball," or "No homework, then no television programs tonight."

6. Try to get your last born's baby book completed before he or she is twenty-one. Life seems to pile up on parents with the arrival of the third and fourth child. Check to see if you're neglecting the last born because you just don't seem to have as much time as you used to. Let other things go if necessary to be sure you provide time for each child.

7. Oh yes—along the way, try to pick out a nice first born for your last born to marry. The odds are high they'll make a great team!

Epilogue

THERE IS STILL ONLY ONE THING YOU CAN'T DO WITHOUT

*i*f you've gotten this far, you are probably a first born who will enjoy reviewing key points. If you are an intrepid middle child or last born, hang in there. I have one or two more stories you may like. First, the key points to remember about birth order:

1. As important as a child's order of birth may be, it is only an influence, not a final fact of life forever set in cement and unchangeable as far as how that child will turn out.
2. The way parents treat their children is as important as their birth order, spacing, sex, and physical or mental characteristics. The key question is: Was the environment provided by the parents loving, accepting, and warm or was it critical, cold, and distant?
3. Every birth order has inherent strengths and weaknesses. Parents must accept both while helping the child develop positive traits and cope with negative ones.
4. No birth order is "better" or more desirable than another. First borns seem to have a corner on achieve-

ment and the headlines, but the door is wide open for later borns to make their mark. It is up to them.

5. Birth order information does not give the total psychological picture for anyone. No system of personality development can do that. Birth-order statistics and characteristics are indicators that combine with physical, mental, and emotional factors to give the bigger picture.

6. Understanding some basic principles of birth order is not a formula for automatically solving problems or changing your personality overnight. Changing oneself is the hardest task any human being can attempt; it takes lots of work.

I've been in the field of psychology and family counseling for more than thirty years. I spent thousands of hours preparing to be a psychologist and therapist. Then God blessed me with opportunities to talk to many thousands of clients—husbands and wives, moms and dads, stepparents, children, stepchildren, divorced people, and other singles—I have pretty well gone the gamut. Yet I know I have not begun to see and hear it all and I also know there is much more that I need to master to be able to do my job better as a therapist and a parent.

I'm sure anyone in any of the helping professions would admit that he or she can never know enough, but at the same time all the years of talking with and listening to people have convinced me that it isn't always *what* you know. Everything doesn't ride on knowledge, skill, and technique.

As I closed the first edition of this book, I observed that you could read all the books, use all the techniques, and say all the right words (you hope), and there is still only one thing that remains absolutely necessary. This one thing is every parent's secret weapon and it works equally well with every birth order. I'm not talking about something you learn in so many lessons like operating a computer or driving a car. No, it's something you actually have at the start and then develop slowly and sometimes painfully. And just about the time you think you are getting the real hang of it, you are back to square one as you realize how basic life really is.

I Thought Our Family Was Complete, and Then . . .

That's really what happened to me when we got our second family long after we thought our days of having children had ended. I'm not sure there are that many people who rear one family of three children and then, in their forties, have a couple more just to be sure they "got it right." So I'd like to share with you what it was like to learn—on two different occasions—that a new little ankle biter was on the way and all those late-night shows that we thought were over would go into reruns.

Just before Christmas in 1986 Sande called the office and surprised me by saying she wanted to take me out to dinner. As we were enjoying our meal, she pulled out a greeting card she had made for me. Because Sande is thoughtful and quite creative, I didn't suspect anything as I read the cover, which asked me:

"Are you ready to change your summer plans?"

"Are you ready to work late?"

"Are you ready to change your work schedule?"

Puzzled, I flipped it open and was greeted by a picture of Santa Claus saying, "Merry Christmas!" In his arms was a little baby with a toothless grin.

As the light began to dawn, I gave Sande a look, and she nodded her head yes. I couldn't help it. I let out a war whoop of joy that startled several nearby diners. The first member of our second family was on her way.

As I contemplated telling our three children the news, I was sure the girls would be thrilled, but I was concerned about Kevey, who was eight years old and about to lose his privileged position as "baby of the family." As it turned out, Holly, just turned fourteen, responded with shocked silence. Krissy, twelve, just clapped her hands over her ears and wailed, "I don't want to hear this! I don't want to hear this!"

I'm still not quite sure why the girls reacted the way they did. Perhaps they were happy with the family the way it was and this was just too much of an unsettling idea. Maybe they were embarrassed because they thought their parents didn't "do that kind of stuff anymore."

When we sat down with Kevey, I was really worried. I considered not telling him—perhaps we could do it later, maybe when the baby was three years old! As Sande and I faced Kevey, I said, "We have something to tell you."

"What is it, Dad?"

While I stuttered around trying to handle the situation as a professional psychologist should, Sande broke in and said, "I'm going to have a baby" (first borns always like the direct approach).

I steeled myself for Kevey's explosion, but all he said was, "Hey . . . that's baaaaad!"

"Baaaaad?" I said puzzled.

"Dad, you know . . . that means gooooood."

"Oh . . . right, of course," I said, acting as if I were current on the latest "in" terms of Kevey's generation.

Giving his mother a hug, Kevey said, "This is great—hey, Dad!"

"Yeah?"

"Can we go to the store and buy some Pampers?"

Kevey was disappointed when he learned we wouldn't need Pampers for at least six months but he was totally cool about no longer being the baby of the family. And in a matter of days, Holly and Krissy began talking to us again. When Hannah Elizabeth arrived, they couldn't wait to get her home from the hospital and start helping with her care.

And their interest wasn't just fired by momentary curiosity. They were always there and ready to help Sande with Hannah, and I really mean it when I say that this little girl had five parents who loved her very much. One of the really poignant proofs of that hangs on our wall in the family room—a framed copy of a poem that Holly wrote to Hannah when she was only two months old:

To Hannah Elizabeth Leman
Born June 30, 1987

> *A child with warm and tender skin, soft and smooth without a flaw,*
> *The small body hasn't experienced life yet . . . just being born*
> *   into it . . . but this is God's law.*
> *The innocence of a child, something we should all have . . .*
> *   something we should strive to be,*
> *An innocent child, fresh in God's sight, as she ventures out*
> *   to experience life.*
> *—Holly Leman, age 14*

But you'll notice that I keep saying Hannah was the first born of our second family. This suggests that there would be still more children even though Sande was forty-two and I was forty-four when Hannah arrived. And, of course, there may be some readers (particularly wives) who are wondering, *Leman, you jerk, why didn't you get fixed?*

Well, let me explain. After Hannah was born, I went in to the doctor to inquire, and he said that it was a rather simple procedure and he was sure I knew all about how it was done. Actually, I didn't and I asked him for a very short course in Vasectomy 101.

"It's very simple. All we do is put a little metal clip here, and a little metal clip there . . ."

Metal clip? That was it for me. Surely we could try to rely on our usual methods of birth control and take whatever God gave us. I say to my shame, as a husband and a therapist, that as many (most?) men do, I've left birth control matters to my wife. I should have been brave enough to endure the metal clips, but as I look back I'm glad I didn't because we have these two wonderful little girls who have brought such joy into our lives.

"Tell Me You're *NOT* Pregnant!"

Five years went by and it looked as if little Hannah would be a combination toy princess of the family who had some first-born—actually quasi-only child—characteristics because of that large gap between her and her older brother. In February 1992, I drove the entire family over to California for a weekend at Disneyland. As we enjoyed the "happiest place on earth," I noticed that Sande, who was usually full of life and all smiles, was just a little distant.

We left Disneyland late Sunday afternoon and, being a typical male, I had visions of "driving straight through" and making Tucson by midnight. We dropped south to Interstate 8 and headed east. As we got to La Mesa, a suburb of San Diego, Sande announced, "We've got to stop, I need something to eat."

"Okay, we can grab something at a drive-in—I'd like to keep going."

"No, I don't feel so good. I need to stop at a restaurant."

As we pulled into a Coco's restaurant, I wasn't real happy because I hated the thought of having all those cars I worked so hard to pass go on by while I was eating! We placed our orders and we were sitting around the table waiting to be served when Sande started to cry. Bewildered, I asked her, "What's wrong?"

All she would say was, "I don't feel so good."

Our son, who was now fourteen and preferred to be called Kevin, observed perceptively, "She's pregnant!"

"You mother is *not pregnant*," I said as I glanced at Sande with a look that said, *Tell me you're not pregnant.*

But Sande nodded her head in the affirmative and more tears began to flow. My wife had announced another baby was coming, but this time no whoop of joy escaped my lips. It was more like a gasp of dismay, and maybe a bit of angry frustration. It turned out she had been pregnant a couple of months and here I was finding out about it at the very same moment as our children! And things didn't get much better when Sande said firmly, "I want you to call the doctor *now!*"

"Doctor Who?" I wondered, and she gave me the obstetrician's name and instructions on what to ask him. She was spotting and was afraid she was going to lose the baby. I went to find a pay phone and made the call. I was lucky enough to connect with the doctor who was very concerned and very direct: "Get her off her feet immediately and to a motel. She needs to rest in bed tonight and then get her here tomorrow just as soon as you can."

I came back to the table and Sande was sitting there—alone. All the children were missing. The thought flashed across my mind: *Have they all run away?* Later I learned that Kevin had taken Hannah for a walk and the two older girls had retreated to the rest room where Krissy spent some time crying and Holly thumbed through the pages of a greater San Diego phone book with no particular purpose in mind whatsoever.

Somehow we finished dinner and went off to find a motel. Even though it was a Sunday night, most of the motels were filled, but finally a Travelodge took us in with only one room and two double beds. I can't say I slept much that night. I kept doing a numbers game in my mind and saying, *She can't be pregnant . . . she can't be pregnant . . .*

I kept mulling over what the doctor had said—the possibility she could lose the baby if she wasn't careful . . . And what about being parents at our age—Sande was forty-six and I was forty-eight. By the time the baby would arrive, she'd be forty-seven and I'd be forty-nine! That meant that I would be almost seventy years old by the time our child graduated from high school!

The next morning it was a somber ride home, as each of us pondered how Sande's pregnancy was going to impact our individual lives. Our two younger ones, Hannah and Kevin, were taking the news in stride, particularly four-year-old Hannah who did not appear to fear dethronement at all. She was already looking forward to having a baby sister to mother.

But Holly and Krissy, nineteen and seventeen at the time, weren't taking this news any better than they had taken the announcement about Hannah five years earlier. They just stared out the window and I was sure they were probably thinking, *Hannah was bad enough but Mom and Dad are STILL doing it even at their age!* I imagined Holly and Krissy getting together and collaborating on another poem, something like:

> *Oh, Mom and Dad,*
> *We love you so*
> *But don't you know*
> *How babies grow?*

We got home in record time and immediately I got Sande to the doctor. After several days of bed rest, we went back in and talked to the obstetrician and by this time I was in a little better frame of mind. Because of Sande's age, this was a high-risk pregnancy. The doctor started going through all the statistics about all of the odds on bad things happening to the baby. In her classic first-born style, Sande just looked at him and said, "Why are you telling us these things?"

The doctor looked at me in a helpless way as if to say, "Can you help me out here, Buddy?"

Then Sande quickly made the doctor understand that it didn't make any difference. Abortion would never be an option; she would go ahead and have this baby.

Only One Thing Remains Absolutely Necessary

Not long after we got back from Disneyland, I had to take a business trip east, and on the way home I stopped in Buffalo as I frequently do to check on our summer home in Chautauqua Lake. While there I dropped in on my life-long friend "Moonhead" and his wife, Wendy. Although the initial shock had worn off, I was still stewing and saying things like, "Holy crow, I'm going to be sixty-seven years old when the child's a senior in high school!" And then Wendy said it all—for me, for Sande, for everyone:

"Can you think of a better family for that little baby to grow up in?"

That stopped me in my baby Cub tracks. I knew in a moment I had to stop holding my own little pity parties. Oh, sure, I had been joking, of course, but behind the jokes was a feeling of, "Why us? Why *me?*"

As for Wendy's question, I had to think about that for a few moments before answering. Surely there were parents who were younger, with more energy, and equipped with strong nervous systems that weren't ready for a one-hundred-thousand-mile recall. But could any family love that little cub more than Mama and Papa Bear Leman?

I said to Wendy: "You're right. You are so *very right.* Thanks—I needed that—I really did."

Wendy had referred to the irreplaceable secret weapon that no parent can do without: unconditional, go-for-broke, no-holds-barred, sacrificial love for your kids—and your mate. From that moment on I began telling myself, *I've got to suck it up . . . I'm Sande's partner . . . her servant. It's going to be tough on her. She didn't expect this either.*

On the flight home to Tucson, I kept trying to think of a way to tell Sande about my new attitude toward the pregnancy. When I left on the trip, I hadn't been that positive or supportive. In fact I had been downright grumpy and I wanted to make it right. When I got home, I found Sande still concerned about the well-being of the baby. I reminded her of the positive report from the doctor after we had gotten home from Disneyland, and then I said:

"You know, I've been a jerk about this—feeling sorry for myself and not being there for you as much as I could have. But when I dropped by Moonhead's place, Wendy set me straight. She really got my attention when she asked me if I could think of a better family for that little baby to grow up in."

For a second I wasn't sure how Mama Bear would receive Wendy's wisdom. But then she smiled back at me with a twinkle in her eye, and I knew that I was forgiven for any self-pitying misgivings that I had had. And I also knew the joy we would experience together was among the greatest gifts God could give us.

I never thought I'd be glad I was such a chicken about metal clips, but in the end my lack of courage paid off. Lauren arrived whole and sound, and has become the capstone of five incredible blessings from God.

No, I'm not going to claim that having Hannah and then Lauren was a piece of cake and Sande and I were both so blessed that we wouldn't trade a moment of any of it for a little peace and quiet. There were plenty of times when we weren't sure we would make it through the night. But make it through the nights we did and once Lauren was six and into school, Sande was once again at the place in life where she could see a little daylight and have a little freedom during the day while *all* her children are at work or in school.

As for me, I have that date with history. It will be 2010. I will be sixty-seven and Lauren, eighteen, will be striding down the aisle to pick up her high school diploma. I confess I try not to think about it, but every now and then I get reminded in interesting ways. Not long ago, I was taking Lauren to school, and as we came up the walk a grandfatherly looking fellow was sitting there sort of leaning on the fender of his car—obviously, waiting for someone. He smiled at me and said, "I've got a grandchild in this school too."

I looked at him and thought I would gently correct his error and so I said, "Actually, sir, this is number five."

"Oh! *Five grandchildren!* Aren't you lucky!"

As I walked into the school with Lauren, I couldn't help but chuckle. Yes, I could argue with him about "looking like a grandfather" (although I supposed I would lose). But one thing is for sure. I *am* very, very lucky—and very, very blessed!

Appendix A

U.S. PRESIDENTS AND THEIR BIRTH ORDER

George Washington—fifth child of father; first of mother; ten-year gap before his birth

John Adams—oldest of three boys

Thomas Jefferson—third of ten; oldest son

James Madison—oldest of twelve

James Monroe—oldest of five

John Quincy Adams—second of five; oldest son

Andrew Jackson—youngest of three sons; two years between him and older brother

Martin Van Buren—third of five; also had three older half siblings; two years between him and older sibling

William Henry Harrison—youngest of seven; oldest son

John Tyler—sixth of eight; second son; two years between him and older brother

James K. Polk—oldest of ten

Zachary Taylor—third of nine; third son; two years between him and older brother

Millard Fillmore—second of nine; oldest son

Franklin Pierce—seventh child of father (sixth of eight in second marriage); one year between him and older brother

James Buchanan—second of eleven; oldest son

Abraham Lincoln—second child of first wife (three total); oldest son

Andrew Johnson—third of three; second son; four years between him and older brother

Ulysses S. Grant—oldest of six

Rutherford B. Hayes—youngest of five; seven years between him and older brother with two sisters between them

James Garfield—youngest of five; five years between him and older brother

Chester Arthur—fifth of nine; oldest son

Grover Cleveland—fifth of nine; two years between him and older brother

Benjamin Harrison—fifth of thirteen (second of ten in second marriage); one year between him and older brother

William McKinley—seventh of nine; at least five years between him and older brother

Theodore Roosevelt—second of four; oldest son

William Howard Taft—seventh of ten (second of five in second marriage); two years between him and older brother

Woodrow Wilson—third of four; six years between him and older brother with one sister between them

Warren G. Harding—oldest of eight

Calvin Coolidge—oldest of two (father's first marriage)

Herbert Hoover—second of three; second son; three years between him and older brother

Franklin Roosevelt—second son (only child of father's second marriage); twenty-eight years between him and older half brother

Harry S Truman—oldest of three

Dwight Eisenhower—third of seven sons; one year between him and older brother

John F. Kennedy—second of nine; second son; two years between him and older brother

Lyndon Johnson—oldest of five

Richard Nixon—second of five sons; four years between him and older brother

Gerald Ford—only child of parents' first marriage (three half siblings in father's second marriage; three half siblings in mother's second marriage)

Jimmy Carter—oldest of four (Billy was the baby)

Ronald Reagan—youngest of two sons; two years between him and older brother

George Bush—second of five; second son; two years between him and older brother

Bill Clinton—only child (mother's first marriage); one younger half brother

George W. Bush—oldest of six

Appendix B

A REVIEW OF *BORN TO REBEL*
BY FRANK SULLOWAY

*O*ne of the most prolific and impressive researchers who has validated birth order is Frank Sulloway, who received a great deal of attention from the scholarly community as well as the general public when his book, *Born to Rebel: Birth Order Family Dynamics and Creative Lives,* was published in 1996. A research scholar at MIT, Sulloway spent twenty-six years accumulating massive statistical evidence to show that there is a real difference between first borns, who tend to be conservative and stick with the status quo, and later borns, who are more open-minded and willing to take risks and explode cherished ideas and theories.

If you care to wade through Sulloway's book, which includes 368 pages of text and 285 pages of appendices with all kinds of scientific data, plus another 159 pages of endnotes and bibliography, you can find thousands of birth-order examples from history that he uses to prove his point. Some are from the past; others are more contemporary.

For example, to illustrate the first born's tendency to be more conscientious, he points out that in Neil Simon's *The Odd Couple,* the fussy "neatnik" was played by two first borns, Jack Lemon in the movie and later Tony Randall on television. And, of course, the easygoing slob was played by Walter Mathau in the movie and later Jack Klugman on TV, both last borns.

Among many current or recent world leaders discussed in *Born to Rebel* are first borns Mikhail Gorbachev, Boris Yeltsin, Bill Clinton, Jimmy Carter, Saddam Hussein, and Jesse Jackson; middle borns Yasser Arafat, George Bush, and Fidel Castro; last borns Ho Chi Minh and Ronald Reagan.

Just a few of the many historical figures he discusses include first borns Winston Churchill, William Shakespeare, George Washington, and Franklin D. Roosevelt (an only child); middle borns Napoléon Bonaparte, Henry VIII, Patrick Henry, and Adolf Hitler; last borns Mohandas K. Gandhi and Voltaire.

In the fields of science and philosophy, Sulloway mentions first borns Albert Einstein, Galileo, and Leonardo da Vinci (only child); middle borns Louis Pasteur, Albert Schweitzer, and Charles Darwin; last borns Copernicus, Francis Bacon, and René Descartes. Copernicus, you will recall, was the scientist who introduced the revolutionary idea that the world was not flat but indeed round and revolved around the sun—he was the youngest of four children. Charles Darwin, the proponent of evolution, and his disciple, Alfred Russell Wallace, were both the fifth of six children.

Sulloway makes a lot out of Darwin's theories in his book. In some ways *Born to Rebel* is an apologetic for evolution and the theory of natural selection. Back in the 1960s when he was a sophomore at Harvard, Sulloway became fascinated with Darwin. He wanted to know more about just how someone who described himself as being rather ordinary and average became one of the most famous scientists in five hundred years by advancing the controversial theory of evolution through natural selection.

As Sulloway continued to study Darwin and thousands of other people, he saw the evidence piling up. He concluded that if you want to predict a revolutionary or a rebel, look at his or her birth order. First borns tend toward being conservative and later borns like Darwin are likely to be freethinkers. And that's where Sulloway got the title for his book—*Born to Rebel.*

As a creationist, I don't share Sulloway's notions that Darwinian evolution is proven by birth-order examples. But creationists and evolutionists alike can clearly see in Sulloway's voluminous research that birth order does have scientific validity as far as characteristics of first borns and later borns are concerned.

As he interacted with the findings of Cecile Ernst and Jules Angst, who severely criticized birth order in their book *Birth Order: Its Influence on Personality,* Sulloway summarized 196 birth-order studies that do meet the standards for what Ernst and Angst would call "properly controlled research." As he worked with these 196 studies, Sulloway classified them according to the five major "personality dimensions" that are used consistently in personality tests administered in different countries and languages throughout the world.[1] This "big five" included openness to experience, conscientiousness, agreeableness, neuroticism (how emotionally stable or unstable someone might be), and extraversion. Out of the 196 studies, 72 of them convincingly confirmed the following propositions:

> *Openness to experience*—first borns are more conforming, traditional, and closely identified with parents.
> *Conscientiousness*—first borns are more responsible, achievement oriented, organized, and planful.

Agreeableness—later borns are more easygoing, cooperative, and popular.

Neuroticism (emotional instability)—first borns are more jealous, anxious, neurotic, fearful, and likely to affiliate under stress.

Extraversion—first borns are more extraverted, assertive, and likely to exhibit leadership.

According to Sulloway's findings, the possibility that 72 out of 196 birth-order studies would confirm these five aspects of the human personality so convincingly by mere chance is less than one in a billion billion.[2]

One of the most convincing pieces of research Sulloway cites to substantiate birth-order effects is the work of Helen Koch, a psychologist at the University of Chicago, who, beginning in 1954, published ten articles after testing the influences of birth order on many different psychological traits. As Sulloway observes: "Koch's study is noteworthy for its sophisticated design. Even today, no study has approached its effects to control for so many compounding variables."[3] Koch used fifty-eight different measures of behavior. Among her findings was that first borns are more self-confident, competitive, insistent on rights, emotionally intense, and upset by defeat. These are all typical traits I have seen in first borns for twenty-five years.

While a lot of the birth-order critics call Sulloway's work "rubbish and poppycock," other scholars say that he's on to something. He has gained the praise of many people who say that the depth and scope of *Born to Rebel* cannot be denied. Heavyweights in the academic community were quoted in *The New Yorker,* giving such praise as: his work "definitely settles the question of birth order's importance in the development of personality"; his work is "completely original and unlike anything I have ever seen." One eminent anthropologist even commented that she thought Sulloway would "join the pantheon of thinkers, like Freud and Darwin, whose work has radically and forever changed the way we look at ourselves and the world."[4]

Even Alan Wolfe, one of the most vociferous critics of Sulloway's book, concedes in his scathing review in *The New Republic:* "Let us concede, therefore, that an important discovery has been announced in this book: Social scientists, as a result of Sulloway's exhaustive statistical investigations, will now have to give the question of birth order its proper due."[5]

But while saying that, Wolfe goes on to declare that Sulloway went too far with his claims about the scope and power of birth order as a final determinant of personality. Wolfe believes that if we are all willing to hear that birth order determines our temperament, ". . . we will have surrendered to a false and awful notion: that who we are can be pinned down and explained by what is least human about us, by a fixed drive put into place at the moment of our birth from which it is futile to try to escape."[6]

I think I can understand Wolfe's concern, but he has nothing to fear from any Adlerian therapist who understands the legitimate part birth order plays in anyone's life. Birth order is simply one of several ways to look at the puzzle known as the human personality. After more than twenty-five years of work with the human personality, I know that it's a good one.

Notes

Chapter 1 *Birth Order—Does It Really Make Any Sense?*

1. See Richard W. Bradley, "Using Birth Order and Sibling Dynamics in Career Counseling," *The Personnel and Guidance Journal* (September 1982): 25. Bradley quotes from the article "Is First Best?" *Newsweek* (January 6, 1969): 37.

2. See, for example, R. L. Adams and B. N. Phillips, "Motivation and Achievement Differences among Children of the Various Ordinal Birth Positions," *Child Development* (March 1972): 157.

3. Sally Leman Chall, *Making God Real to Your Children* (Grand Rapids: Revell, 1991); *Mommy Appleseed* (Eugene, Ore: Harvest House, 1993).

4. See Walter Toman, *Family Constellation* (New York: Springer, 1976), 33.

5. Ibid., 5.

6. See James H. S. Bossard, *The Large Family System* (Philadelphia: University of Pennsylvania Press, 1966), 79.

Chapter 2 *But, Doc, I Don't Fit Your Birth Order Mold!*

1. Tom Peters, "'Personality' Has Southwest Flying above Its Competition," *Arizona Daily Star,* 26 September 1994, p. B4.

2. Quoted in Kevin Leman, *Winning the Rat Race without Becoming a Rat* (Nashville: Thomas Nelson, 1996), 70.

3. "Former Arizona Governor Gets Two and a Half-Year Prison Term," *Los Angeles Times,* 3 February 1998, p. A13.

4. Bradford Wilson and George Edington, *First Child, Second Child* (New York: McGraw-Hill, 1981), 259.

5. Ibid., 282.

Chapter 3 *What's Parenting Got to Do with It?*

1. Lee Iacocca with William Novak, *Iacocca* (New York: Bantam, 1986), 18.

2. Ibid.

3. Adapted from Leman, *Winning the Rat Race,* 152–53.

4. Statistics provided by the Stepfamily Association of America, Inc., 215 Centennial Mall South, Suite 212, Lincoln, Nebraska 68508-1834.

5. Barbara Hustedt Crook, "His, Hers, Theirs—Buy Nuclear Family Ties," *Cosmopolitan* (August 1991): 76, 78.

6. Adapted from Kevin Leman, *Living in a Stepfamily without Getting Stepped On* (Nashville: Thomas Nelson, 1994), 23.

7. For example, see the work of Carmi Schooler, "Birth Order Effects: Not Here, Not Now!" *Psychological Bulletin* 78, no. 3 (September 1972): 171–72. Schooler concluded that ". . . scores for different birth ranks show no significant difference" and that there is good reason to doubt ". . . the importance of birth order as a determinant of behavior."

8. Cecile Ernst and Jules Angst, *Birth Order: Its Influence on Personality* (New York: Springer-Berlag, 1983), 242.

9. Joseph Rodgers, psychologist at the University of Oklahoma, who was quoted by Geoffrey Cowley, "First Born, Later Born," *Newsweek* (October 7, 1996): 68.

10. UCLA sociologist Judith Blake's findings were noted in Kenneth L. Woodward with Lydia Denworth, "The Order of Innovation," *Newsweek* (May 21, 1990): 76.

11. Leman, *Winning the Rat Race,* 17.

12. Ibid., 118.

13. Ibid.

14. Robert S. Boynton, "The Birth of an Idea," *The New Yorker* (October 7, 1996): 72.

15. Frank J. Sulloway, *Born to Rebel: Birth Order Family Dynamics and Creative Lives* (New York: Pantheon, 1996), 353.

16. Ibid., 72–74.

Chapter 4 *First Come, First Served*

1. Only children are sometimes called "super first borns" because they have many similar characteristics that are exaggerated to some degree. That and other differences between only children and first borns will be discussed in chapter 7.

2. We affirm Dr. Leman's lack of editorial comprehension. (The Editors)

3. Harvey Mackay, *Beware the Naked Man Who Offers You His Shirt* (New York: Ivy Books, 1990), 24.

4. See Leman, *Winning the Rat Race,* 64.

5. Ibid., 26.

Chapter 5 *Just How Serious a Problem Is Perfectionism?*

1. Jane Goodsell, *Not a Good Word about Anybody* (New York: Ballantine, 1988), 46, 50.

2. Kevin Leman, *When Your Best Is Not Good Enough* (Grand Rapids: Revell, 1997).

3. Material on Einstein, Churchill, and Picasso from Miriam Adderholdt-Elliott, *Perfectionism—What's Bad about Being Too Good?* (Minneapolis: Free Spirit, 1987), 18–20.

4. Leman, *When Your Best Is Not Good Enough.* Kevin Leman, *Women Who Try Too Hard: Breaking the Pleasing Habits* (Grand Rapids: Revell, 1987).

Chapter 6 *Moving from Perfectionism toward Excellence*

1. Adapted from Leman, *Winning the Rat Race,* 125–27.

2. Adapted from David Stoop, *Self-Talk: Key to Personal Growth* (Grand Rapids: Revell, 1982), 120.

Chapter 7 *Lonely Only, Super First Born*

1. Toni Falbo, "Does the Only Child Grow Up Miserable?" *Psychology Today* (May 1976): 60.

2. Alfred Adler, *Understanding Human Nature* (New York: Faucett World Library, 1927), 127.

3. Adapted from Leman, *Winning the Rat Race,* 21–22.

4. My official title is "Family Psychologist and Consultant to ABC's *Good Morning, America.*"

5. Karen Peterson, "Kids without Siblings Get Their Due," *USA Today,* 1 March 1993, p. 1D.

6. "Only Children: Cracking the Myth of the Pampered Only Misfit," *U.S. News and World Report* (January 10, 1994): 50.

7. Peterson, "Kids without Siblings Get Their Due," 1D.

8. This is a paraphrase of what Adler said. See Lucille K. Forer with Henry Still, *The Birth Order Factor* (New York: David McKay, 1976), 255.

9. Adapted from Leman, *Winning the Rat Race,* 146–51.

Chapter 8 / Never Did Get No Respect

1. Because Dr. Leman is a baby of the family, we counted for him and learned that even in this new revised edition of *The Birth Order Book,* the middle children, indeed, still got the fewest pages. Sorry! (The Editors)

2. Wilson and Edington, *First Child, Second Child,* 92.

3. Forer, *The Birth Order Factor,* 77.

4. Eleanor G. Neisser, *Brothers and Sisters* (New York: Harper, 1951), 154, quoting Eleanor Estes, *The Middle Moffat.*

5. Wilson and Edington, *First Child, Second Child,* 95.

6. Donald J. Trump with Tony Schwartz, *Trump: The Art of the Deal* (New York: Random House, 1987), 3, 43–44.

7. Wilson and Edington, *First Child, Second Child,* 99.

8. Ibid., 104.

9. Ibid., 103.

10. Alfred Adler, *The Individual Psychology of Alfred Adler,* ed. H. L. Ansbacher and R. R. Ansbacher (New York: Harper & Row, 1956), 379–80.

11. Quoted by Irving D. Harris, *The Promised Seed* (Glencove: The Free Press of Glencove, 1964), 75.

12. Pam Hait, "Birth Order and Relationships," *Sunday Woman* (September 12, 1982): 4.

Chapter 9 *Born Last but Seldom Least*

1. Wilson and Edington, *First Child, Second Child,* 108.

2. Mopsy Strange Kennedy, "A Last Born Speaks Out—At Last," *Newsweek* (November 7, 1977): 22.

3. Wilson and Edington, *First Child, Second Child,* 109.

4. Ibid., 108.

5. See also my book *Parenthood without Hassles* (Eugene, Ore: Harvest House, 1979): 11.

6. Ibid., 12.

7. See Wilson and Edington, *First Child, Second Child,* 109–10.

Chapter 10 *How to Let Your Birth Order Work for You in Business*

1. For a complete discussion of using birth order knowledge in business, see Leman, *Winning the Rat Race without Becoming a Rat,* from which this chapter was adapted (see especially chapters 4, 5, and 6).

2. Harvey Mackay, *Swim with the Sharks without Being Eaten Alive* (New York: Ivy Books, 1988), 23.

Chapter 11 *Birth Order Marriages Aren't Made in Heaven*

1. See Toman, *Family Constellation.* Toman studied three thousand families before coming up with his conclusions. In a smaller study, Dr. Theodore D. Kempler, University of Wisconsin, researched 236 business executives and their wives and also discovered that certain birth order combinations made better marriages than others. The smaller study is documented in Lucille Forer's book, *The Birth Order Factor,* 187–88.

2. Kevin Leman, *Were You Born for Each Other?* (New York: Delacorte, 1991).

3. Toman, *Family Constellation.*

Chapter 12 *I Only Count When . . .*

1. Much of the material in this chapter on life-styles and life themes is adapted from Leman, *Living in a Stepfamily,* see chapters 6 and 7.

2. Alfred Adler, *The Practice and Theory of Individual Psychology* (London: Routledge & Kegan Paul, 1923), 3.

3. Adler, *Understanding Human Nature,* 31.

4. Rudolph Dreikurs, *Fundamentals of Adlerian Psychology* (Chicago: Alfred Adler Institute, 1953), 35.

Chapter 13 *Why Reality Discipline Works with Any Birth Order*

1. Adapted from Leman, *Living in a Stepfamily,* 205–6.

2. Kevin Leman, *Making Children Mind without Losing Yours* (Grand Rapids: Revell, 1984), 11.

3. Adapted from ibid., 27–28.

4. For more on the difference between reality discipline and authoritative parenting versus other styles of parenting, such as authoritarianism, see my new curriculum book *Becoming the Parent God Wants You to Be* (Colorado Springs: NavPress, 1998). Based on *Making Children Mind,* this book creates discussion situations for parents to interact together on right and wrong ways to raise children, including such systems that demand instant obedience from children who are given three ways to respond to the parent: "Yes, Sir," "No, Sir," and "May I appeal to you, Sir?"

5. Leman, *Making Children Mind,* 71–72.

6. See Beth Brophy, "Because I Said So," *U.S. News and World Report* (November 10, 1997): 71.

7. For more on this, see *Making Children Mind,* 70.

8. This statement is attributed to Josh McDowell, author and widely known speaker at high school and college campuses across the United States and in other countries. Josh is the father of three children.

9. See Leman, *Making Children Mind,* 88–89, 109.

10. Ibid., 115–16.

Chapter 14 *Flaunt Your Imperfections*

1. See Leman, *Making Children Mind,* 88.

Chapter 17 *Helping the Family "Cub" Grow Up*

1. Wilson and Edington, *First Child, Second Child,* 110–11.

2. Neisser, *Brothers and Sisters,* 165–66.

Appendix B *A Review of* Born to Rebel *by Frank Sulloway*

1. Sulloway cites several different sources concerning the use of the "big five" in personality tests throughout the world. See Sulloway, *Born to Rebel,* 68.

2. See ibid., 72, and especially the table on p. 73.

3. Ibid., 75.

4. Boynton, "The Birth of an Idea," 74.

5. Alan Wolfe, "Up from Scientism," *The New Republic* (December 23, 1996): 32.

6. Ibid., 35.

Other resources by Dr. Kevin Leman

Audiotapes:
Why Kids Misbehave and What You Can Do about It
How to Make Your Child Feel Special
Keeping Your Family Together When the World Is Falling Apart
Living in a Stepfamily without Getting Stepped On

Videotapes:
Raising Successful and Confident Kids
How to Get Kids to Do What You Want
Why Kids Misbehave
Living in a Stepfamily

Video series:
Making Children Mind without Losing Yours (Christian—parenting edition)
Making Children Mind without Losing Yours (secular—public school teacher edition)
Making the Most of Marriage
Single Parenting That Works!
Bringing Peace and Harmony to the Blended Family

Founder of MatchWise.com, internationally known Christian psychologist, award-winning author, radio and television personality, and speaker, **Dr. Kevin Leman** has ministered to and entertained audiences worldwide with his wit and commonsense psychology.

Best-selling author Dr. Leman has made house calls for *Focus on the Family* with Dr. James Dobson as well as numerous radio and television programs, including *Oprah, American Morning*, CBS's *The Early Show, Today*, and *The View*. Dr. Leman has served as a consulting family psychologist to *Good Morning America*.

Dr. Leman is the founder and president of Couples of Promise, an organization designed and committed to helping couples remain happily married. His professional affiliations include the American Psychological Association, the American Federation of Radio and Television Artists, the National Register of Health Services Providers in Psychology, and the North American Society of Adlerian Psychology.

Dr. Leman attended North Park College. He received his bachelor's degree in psychology from the University of Arizona, where he later earned his master's and doctorate degrees. Originally from Williamsville, New York, he and his wife, Sande, live in Tucson, Arizona. They have five children and one grandchild.

For information regarding speaking availability, business consultations, or seminars, please contact Dr. Leman at:

Dr. Kevin Leman
P.O. Box 35370
Tucson, AZ 85704
Phone: (520) 797-3830
Fax: (520)-797-3809
Web site: www.realfamilies.com
　　　　　www.matchwise.com

Books to nurture YOURSELF, your MARRIAGE, and your FAMILY

Bring out the best in your kids with Dr. Kevin Leman's 7 principles of "Reality Discipline" —a loving, no-nonsense parenting approach that really works.

With candor and humor, this book teaches you how to build communication, affection, and consideration in your marriage to make it more emotionally and physically satisfying.